The Automotive Gray Market

ALSO BY JOHN B. HEGE
AND FROM McFARLAND

The Wankel Rotary Engine: A History
(2002; paperback 2006)

The Automotive Gray Market
An Inside History

JOHN B. HEGE

McFarland & Company, Inc., Publishers
Jefferson, North Carolina

Library of Congress Cataloguing-in-Publication Data

ISBN (print) 978-0-7864-6373-2
ISBN (ebook) 978-1-4766-4410-3

British Library cataloguing data are available

Library of Congress Control Number 2022010131

© 2022 John B. Hege. All rights reserved

No part of this book may be reproduced or transmitted in any form or by any means, electronic or mechanical, including photocopying or recording, or by any information storage and retrieval system, without permission in writing from the publisher.

Front cover: 1979 Lamborghini Countach LP400S (photograph by Michael Jörgens); carburetor parts diagram for Countach engine (Automobili Lamborghini S.p.A.)

Printed in the United States of America

McFarland & Company, Inc., Publishers
Box 611, Jefferson, North Carolina 28640
www.mcfarlandpub.com

Table of Contents

Preface   1

Introduction   5

1. Congress and Cars   7
2. Small Importers and Their Reactions   17
3. The First Compliance Shops   28
4. Making Them Pass   47
5. The Stoichiometric Closed Loop Electronic Feedback Controlled Breakthrough   66
6. The Boom   78
7. More Fuel on the Fire   89
8. In the Workshop   98
9. The Independent Labs   113
10. The Shine Rubs Off   128
11. Meanwhile, at Lamborghini   133
12. The Factories Push Back   143
13. An Inaction of Congress   156
14. The Market Winds Down   164
15. Lessons of the Gray Market   171

Chapter Notes   175
Bibliography   177
Index   181

Preface

I learned about the automotive gray market the same way most everyone else did, through the automotive press. As a young man in the 1970s, I loved sports cars and enjoyed reading about exotic, outrageously expensive imports that I would most likely never get to drive, much less own. My friends and I would talk for hours about the recent developments in automobiles as though they were an important part of our lives, easily ignoring the fact that none of us could afford much more than a worn-out Volkswagen.

The big news of the decade was that the times they were a-changin' and a new set of rules was coming out of Washington forcing drastic change in the automotive industry. By the mid–1970s some foreign automakers had already thrown up their hands and abandoned the American market rather than bear the burdens imposed on car makers by an increasingly socially aware government. Even though I was only 16, I was outraged at the idea that masterpieces like the Maserati Bora or the then-concept Lamborghini Countach were not going to be available for sale in America.

A few years later, having finished high school and found work as a mechanic in a series of independent import repair shops, I kept up my reading of automotive journals and learned that a few small shops around the country were attempting to modify some of these forbidden cars to bring them into compliance with U.S. standards. This was exciting news for me, even though the chances of my even being on the same side of a fence with most of these cars were no better than they were years before. It was fun to talk about, fun to form theories, make projections, speculate about future developments the same way it's fun to talk about sports teams as though your opinion is important all the while knowing that you will never be involved.

Of course, I dreamed of working in one of these upstart "compliance" shops, but I imagined that these guys were all engineers with multiple degrees carrying clipboards and wearing lab coats with pocket protectors. I never suspected that I would be qualified to do that kind of work. I was wrong on all counts.

Maserati Bora showing DeLorean-style side marker installation. Because this was a 1972 model, there was little modification needed beyond side markers, seat belts, and a few labels on the dashboard (private collection).

Years went by and the increase in "direct imports" escaped my notice, until one day I heard about a man in a neighboring town who was aspiring to import Lamborghinis. I figured "what the hell?" and I wrote him a letter explaining how much he needed me to work in his shop. Much to my surprise, he responded and invited me to come by for an interview that was the beginning of my two-year tour in the gray market. It was a short time in my career where I learned a lifetime's worth of lessons about people, money, corruption, government, and incidentally, about automobiles.

When I began work on this project, I looked up some old colleagues from 25 years ago and found that most just weren't interested in talking about those days. My time in the gray market was spent on the ground floor, in the workshop or on the road. (There was a lot of travelling involved.) My associates and I were mostly working-class people who had become involved in a shady business thinking they were just taking a regular job. As they became more deeply involved, they began to understand that some of the things that were happening in the shop and in the labs could potentially get them in trouble with the feds and when the whole thing was over, and the smoke had cleared, they were happy to be done with it.

This work is not intended as an exposé or an indictment of any individual or business. It's more of a memoir. Much of the material comes from my own personal experience, conversations, and observations of a truly outrageous period in the imported car business. In some places I have changed names and been deliberately vague about locations of actual events in order not to make the actual individuals uncomfortable. I hope that old colleagues of mine, reading this work will simply smile to themselves when they think of the times we had.

Introduction

During the late 1960s and through the seventies, the automobile industry was going through drastic changes. Increasing social awareness led to government imposed regulations on automobiles sold in the United States regarding safety in a crash and exhaust emissions. Car companies who wanted to play in the world's largest automotive market complied, but the modifications required were costly. The regulations imposed by Congress were designed to become more and more stringent with each passing year in order to take advantage of improving technology. So, the effort required to build a compliant car became greater and more expensive year by year.

Some of the smaller foreign companies, makers who had never enjoyed large U.S. sales, decided it wasn't worth the time and expense to produce a model for export to the U.S. and simply discontinued sales in America; others offered only certain models for the American market. Often the cars that they declined to sell in America were considered to be the more exciting high-performance models that were popular among the wealthy and coveted by the more average car enthusiasts. Making them unavailable only made them more desirable.

During the seventies, a few ambitious souls saw this as a new opportunity and the first "compliance" shops opened. These shops would undertake the necessary modifications of non–U.S. model cars and then petition the government agencies to allow them to be sold in the U.S. market. The automotive gray market was born.

The number of cars brought into the States through such "Direct Importers" probably would never have amounted to much had it not been for a glitch in the international economy that took place in the first half of the 1980s. Many people remember the runaway inflation and high interest rates of the Carter years. Those interest rates made American dollars very valuable in foreign markets, nearly doubling the buying power of an American shopper overseas. Soon people realized that they could travel to Germany, buy a top-of-the-line Mercedes or other luxury car, ship it back to the States, and even after paying the cost of the shipping and compliance work, save thousands of dollars over the dealer's price for the same car.

It became trendy among the class of young professionals recently dubbed "yuppies" to import their own luxury car. Soon tourist magazines were publishing articles about taking a European vacation and bringing home a new car. Independent car dealers were bringing in cars by the truckload and circumventing the established dealer networks. In 1985 alone, over 60,000 cars were imported through "gray market" channels, causing anger and frustration among the established dealer networks and an overwhelming backlog of paperwork for government agencies that had been designed to handle only a small fraction of the incoming applications.

This is the story of the rise and fall of the gray market, covering a period of around twenty years from its emergence to its final or near final suffocation under a mountain of government paperwork and legislation. Though it probably could never have been predicted, hindsight more likely brings a chuckle and a response of "Of course it happened! How could it not?" Automobiles have been an American passion since their invention and anything that happens in the American automotive market always happens in huge numbers and brings huge consequences.

1

Congress and Cars

To be sure, the Countach was a stunning car. The first preview came at the 1971 Geneva Motor show. It was a concept car, a kind of mission statement displaying to the automotive world the intentions of its parent company, Lamborghini. It was an outrageous statement to be made by the small sports car company started by an Italian tractor builder only eight years before. They had only been building cars since 1963 and could only produce a few of their hand-made cars each year. But the cars that they did build and deliver to their customers were creative, exciting, fast, and attracted attention everywhere they were seen. Consequently, they had little trouble selling them as fast as they could make them.

The car was engineered and styled like nothing anyone had ever seen. Trapezoids were the recurring theme in the body, kicking off a trend of sharp angles and straight lines in auto bodies that would continue for nearly two decades. The doors, instead of swinging out like a conventional car or up like a "gull wing," pivoted up and forward from a single point, resembling nothing as much as the wings of a beetle preparing for flight. The engine was center mounted, of course, between the axle lines, as was the accepted practice among many high-end performance car builders of the time but there was an added kink: the engine was turned around backwards, with the crankshaft pulley end at the rear of the car and the flywheel and clutch toward the front. The transmission was mounted forward of the engine so that the tail of the transmission was right beside the driver and the shift lever sprouted right up out of the gearbox, easily to hand. Power was then transferred to a shaft running parallel to the engine and rearward to the final drive unit just below and to the rear of the "timing" end of the engine. According to Lamborghini, this gave the car an almost perfect 50/50 weight distribution.

The proposed power plant was a 3.9-liter V12 with four camshafts and fed by six two-barrel carburetors. Its predicted output of 375 HP put it right in the range of 100 HP/liter that was considered state-of-the-art for a production car at the time and suggesting a possible top speed of near 200 MPH.

1985 Lamborghini Countach. Photograph shows the aftermarket side markers and an installation of a rear bumper from a Chevrolet Celebrity (private collection).

But the most outrageous thing about the Countach was that it would not likely be available in America. Had it been conceived a few years earlier there could have been a chance, but the at the time of its conception under the pen of Paolo Stanzini, the Countach flew in the face of the recent social consciousness that was beginning to emerge in the United States. Showing little apparent regard to passenger safety in the event of a crash and less toward the content of the exhaust, the design of the car was in violation of several laws already on the books and even more to come.

In the latter half of the 1960s, America had begun the process of cleaning up her act. For several decades people who lived in large population centers had begun to notice that things were getting pretty dirty. The air was getting foul and dark and more and more the rivers and streams were becoming incapable of supporting life. It wasn't hard to see the source of the trouble: major industries, manufacturers, and automobiles were fouling the nest. Factories and cities were dumping their wastes into the air and the rivers without a thought of treating it in any way and automobiles belched and leaked anything they didn't consume, leaving trails of soot or smoke and a mist of oil products in their wake.

For Americans, the sixties were about self-discovery. It was a time of looking at ourselves, our habits, our government, and trying to break some of the old self-destructive habits that had been developing since the beginnings of industrialized times. At least that's the way it began. Alongside television ads instructing citizens how to protect themselves from nuclear attack by ducking under the furniture were anti littering ads featuring crying Indians and public awareness ads showing cartoon children swimming in polluted water. Clean air and water were becoming *the* issue of the time and the politicians in both of the major parties were taking notice.

Long before the American public had begun to ponder complex issues such as the implications of climate change, the idea of pollution control was just a question of not being poisoned. Everyone knew that you couldn't survive for long in a closed garage with a running car, but the sky was big and for most people it was difficult to imagine that automobiles could have a significant impact. Even when it was becoming obvious, however, it was not an issue individuals could be expected to resolve with respect to their personal cars.

There had already been a few good wake-up calls. Much like the storms of the dust bowl years, there were portents of environmental calamity if serious changes were not made. In December 1952, London was trapped under a smoke-filled fog that reduced visibility to about three feet. Londoners were accustomed to heavy fog, but this time was different. A "thermal inversion" trapped a layer of air over the city for five days causing smoke and soot from factories, home chimneys, and auto exhausts to build up rather than blow away as usual. The *Manchester Guardian* reported that the midday sun "hung sulkily in the in the dirty sky with no more radiance than an unlit Chinese lantern." Hospitals quickly filled with patients suffering from respiratory disorders and deaths rose sharply. In a later analysis, the British Committee on air pollution estimated that during the time of the smog event there were 4000 more deaths in London than normally would have occurred.

Similar events were taking place with some regularity. New York City was trapped under a ten-day inversion in 1953, and later for four days in 1963. London was again darkened by smog in 1956 and 1962. Other major population and industrial centers suffered under their own smoke as well. Los Angeles became famous for a seasonal blanket of brown smog that hung over the city for most of the year, a result not so much of the soot from factory smokestacks as from an accumulation of the exhaust products of a booming population of cars.[1]

The first national legislation to deal with the issue in America took place with the passage of the Air Pollution Control Act of 1955. This was a gentle nod toward the problem that provided federal funds to research the scope and sources of air pollution. In 1959 California took up the lead by creating the California Motor Vehicle Pollution Control Board, assigning them the task of testing vehicle exhausts with the goal of setting appropriate standards. California would continue to run ahead of the federal government in anti-pollution legislation, eventually leading Congress to look toward that state as a pilot program for potential changes in national regulations.

In 1961, California introduced their first pollution control measures for cars. Researchers had recognized early on that most of the offensive vapors emitted by cars came not from the tailpipe, but from the crankcase vent. The crankcase is the part of the engine containing the rotating parts. It's isolated from combustion in the cylinders by the piston rings, which inevitably will leak to some degree. This "blow-by" can result in high pressures in the crankcase that have to be relieved somehow. Up until that time, automakers dealt with the problem via a "road draft tube," an open vent that hung under the car into the airstream of the moving car. The end of the tube was chamfered so that the passing air from the motion of the car would draw the crankcase fumes out of the pipe and create a slight atmospheric depression in the crankcase—an elegantly simple solution whose only downside was that it belched an oily vapor into the air and left a film of oil on the road surface and on the underside of the car. This accumulated film was bad enough that motorcyclists were trained to ride not in the center of the lane, but on one side or the other to avoid the slippery stripe left by the passing cars. When rain came, the air pollution quickly became a water pollution problem, as the film of oil was rinsed off the highways and into the storm drains, rivers and streams. People who remember life in the sixties will recall the swirling rainbow-colored film on the roads that always accompanied the start of a rainstorm, as accumulated oil washed into the environment.

A new device, tagged the "Positive Crankcase Ventilation System," included a simple and inexpensive series of pipes and valves to divert the crankcase fumes into the intake airstream of the engine. This achieved the needed pressure relief in the engine but burned the fumes from the vent instead of releasing them into the atmosphere. It was a small measure that achieved big results and starting with the 1963 models, California stated that Positive Crankcase Ventilation (PCV) would be required equipment on cars sold in that state.

The federal government was far less decisive, but they did eventually tag along. In 1963, Congress passed the Clean Air Act, which gave the Department of Health Education and Welfare the job of studying the pollution problem and making recommendations for improvements. In their initial report, HEW was not shy about recommending national standards to reduce hydrocarbon (HC), carbon monoxide (CO) and nitrogen oxide (NOx) emissions from auto exhausts, saying, "Considering the present extent of automobile air pollution and the speed at which it is growing, effective control of these emissions is needed now. Although there is much to learn, control measures should not be delayed pending completion of the needed research."[2]

For the time being, this statement reflected the position of President Lyndon Johnson's administration. He later reinforced that position in a speech about protecting the natural beauty of the United States. However, when hearings convened later that year to discuss a clean air bill that included national standards and requirements for automakers to follow, HEW appeared to back off from their previous position, and recommended voluntary compliance measures while waiting for the numbers to come in from California's experiment with regulation. Congressmen were noticeably confused and frustrated by this unexpected reversal by HEW and presumably the White House, but went on to pass the bill anyway, leaving the Johnson Administration to deal with the inevitable criticisms about being in the pocket of the auto industry. This sort of political squabbling could be counted on to accompany any attempts at pollution control in the future.

The political faux pas notwithstanding, the Motor Vehicle Pollution Control Act of 1965 was historic in that it was the first national legislation specifically regulating emissions from automobiles. By itself, it wasn't a big burden on the automakers—it only codified standards they already had to meet to sell cars in California. In fact, they preferred a national law because they saw the alternative as fifty different sets of standards from individual states. But inevitably, more laws would follow with the passage of the Air Quality Act of 1967 and later, the Clean Air Act of 1970 which created the Environmental Protection Agency under the pen of Richard Nixon. The EPA, as it came to be known, took over the task of enforcing the new laws and created a schedule of ever-increasing regulation of HC, CO and NOx for the coming years. Expressed in terms of grams per mile, the schedule called for the reduction of the offending gasses by 90 percent between the model years of 1970 and 1976. It was a lofty goal, and American automakers were quick to protest that they had neither the money nor the technology to meet these standards. Their knee-jerk reaction to the new rules was to spend millions on lawyers and lobbyists in attempts to ease their regulatory burden, sometimes successfully: in 1973 they were able to persuade the EPA to defer the 1975 and 1976 standards for one year or face a "collapse of the automotive industry."

Curiously, some of the larger import automakers seemed to have little trouble bringing their models up to standards. It may be that they were not savvy enough with the American political system to place their bets on changing the law; so rather than spending their money on lawyers and lobbyists they instead invested heavily in research and development.

Despite the automakers' protests, for the first few years the regulations were not so much of a burden, the fact being that cars of the sixties were so filthy that it didn't take much to clean them up quite a lot. Like the PCV system, initial solutions did not require a great deal of hardware or technology. Beginning in 1971, automakers were required to install closed fuel systems or *Evaporative Emission Control* systems. Evap systems, as they came to be called by auto mechanics, were required because the EPA recognized that fuel vapors evaporating, for example, from a car parked in the hot sun were also a significant source of hydrocarbon pollution. Evaporative control was achieved by replacing vented gas caps with sealed ones and venting the fuel tank and carburetor bowl through a series of tubes and valves to a canister full of activated charcoal pellets. In a parked vehicle, the charcoal absorbed the vapors as long as they were not excessive. When the engine was running, air was drawn through the charcoal into the engine, purging the vapor from the canister. The result was that cars sitting in a sunny parking lots didn't smell like gasoline anymore.

Again, the real cost of the evap system wasn't very large, and it didn't affect the performance of the car. But it was a little more complicated than the PCV and it had its occasional problems. Most often though, those problems were a result of misconnected vacuum and vent lines, work done by owner-mechanics or even by professionals who didn't understand the operation of or even the need for the system.

While the automakers may have felt that they were being unfairly overburdened by the new law, auto mechanics, struggling to understand the outbreak of unexplained devices found under the hood, developed their own opinion of the new automotive legislation. There was little or no training available at the time to prepare for the tangle of vacuum lines and mysterious devices that were beginning to clutter engine compartments. As the years passed and emission regulations continued to tighten, the control systems became more and more complicated. Drivability issues and bizarre new symptoms were cropping up in relatively new cars. Tune-up specifications didn't make sense anymore. The practice of retarding ignition timing—setting it to fire the spark plugs just *after* the pistons had already begun their power strokes—and allowing a vacuum advance device to adjust ignition timing according to engine RPMs was against all conventional wisdom. Many mechanics dealt with these new problems with radical surgery. The offending components were removed, and the engines tuned back to more conventional settings. It worked for the first few years. It was a form of denial, returning things to the way they used to be back when things were easier to understand. Mechanics just swept the problems under the rug while hoping that all this emission control nonsense would turn out to be just a passing fad. The customers wanted their cars fixed quickly, and in most cases, they didn't care what went on under the hood as long as the car worked the way they expected. Given the choice, customers frequently chose to have troublesome components removed or blocked off rather than deal with the expense of replacing an obscure black box. Just as often, components were removed without the owner's knowledge or consent. But nobody was checking the tailpipe emissions yet, so across the country an emission controlectomy became standard operating procedure.

Aside from the annoyance felt by auto mechanics, the first changes required by the new U.S. policy didn't really put anybody off too much, and the manufacturers were ready to comply. For that matter, the new, cleaner upgrades made enough sense for all markets that some manufacturers made the changes to cars for all their international markets so there wasn't any need to build a special model for the United States alone. In other cases, since the new emission control systems used just a few add-on parts, the carmakers simply left off the additional pieces required for the U.S.

But it wasn't just emission controls that constrained auto-makers in the sixties. Americans were becoming more and more safety conscious as well. Warning labels were appearing on plastic dry cleaning bags and there was talk about making medicine bottles more difficult to open. In 1966 a little-known lawyer named Ralph Nader authored *Unsafe at Any Speed*, a book mostly about the 1963 Corvair, but also covering other automobiles. The book focused on faulty and unsafe design features of recent automobiles and on the industry's resistance to fixing them. Nader's book launched an era where the public would consider it the responsibility of the government to protect them from faulty merchandise of any kind. Also in 1966, another new arm of the government, the Department of Transportation (DOT), was formed and its subsidiary, the National Highway Traffic Safety Association (NHTSA), was created for making rules to make car crashes more survivable.

Though it wasn't as high profile as air pollution, Congress had been kicking around the idea of auto safety regulations throughout the sixties and had helped to fund a number of studies. Grad students and researchers around the country had been given the entertaining job of crashing cars full of anthropomorphic dummies into barriers at highway speeds. While the results may not seem too surprising by current standards, these tests led to basic changes in the accepted schools of thought about what it takes to survive a crash. Up until formal testing was done, it was assumed that the best way to survive a high-speed crash was to be thrown clear of the vehicle. When crash testing began in the laboratory, however, it was found to be safer to stay inside the car and the focus was turned toward making the environment inside the car as safe as possible.

For a driver belted into his seat, the most dangerous part of an early (pre-1968) car was the steering column. In most cases, the steering column was a long tube that extended from the steering wheel to the steering gear box mounted somewhere near the front of the vehicle. In a crash that was sufficient to distort the front of the car, the steering box with its column would be displaced toward the rear, often impaling the driver in the chest. The solution was to build the steering shaft in several pieces designed to break away or collapse like a telescope in the event of a crash. This idea was accepted without much resistance by the car companies and General Motors announced that they would be fitting collapsible steering columns to their 1967 model cars voluntarily. Other makers quickly followed once the feature became mandatory.

Another fundamental change in design that was gaining popularity was the dual braking system. It was an improvement over previous brake systems in that a hydraulic leak anywhere in the system would cause a partial, but not a total failure. Because it had two separate hydraulic circuits, one circuit could fail and still leave the driver with some braking power. The dual circuit system required changes only to the master cylinder design and had already been adopted by several companies before it too became mandatory in 1968.

Many styling features of cars were destined to fall to the legislative axe. Some interior elements, such as control knobs and instrument panels, sported sharp edges and spiked centers that would rip the flesh of anyone unfortunate enough to have their bodies slammed into them. Those shapes would have to be rounded off, and protruding devices like door handles would have to be recessed into the surface where they were mounted.

Most of the recommendations that came across the table were practical and inexpensive, and since nobody could look good arguing against building a car in which a 30 MPH crash need not be fatal, the automakers swallowed many of these mandates quietly. But some of the recommended changes, protested industry officials, illustrated researchers' lack of knowledge of the car business. For instance, a proposed requirement that interior surfaces be painted with non-reflective colors seemed sensible enough, but Ford painted its pickup trucks inside and out at the same time prior to final assembly. So compliance with this one standard would have required a major change in production process costing about 15 million dollars.[3]

While they might have had some valid arguments against certain mandatory requirements, the auto industry in America shot themselves in the foot and ended up with the public image of a bumbling bad guy when news leaked out that General Motor's response to criticisms leveled by Ralph Nader was to have him followed. Shortly after the publication of Nader's Book, GM's General Counsel, working through a Washington lawyer, engaged a detective agency to investigate Nader in the hopes of finding some way to discredit him. Not being able to find anything useful, the agents allegedly resorted to harassment including surveillance, late night phone calls, and attempts to lure him into compromising situations with young women. An account of the investigation was published in the March 12, 1966, issue of *The New Republic* that was widely quoted in the press, and two senators requested a Justice Department inquiry into the affair. Having essentially been caught red-handed, GM President James Roche, testifying before a committee, had to admit that General Motors was responsible for launching the investigations, saying, "In the process of ordering a formal statement denying our involvement, I discovered to my dismay that we were indeed involved."[4]

Details of the harassment were never proven, and no charges were filed, but the affair left GM with even less credibility than before and their investigation, instead of besmirching Nader's reputation, only succeeded in boosting his image and launching his career as a consumer rights and safety advocate—a career that would see him make several attempts at an independent run for the presidency.

If the auto industry in America ever had a chance of putting up a good case against mandatory safety standards, it was gone after the Nader affair and Congress unanimously passed an auto safety bill in August of 1966. The bill required the Secretary of Commerce to issue safety standards for the automakers by January 31, 1967, to take effect no later than one year afterward. Among items on the list of expected regulations were tire load standards, dual braking systems, collapsible steering columns, anchorage for lap and shoulder belts, headrests, rear window defoggers, recessed controls and handles, stronger door latches and hinges, and rupture-resistant fuel tanks and fuel lines. Two months later, by yet another act of Congress, the Department of Transportation was created and took over the job of issuing and enforcing safety standards for upcoming car models. The newly formed DOT and NHTSA became the final authority on automobile safety. (Throughout this text, the terms DOT and NHTSA are used interchangeably because that's how they were used in the gray market shops, and simply because DOT rolls off the tongue more easily than NHTSA. But it was the NHTSA that made most of the rules and it was their office that processed the paperwork for automobile conversions.)

By 1970, Congress had thoroughly insinuated itself into the automobile industry. The two new agencies were now in place to manage safety and pollution regulation and new standards for each model year would be put in place by those agencies periodically, without the passage of additional legislation. Now that the legal mechanisms were in place, other interests, like the insurance industry, were able to weigh in and promote changes, such as the 5 MPH safety bumper required in 1974, which didn't save lives but was supposed to save insurance companies a great deal of money. In some cases, accusations were cast about that some parts suppliers had lobbied to have certain requirements laid down to guarantee their parts market. None of this was new to the world of government intervention in business, but people inside the automotive industry constantly argued that their field was too complicated for the government agencies to fully understand, and that Congress was likely to make laws based on bad advice. One automotive journalist, protesting Congress' lack of knowledge of their subject, remarked that if Congress were to learn that manufacturers were not putting flies in their flywheels, they would next year pass legislation dictating the number and quality of flies to be used henceforth.

Year after year the regulations became tougher and tighter. The book of laws governing automobiles was growing thicker and thicker and it was becoming more and more expensive to build a car to be sold in the American market. Emissions research was very expensive, and the devices and modifications that were required drove up the cost of the cars. Early safety regulations were not too cumbersome, but later requirements like bumper strength often required major changes to the body and frame design. In many cases the maker was required to crash test their cars to satisfy the DOT. This was a minor expense for a company that built hundreds of thousands of cars, but a burden for a company that sold only a few hand-built cars per year. The major importers had to play by the rules, the American makers tried diligently to change the rules, and many of the minor importers simply pulled out of the United States altogether.

2

Small Importers and Their Reactions

Traveling in any major American city in 1970, you might have seen car dealerships for brands that would be well forgotten by 1990. The U.S. marketplace had seen hundreds of car manufacturers come and go through the decades and though the major domestic makers had been whittled down to the big three (GM, Ford and Chrysler) and their brands, numerous import brands had flowed into the market during the sixties to satisfy car buyers looking for something different. Of course Volkswagen from West Germany made their presence well known early and, inspired by their success, other makers of small, inexpensive cars began to ramp up their plans to sell cars in the American market. Import car dealerships popped up all over the place during the 1960s. They were usually piggybacked onto an existing American car dealership as an alternative for buyers, some backed by the major American counterparts. Chrysler was involved with Simca of France. AMC was in bed with Renault, also of France. General Motors was bringing in German Opels and selling them at their Buick dealers, and Ford was producing cars in England and dabbled with importing some of the "sportier" models. Mercedes was involved with Studebaker for a time, their relationship ending with the failure of the latter. But as the market for imports grew, some of the major makers, particularly those from Japan, began to show up in stand-alone dealerships.

While the new series of regulations handed down from Washington posed a problem to major car companies, they were devastating for the smaller players. With the DOT spelling out requirements for crashworthiness, many of the tests that were required for verifying compliance with the new regulations resulted in the complete destruction of a completed car, often multiple examples. A company that produced cars numbering in the hundreds of thousands could spread out the expense of destroying a few copies well enough to make it bearable, but a small sports car company that only produced a few cars each year could hardly afford to sacrifice completed examples on the altar of the newly created National Highway Traffic Safety Administration. For this reason, Congress amended the safety act, installing a possible exemption for producers of less than 500 cars a year. The amendment made it possible for ultra-small companies like Avanti Motors, who built hand-made Studebaker Avantis after the larger company's demise, to continue to sell their cars in the United States. But there were plenty of other companies that came in just above the 500 car per year mark that still found the new regulations burdensome.

To make things even harder, nobody really knew when the rules were going to change. The NHTSA had the power to write the rules and some of their proposals bordered on the absurd. In December of 1970 they proposed a law requiring that the maximum speed of any new car be limited to 95 MPH, and furthermore that the horn and four-way flashers be automatically activated when the speed of the car exceeded 85 MPH. Fortunately the rulemaking process involved their proposing new legislation and then putting out there for consideration and comment by all interested parties before becoming law, and that one didn't make it to the code.[1] But with ideas like that coming out of Washington on a regular basis, and knowing the unpredictable nature of the lawmakers, carmakers were justifiably apprehensive about what was likely to come next and how it might affect their place in the market.

The British had been well involved in America for decades, with large luxury sedans and GT cars like the big Jaguars and with pint-sized roadsters like Austin-Healey, MG and Triumph. While their sales may have only been a small bump on the graph in the U.S., those sales represented a significant portion of British motor production. With annual production numbers in the tens of thousands, they had never been major car producers by world standards and many of their models rolled off the assembly lines painfully slowly. But the American appetite for their courtly sedans and small open roadsters was strong enough, and for years they sold well enough to justify the investment necessary to stay in the U.S. market.

All the British automakers had been running on the financial ragged edge for most of the 1960s. Who or what may have been responsible would depend on who was describing the problem. Some of the often-cited issues were bad market research, erratic suppliers, an apathetic work force or poor management and all of these played a role in the eventual fall of the English automakers. International sales continued to fall into the 1970s and their production costs continued to rise until they survived only by consolidating their markets and buying each other. Austin, which was already part of BMC (British Motor Corporation), purchased MG. BMC joined with Jaguar Cars to form British Motor Holdings in 1966. British Motor Holdings became British Leyland Motor Corporation (BLMC) in 1968, of which

2. Small Importers and Their Reactions

Triumph was a part. By 1975, when during yet another crisis they sought and won British government subsidy, most of the competing brands in England were all part of the same company which became known as British Leyland.

One of the British Leyland brands, MG had been successfully selling open roadsters to the Americans for 20 years. They had made a couple of attempts at selling small front-wheel-drive economy cars, but they were largely unsuccessful, scattering the American market with just a few thousand examples. But MG had been fairly successful (by British standards) selling Americans their B model in about the same design for a decade before they were compelled to upgrade it to the new safety and emission standards taking effect in the '70s.

In its original trim the MGB had been a neat and quick little dual-carburetor, 100 HP roadster weighing slightly over 2000 lbs. Starting in 1971, as the small company attempted to come into line with the new American emission regulations, the compression ratio was lowered from 8.8 to 8.0:1 and the camshaft timing and fuel mixture were dialed back, making the car less and less powerful with each passing year. To make matters worse, safety regulations required adding more weight to the car in the form of bumper and door reinforcement, and interior padding so as the power decreased, there was more and more weight for the engine to move. By 1980 the "B" choked down to a single carburetor and equipped with the entire menu of add on emission control devices developed by Detroit, auxiliary air injection, exhaust gas recirculation (EGR), catalyst, and even an electric heater element for the intake manifold. In that trim it only had 62 HP to move its now 2,400-pound bulk.

The same occurred with the MG Midget, which was a re-badged Austin-Healey Sprite. Like the B, the Midget was a design that was already outdated by 1970 and, with its modified tractor engine, did not lend itself well to the changes that the new rules required. In 1972 the 1275 cc engine made 65 HP; 1973 and '74 saw the car gain an air pump system, but engineers were not able to bring that engine into compliance with 1975 U.S. specifications, so a 1500 cc engine was borrowed from the Triumph Spitfire to make the car marketable in America. Even though the engine was larger, in U.S. trim it still only produced 65 HP.

At the behest of the American insurance companies, new standards were issued for 1974 dictating bumper height and impact resistance. This also was a big challenge for MG because the lightweight unit body did not hold up well in crash testing. The original nose was minimalist, trimmed in chrome and quite attractive, but it did little to protect the car from someone parallel parking by the Braille system. The engineers couldn't find much to work with in the existing structures of the cars, so the nose and tail of both the B and Midget were fitted with ungainly looking black rubber covered battering rams and the suspension was raised by 1½ inch to meet the standard height specs.

By 1975, with not enough power to compete with a Volkswagen, and poor handling due to the heavy weights on either end *and* the raised suspension, MG's only models had little or none of the qualities that had made them popular in the past. The time would have been ripe for a new model car that had many of the necessary changes designed in instead of added on, but British Leyland didn't have the funds to design and develop a new MG. So as sales dropped off, the management decided to cut MG loose in hopes of saving the other brands. In September of 1979 they announced the end of the MG brand.

Triumph's story was not much different from that of its stepsister. They had been selling their cars in America for decades. Offering a larger range of models than MG, they enjoyed a comfortable little niche market with cars like the TR4, TR 250 and later the spitfire, GT6 and TR6. Like MG, Triumph's American sales were not large by U.S. standards, but they were important to the company's survival.

Triumph's largest market was in California so to continue to sell their cars there, they had also to meet the new California emission standards which were a few years ahead of the rest of the U.S. With little in the budget for research and development, like MG they adapted the cars that they already had by applying the same technology that they saw the major American manufacturers using. Unfortunately, these technologies robbed an engine of a large part of its efficiency, a fault which could be tolerated on a large displacement V8 or even on a six but left little to work with on a four-cylinder engine of two liters or less.

Auxiliary air pumps began to appear in 1968 and as standards became tighter, cars formerly equipped with SU carburetors were re-fitted with their evil cousins, Zenith-Stromberg carburetors, for more control over the fuel mixture. The Spitfire model went from twin carbs to a single. Bumpers were also modified to American specs, but far more gracefully than had been the case with MG.

British Leyland had higher hopes for the future of Triumph than for MG, so they authorized construction of an entirely new car to meet the changing market. The TR7 appeared in the U.S. in 1975. Looking nothing like anything Triumph had done before, it had a wedge-shaped styling theme that was going to be popular among car makers for about a decade. Initially the TR7 abandoned the open roadster motif and had a well-supported roof structure because makers were anticipating that Washington would soon be issuing roll-over standards. With impact safety bumpers and other crash protection features already incorporated into the body design and a recently developed overhead camshaft two-liter four-cylinder, Triumph hoped the new car would do well in the highly regulated markets of the future; and it might have, but for relentless labor problems that led to quality issues in the new car. The TR7 and its V8 powered cousin, the TR8, earned a reputation for very poor reliability early on and never became the success in the U.S. that British Leyland had been counting on.

By 1980 the only other car Triumph had in the U.S. market was the Spitfire, which like the MG had lost considerable power and gained weight as a result of its federalization. Sales had dropped off drastically and Leyland lost hopes of saving the brand. The last Triumph rolled off of the line in late 1981.

Whether Triumph or MG would have been able to survive had it not been for the U.S. government regulation of the automobile market is open to speculation. Both companies were regularly besieged with labor problems during the '70s and at times they were lucky to get a car off of the line at all. There had in fact been a joke going around the management that their line workers "didn't punch a clock, they signed the guest register." In the face of that and other financial problems, the necessary time and funding for properly developing and building a car for the new market just weren't there so while it may have been doubtful that they would have survived anyway, the burden of the new U.S. legislation which severely affected their sales in a vital market could easily have been the final nail in the coffin.

Jaguar had always depended largely on U.S. sales as well and had to take steps to build compliant cars, but because their models were large sedans and sports cars with big six and later, twelve-cylinder engines, their performance, while it suffered in U.S. trim, was still comparable to their large American counterparts. The technology used to meet the tailpipe specifications was largely borrowed from the American car companies with the exception of the Zenith-Stromberg side-draft carburetor. These carburetors, built specifically for emission control applications, were universally replacing the ubiquitous SU carburetors formally found on most British powerplants almost invariably resulting in a 10 percent or more decrease in power output. But the Jaguars sixes held up fairly well under the modifications, largely because they had early on adopted a very efficient hemispherical combustion chamber shape that promoted complete combustion under most conditions. Because their engines didn't produce as much of the offending gasses to begin with, they didn't require as much tampering after the fact to clean them up as their American competition.

Jaguar adapted fairly well to the American regulations continuing to build the XJ6 sedan and E type roadster that they had been building for a decade. The body styles lent themselves far better to the addition of the required impact absorbing bumpers and while they were arguably less attractive in U.S. trim, they still managed to sell enough cars to maintain interest. In 1976 they replaced the E-type with the XJS, a two seat hard top GT style car built with the American market in mind. While roll-over safety requirements had not yet been handed down from Washington, Jaguar, like most manufacturers, expected them and were phasing out their convertible models. The XJS was powered by the same V12 engine that had been used in the XJ12 sedans and in some of the E-types. At 244 HP, any power loss associated with emission devices was hardly noticeable from the driver's seat and the car performed well in U.S. trim.

Jaguar and other manufacturers began to see the advantage of fuel injection over carburetors in the early seventies. A carburetor, no matter how complicated, was still little more than a fuel nozzle placed in the airstream of the intake from which fuel was drawn and hopefully, atomized. Any number of conditions, temperature, barometric pressure, engine load or speed could affect the efficiency of that operation and engineers had been forced to add layers and layers of devices to compensate for those changes. Recent improvements in microcomputer technology were making electronically controlled fuel injection feasible and many of the import car makers were discovering they could control engines far more precisely with the new systems under development by automotive electronics companies like Bosch. The additional layer of control not only improved performance and fuel economy but provided a noticeable edge in controlling emissions. Bosch injection systems replaced the Zenith carburetors on the Jaguar twelve-cylinder engines in 1975 and the six-cylinder engines in 1979 giving the maker a technological advantage over the American luxury car makers.

Thus equipped, Jaguar was able to continue to sell their cars in the U.S. market. Like the other Leyland companies, they continued to have labor and quality issues, but were able to avoid the fate of MG and Triumph.

The French had been in the U.S. market in small numbers since after World War II. But didn't seem to rely on U.S. sales to keep them afloat. Citroën in particular, while widely popular in Europe and in French colonial territory, was never much more than a curiosity in the United States having a reputation as strange looking car driven by quirky college professors and their ilk.

Citroën's first encounter with American regulations occurred in 1967 with the issuance of crash survivability standards. Since the end of World War II, they had been producing an ultra-light, ultra-cheap car powered by a two-cylinder air cooled engine. The car was wildly popular in post-war Europe and sold some copies in the U.S. though it never gained more than a cult following here. The 2CV as it was called was little more than a four-door go-cart and stood no chance of surviving the required crash testing now required by the U.S. government, so Citroën simply stopped offering the 2CV in the United States.

Citroën next ran afoul of U.S. regulation when they decided to upgrade the type of hydraulic fluid they used in their "D" models' integrated brake-suspension system. Among the new highway safety laws was a rule aimed at standardizing brake hydraulic fluid in cars in to prevent damage to braking systems by use of the wrong type of fluid. The D Models (ID 19 and DS 21) had a very sophisticated hydraulic system that integrated the brake, suspension, power steering, and in some cars shift control systems. Citroën had been using conventional brake fluid in their cars and because conventional fluid is hygroscopic (moisture-absorbing) in nature they had been experiencing problems with corrosion in their hydraulic systems as a result. They found that they could make the hydraulic systems much more reliable by changing the system over to a different fluid. While the mineral oil-based fluid that they chose was superior to conventional brake fluid in many ways, it was not compatible with the seals of a brake fluid system nor could the seals in a mineral oil system tolerate the presence of brake fluid. In the words of the Citroën owner's manual, "introduction of the incorrect fluid into the reservoir will destroy the vehicle hydraulic system quickly and completely."

Citroën made the change in their hydraulic fluid for the 1967 model year, but while the new fluid made the cars more reliable, it did not meet the standards as spelled out by the DOT, so they were not able to import cars so equipped into the United States right away. So for the model year of 1967 they produced "brake fluid" cars for the U.S. and "green fluid" cars for the rest of the world while they waited on the paperwork necessary to grant them an exemption to the rules. The exemption was granted in 1968 and from that point forward, Citroën made only the "green fluid" cars.

Citroën continued to import their "D" models into the 1970s, when they again found themselves at odds with the legislators. The new bumper regulation that took effect beginning in 1974 not only established requirements for damage control, but it also dictated a "crash zone" from 16 to 20 inches above the ground. Other manufacturers dealt with this issue by attaching large pieces of hardware to cover the required area or even by changing the suspension height as with MG, but the Citroëns' suspension height was not fixed because of the hydraulic suspension system. In fact, the ride height was controllable from the driver's seat. But the most serious issue was that the suspension would gradually leak down when the car was shut off. How long it took to leak down depended on the condition of the car. If the hydraulics were in good shape, it could stay up for eight hours or more. But when the suspension was flat, the bumpers were only about a foot off the ground, leaving parked cars vulnerable to serious damage from the kind of low-speed bumps encountered in parallel parking. This problem affected their new GT car, the SM, as well as all the D models as they were also equipped with their trademark suspension system.

So, Citroën pulled out of the U.S. at the end of the 1973 model year. Their sales in America had never amounted to much to begin with, and bringing the bumper height into compliance would have involved fundamental changes to their cars. Building a completely different car just for the U.S. market didn't make sense anymore.

Ironically, Citroën was one car maker who had focused on safety long before it became fashionable in the U.S. Their integrated suspension and braking system made the car much more maneuverable in extreme conditions and prevented the kind of weight transfer that could easily lead to rear wheel lockup under hard braking. They harped on this feature strongly in their advertising, considering safety to be an important selling point. One of their ads showed a car having a front tire blow-out while the car was travelling between two tractor-trailers at sixty miles per hour. The driver easily brought the car to a safe, controlled stop. Additionally, the car's interior was designed to minimize injury in the event of a crash, particularly the steering wheel which had a single bent center spoke that prevented the impaling of the driver on the steering shaft in the event of a frontal impact. Seat belts were installed long before they were a gleam in the eye of the DOT and the interior handles and controls were not of the type that can cause additional injury to a person who is flung about the interior of the car. Citroën was unwilling to modify the car to meet the low-speed crash standards because they said making the changes would actually make the cars *less* safe in the event of a high-speed crash. The front of their cars contained a certain amount of "dead space" that was designated as a crush zone to absorb the energy of a crash and strengthening that space would defeat the purpose. In short, the big Citroëns were everything that the safety people wanted, just not the way that they wanted it.

Renault was another French company that was familiar to Americans until the eighties. They had been a major automaker in Europe for decades and had always been active in racing, but their early forays into the American market with small rear-engined cars like the Dauphine were mostly disastrous. But they continued to hang on to a small niche of the market selling their cars to people who wanted something different just because it was different. Even the company admitted that their early cars were poorly suited to Americans by promoting the 1968 R 10 as "The Renault for people who swore they would never buy another one."[2] Their cars of the sixties and seventies were mainly small, rear engine cars, later turning to front wheel drive long before it became popular in America, but probably their most interesting entry into the American market was the R5.

Commonly marketed as the Le Car, the R5 was introduced to the

2. Small Importers and Their Reactions

Renault R5 Turbo. Like the Countach, the R5 was a poster child of the automotive gray market. The car was not available for sale in the U.S. except through gray market dealers and was barely available at all because of very low production numbers. Renault never meant for it to be a production car and only made enough "street" models to meet homologation requirements of international racing bodies (author's photograph).

U.S. in 1976 as a very basic economy car already wildly popular in Europe. Though it only made 58 horsepower, thanks to an event called the Le Car Challenge it came to be perversely regarded as a performance sedan. The Le Car Challenge was a showroom-stock racing series accessible to anyone who could afford a $3,500 R5. Safety modifications, such as a full roll cage, were required, but no performance modifications were allowed, so the competition became one of guts and skill rather than of money and technology. The races were surprisingly exciting to watch, as the cars all had roughly the same performance characteristics. Top speed was about 87 MPH and it took a long time to get there, so once top speed was attained, slowing down for turns was not considered an option. Drivers could only change position by nudging other drivers off the line. Cars often went tumbling off the track like soccer balls, with the drivers emerging from the inverted vehicles fifty yards or more from the track and shaking their fist at the competition. The R5 challenge went a long way toward promoting Renault in this country.

Out of this madness sprang the R5 turbo. This was a rally car built around the R5 shell but equipped with a 1400 cc turbocharged engine mounted where the back seat would normally be. Renault built 3576 examples of the R5, enough to homologate it for racing, but because of American safety and emissions rules they never intended it to be sold in the U.S. Thanks to its almost legendary performance and its unavailability in America, examples of the R5 turbo became highly coveted among sports car enthusiasts and as such it, was destined to become one of several gray-market poster children.

But it was the Italian cars that really inspired the independent importers. Ferrari, Maserati and Lamborghini were relatively small sports car companies whose road-going car production was sometimes too high to qualify for exemption, and too low to justify the necessary development work to comply with U.S. laws. Ferrari started as a builder of race cars and went into production of road cars to support the racing endeavors. Their U.S. sales were small, funneled through only two dealers until Fiat purchased 50 percent of the company in 1969. At first Fiat didn't meddle in Ferrari, but the purchase meant they would have funds for future development and factory improvements, meaning Ferrari could begin to produce cars in greater numbers. The people at Fiat saw some potential in the U.S. sports-car market and wanted Ferrari to build a "world market" car that would qualify for sale in the U.S. and other countries that might install regulations of their own in the future. That car was the 308.

The 308 was a departure from earlier Ferrari practice in that it was powered by a V8 rather than a 12 and had the engine mounted transversely behind the passenger compartment and in front of the axle. The mid-engined configuration was lifted from racing experience and was becoming popular among wealthy sports-car enthusiasts because of the improved handling characteristics it afforded. The chassis had the necessary strengthening built in for crash resistance so that cars built for the U.S. needed only to have stronger bumpers with shock-absorbing equipment attached in place of the lighter European version. Ferrari originally imported the 308 Mondial, which was a four-seat interpretation of the car, but the following year they began marketing the 308GTB, a two-seat targa top version.

Ferrari marketed a handful of front-engined V12 cars in the states as the seventies began, but as the Federal regulations became tighter and tighter, they simply let the non-complying models drop out until 1975 when the only car left for sale in America was the 308.

Lamborghini had been running on the financial ragged edge since their beginnings and was severely challenged by the new regulatory environment. Wanting to sell cars in the U.S., they also applied for a stay postponing the 1975 emission standards to 1976 and it was granted, but their forays into the United States were still sporadic depending on whether they had enough financial backing to be able to import cars at all. They had been teasing car enthusiasts with a concept car called the Countach for three years, but by the time it went into production in 1974 only a handful were sold in the U.S. through official channels. For the first four years of production (1974–1978), only about 150 Countach models were built and, since Lamborghini had not certified the car for the U.S. and had been running on temporary exemptions, by 1977 no factory U.S. versions were available.

So by 1976 the market was well primed. Wealthy Americans had been enjoying the most exciting cars that Europe had to offer for over a decade and one by one the government was taking them off the shelf, essentially saying that they were too dirty and dangerous to allow their citizens to own them. Outraged and frustrated, would-be buyers of exotic machinery began to look around for an alternative. Once it became clear that there was money to be made by finding a way to get these cars onto the market, there were plenty of enterprising souls willing to take on the challenge.

3

The First Compliance Shops

As safety and emission regulations became stiffer and stiffer with each passing year, and with the smaller companies dropping out of the U.S. market one by one, the selection of performance cars available to American buyers was thinning out badly. Sports car enthusiasts in America began to feel cheated. Europe had long been the source of the "other" performance cars—cars that appealed to drivers who were not excited by monstrous engines and tire-smoking torque and wanted lightweight, responsive speed. American cars were large, heavy, and powerful and their fans loved to make the tires smoke and feel the 'g's as the forward acceleration pressed them back into their seats. But when the time came to change course or slow it down, the excitement could quickly change to fear as they tried to bring the beast under control. The European sports cars that made inroads into the U.S. market during the 1950s and '60s gained a large following for their superior handling and braking if not their acceleration, even though it may not have been enough to sustain the handful of companies that made them. Those drivers looking to European importers for these alternative performance cars in the 1970s were having their choices narrowed down by what most considered an increasingly meddlesome government. This kind of thing was fairly unprecedented by any memorable act short of prohibition and car enthusiasts of means were not inclined to take it quietly. Mechanics were showing their contempt for emission controls by stripping off any extraneous parts that got in their way, and they were getting away with it. But actually importing a car that didn't comply with the new rules meant getting the car past customs.

Of course, sports like blockade running and getting one over on the man run deep in the American psyche, and that only added to what was already a severe temptation. And many car enthusiasts in the seventies loved to drink beer and fantasize about loading shipping containers with European sports cars and shipping them over labeled as furniture. But short of actually doing the deed and smuggling the cars across the borders (some of that was already happening) sports car lovers knew that it was going to be necessary to find some loopholes in the laws and exploit them.

3. The First Compliance Shops

By making Ferrari, Lamborghini, Lotus and other exotic cars unavailable in America, the government chiefly succeeded in making them more desirable. After all, part of the fun of owning an exotic sports car was in the bragging rights that came with it. If a Ferrari 400i and a Lamborghini Countach were unavailable through the normal legal channels, then the ownership of one went that much further to demonstrate well-connected wealth. Consequently, wealthy car lovers and ambitious dealers quickly set out to circumvent the laws as soon as they went into effect exploring any alternative means to obtain the car of their dreams.

Buying a car overseas, particularly in European countries, was not an uncommon practice in the early seventies and there were plenty of businesses designed to help a customer do just that. For tourists with the means, it was considered a fun part of a European vacation to fly into the city where delivery had been arranged, buy the car and drive it while on holiday, and bring it home when the trip was over. Agents to help customers choose, buy and arrange for overseas delivery had been in business long before Congress became involved with regulating automobiles. But to continue to do business, they were finding they would have to adapt to a plethora of new rules that were constantly in flux, changing with the minds of administrators at the EPA and the DOT. With the implementation of the Clean Air Act of 1972 and the National Highway Safety Act of 1966, the government declared the importation by individuals of automobiles that did not comply with the new regulations to be illegal, but after the original acts, they later installed provisions that made it possible for anyone with the means, the know-how and the tenacity to do so in a legal fashion. But in typical bureaucratic style, they set up a labyrinth of paperwork for potential importers to negotiate. Those automotive brokerage operations originally built around the international private market found their business taking a turn for the worse. Some of them gave out—the ones that survived learned to adapt.

Up until 1968, an American returning home with a car in tow had little more to deal with from U.S. Customs than they would with any other large piece of luggage. They simply stated the value of the car, paid the duty on it and moved on through. As of '68, however, things began to change. Upon returning to the States with a new or used car, the trip through customs could be easy or hard depending on the car. A broker or car-buying tourist who wanted to make the least trouble for himself would have chosen a car that was built for the U.S. market to begin with. By law, such cars had metallic labels attached in conspicuous locations, usually under the hood, by the manufacturers representing them as such. These cars sailed past customs with little more than a glance. The next best thing was a car that, while not certified for the U.S., was equivalent to a similar model that had been. Proving as much required little more than a letter from the factory stating that the car was in fact what the owner was representing it to be. Failing that, the importer could submit paperwork and photographs that established that the cars were identical in all the important areas. But whether by accident or design, some individuals were more adventurous in their automotive tastes and were determined to import cars not originally destined for the United States.

At first it wasn't that difficult, some car buyers even pulled it off without realizing what they had done. Of course, not everybody was acquainted with the changes in the laws at first, and if they showed up at customs with an unqualified car, the problem was theirs alone. In the major port cities, the officials were well versed in the new laws and armed with lists of cars and serial numbers that did not qualify. They rigorously defended the U.S. borders against dirty and unsafe cars. But in the early 1970s the borders with Mexico and Canada were still fairly porous and before the installation of advanced computer networks, it was practically impossible for customs to keep track of an automobile that had been driven across the border, so some of the less noticeable examples were still leaking through. Cars could be driven in from these countries sporting a foreign license and then quietly change hands in the States. Or a sneakier buyer might carry a U.S. plate across the border, attach it to a car in Canada or Mexico, then drive it back as if nothing were amiss. At that time, before the rise of international terrorism, it was possible to cross the Northern and Southern borders without even showing your registration.

Attempts to license cars brought in this way might have raised some eyebrows in major U.S. cities, but there were still plenty of backwoods towns where the local title and tag office shared space in the back of an auto parts store, and in such venues it was sometimes possible to register a car that may not have been on the bureaucrats' lists. There's one legendary case of a European count who purchased a Porsche 917 CAN-AM racer in 1971 and had it fitted with road-going lights and other equipment. He was unable to license it for street use in any country in Europe, but still managed to register the car in Alabama. His was a unique case in that he was a foreign national, but his story was well documented in the press and cited as an example of what wealth and influence could accomplish. Meanwhile other less noteworthy examples—like later British Minis, still available in Canada but not in the U.S.— streamed over the border attracting far less attention. I personally serviced a customer's brand new 1978 Mini while living in a small town in the mountains of Western North Carolina. He had no idea that the car was illegal in the U.S. and expressed surprise when the fact was explained to him. He reported that he bought the car while visiting Canada and simply drove across the border. After arriving home, he applied at the local agency for a title and license. The people at the agency could not find his car on their lists, but assumed it was an oversight and issued a title anyway.

Stories like that couldn't help but make their way to the automotive press and went a long way toward inspiring car enthusiasts to try to pull something off—and prompting officials to tighten up their game a bit. It may never have occurred to the sports car crowd that their declared enemies in officialdom were reading the same journals they were, so it perhaps came as a surprise when a letter from the director of the Office of Compliance of the National Highway Safety Bureau showed up in the pages of *Road & Track*, in response to a 1971 article telling the story of Jeff Johnson and his Lotus Super Seven.

Johnson had purchased the car through an agent in England and had it flown to Denver. Many of the auto importation procedures were still new and enforcement was relatively lax, so rather than being stopped at the point of entry, he was able to pay the necessary taxes and take the car home. He registered the car in Denver and later received a form from U.S. Customs. The form listed several options for the owner to declare either that the car was in compliance with import regulations or why it was not and what would be done about it. Rather than choosing one of the available options, Johnson crossed through the stated options and wrote in "Not imported for re-sale" and sent the form back.[1] Certainly, this was not the end of the story though the later details with respect to Mr. Johnson and his Lotus were not published. Shortly after publishing the article, a letter arrived at the offices of *Road & Track* from Francis Armstrong, who identified himself as the director of the "Office of Compliance." Armstrong informed readers they should not be encouraged by Mr. Johnson's example. He went on to say,

> Alteration of the import form is not permitted, nor is importation *Not for Resale* an allowable exemption under the joint Department of Transportation-Bureau of Customs importation regulations. Importation of a non-complying motor vehicle is a violation of the National Traffic and Motor Vehicle safety Act of 1966 rendering the importer liable to a civil penalty of up to $1000. Foreign diplomatic or military personnel may temporarily import non-complying vehicles for the duration of their assignment after filing a declaration that the importation is for purposes other than re-sale, but this exception is not available for American Citizens resident in the United States.[2]

Road & Track published the letter in the subsequent issue without additional comment.

While Armstrong's letter and the rules stated therein may have been discouraging for some enthusiasts, for many others it still represented a challenge and the ultimate reward, owning and driving a car that practically no one else could have, was too much to resist. Jervis Webb was one such individual.

Webb was a long-time Morgan enthusiast and was frustrated that Morgan, an ultra-low volume British sports car maker of hand-built cars, had chosen to abandon the United States market in the face of all their new laws for carmakers. Morgan had been building sports cars since 1913, and by the 1970s, had done little towards modernizing their cars or their production methods. Their frames were simple channel steel ladder-type structures, much like the cars of the 1930s, and the bodies were largely made of sheet steel panels bolted or riveted to plywood forms. Most of the driveline components were off-the-shelf parts built by other manufacturers, often Ford. They were old-world cars that gave not even a nod to developments in the automobile industry over the last fifty years—and that was their charm. They had imported a few cars during the early seventies, but like many manufacturers they could not be bothered to build a special model to meet the U.S. standards as they stood in 1975. Webb wanted a new 1975 Morgan and he reckoned that he was possessed of enough engineering know-how, funds and determination that he could successfully take on the project of importing one himself.

Before purchasing a car, he contacted the NHTSA and they informed him that as long as he saw to it the car had all the required bells and whistles it could be imported into the States. Those bells and whistles ran from such trivial items as a label on the dashboard explaining the shift pattern, to items requiring major modifications to the car, like impact-absorbing bumpers and a collapsible steering column. The NHTSA verified for Webb that he could satisfy their requirements by replacing various non-compliant parts with pieces of other cars certified for the U.S. by their respective manufacturers. This meant, for example, that a collapsible steering column appropriate for a 1975 MG certified for U.S. import, installed on his Morgan in place of the original equipment, would render the Morgan compliant with the steering column requirement. Likewise, bumper systems with their appropriate battering rams and shock absorber mounts taken from a compliant vehicle and properly mounted to the Morgan's chassis would satisfy the low-speed impact requirement without a physical crash test being necessary.

The EPA was not nearly as helpful and his first contact with them found their representative saying that the car could not be made to comply because it was not a model that had ever been certified for the U.S. by a manufacturer. But Webb was persistent and engaged a lawyer to research the statutes and obtain a letter from the agency that verified that at that time it was in fact legal for individuals to modify and test a car that had not been certified by a maker. With these assurances in hand, he ordered a new 1975 Morgan 4/4.

Morgan had the tradition of offering their cars with a variety of powerplant options, and Webb chose the 1.6-liter Ford Kent engine that Ford

3. The First Compliance Shops 33

had used in earlier U.S. Pintos and Capris, thinking he should be able to install the equipment used on a 1975 Pinto 2.3 engine to bring his car easily into line. This meant installing an auxiliary air pump and the necessary plumbing to get the air into the exhaust headers and finding an appropriate place for the catalytic converter on an extraordinarily low-slung car (it ended up under the left front fender). Various evaporative emissions pieces were also lifted from American models to complete the task. To make a long story short, with the proven equipment in place, Webb's car passed its first test at Olson Laboratories, an independent facility approved by the EPA to perform the federal test procedure (FTP).

So, following completion of the mountain of paperwork involved, the Morgan became a legal resident of the United States. That having been done, the owner estimated his investment at $2500 plus 400 man-hours of labor. If one were to assign a $12/hour figure to the labor, which was an appropriate charge in an automotive garage in 1975, total investment would be as much as $7300. Considering the car cost $6200 new, Webb's reward was purely personal rather than financial. Making it easy to resist the temptation to make a business of importing non-compliant cars[3]

Webb's Morgan was actually a best-case scenario. There were easily as many unsuccessful attempts to import non-compliant cars as there were successes. Even for car buyers who wanted only to bring in an ordinary passenger car that needed minimal modification, simply completing the necessary paperwork proved too much for the uninitiated, so agencies, most of whom were already in the business of helping customers find and import cars from overseas, began offering to navigate the process for a fee. For a price that depended on the amount of work that needed to be done, the owner would be relieved of the burden of the paperwork and decisions about contracting modifications and could await delivery of their car in a U.S. street-legal form. It wasn't a common practice in the seventies and there were few shops that could be contracted to do the modifications, except where the price of the car was high enough that the cost of modifications seemed comparatively small.

Of course, when there are large amounts of money at stake, there are always shady operators looking for a chance to pocket their share, and the gray market business started attracting that type early on. Would-be buyers were only slightly acquainted with the rules, and knowing that they were already running in the margins of the law by trying to acquire a car that was officially proscribed by the U.S. government may have made them less cautious than they might have been. *Car and Driver* magazine published just such an example in 1978. The story told of a car enthusiast who preferred anonymity who purchased a Maserati Ghibli from a well-known exotic car dealership in the Northeast. Maserati's Ghibli was a high-performance

Italian sports car equipped with a powerful but fragile four-camshaft, five-liter V8 engine. Not long after bringing it home the car became troublesome. The engine overheated, the transmission slipped and various devices stopped working. The buyer had thought the car was under warranty but found no one that would honor it. He had repairs done but had to pay for them himself. Within a year the car the car was scrapped. It had caught fire on three separate occasions, lighting up at the turn of the key. The first two fires were minor, but the third pretty much wiped the car out, eventually resulting in a total loss. Having been under the impression that the car was new, he became suspicious about its origin. When he began studying the car more carefully, he realized that the serial numbers on the engine and chassis didn't correspond to his documentation. He contacted the DOT and they inspected the car to find that it was and never had been in compliance with DOT laws, which brought in Customs and they stated that there was no record of the car ever having crossed the border.

It was not a unique case, at the time Customs had some 30 other cases under investigation in California alone.[4] During the 1970s and '80s it could be argued that in spite of the gray market rules, it was easier to dispose of a stolen car by shipping it to the United States than it was to try and launder it in its native country. European authorities had been struggling with car theft for decades and had tons of bureaucratic protections that made it extraordinarily difficult to pass off a car without the proper papers. With the emerging market for exotics in the U.S., and a number of players that didn't mind working around the rules, shipping a stolen car to the States and titling it through the bonding and conversion process became a common method for laundering ill-gotten wheels.

Due Process

For a car owner who wanted to negotiate the process and bring a car in legally, Customs and their adopted siblings, the EPA and DOT, had developed the procedure. When a car came into the port of entry, the owner or agent first had to fill out a pair of customs forms indicating in which of nine categories a car fell. Category 1 specified that the car was manufactured on a date before January 1, 1968, when there were no applicable standards in effect. Customs officials were supposed to be equipped with lists of serial numbers of various manufacturers to help them determine if the car was in fact the age the importer claimed it to be. Of course, numbers can be altered and some no doubt were, but understandably there aren't any official records depicting how many times that dodge was employed.

Category 2 stated that the car was in compliance with all the applicable regulations in effect at the time of manufacture. Most manufacturers who sold cars in the U.S. could offer U.S. compliant cars at any venue including any in the country of origin and a buyer interested only in convenience would choose one of these cars. A U.S. compliant car could be easily identified by buyers and customs officials by the label affixed at the factory designating it as such and customs officials were also equipped with lists of serial numbers for cars that had been approved for U.S. markets to help them spot a car that had a false label attached.

The easy part ended there. Category 3 stated that the car in question was not in compliance with the laws but would be modified to bring it into compliance. The importer had 90 days to bring the car into line and had to submit paperwork explicitly describing the modifications done and identifying the contractor who performed the work. Category 3 was where the compliance shops would find their market.

The other six categories were exceptions to the rules. Option 4 said cars could be brought in if they were intended solely for export. Option 5 was for non-residents of the U.S., who could import cars for personal use and drive them for up to one year, provided they didn't re-sell them. Option 6 said that diplomatic personnel and members of armed forces of foreign countries could also bring in their own cars provided they would not be re-sold. Option 7 included race cars, show cars, test and experimental cars. Experimental cars could be "tested" on public roads for up to a year. Eight was for vehicles never intended for highway use and Option 9 was an exception for "incomplete" vehicles. Option 9 was tested with some regularity by persons trying to import cars by dismantling them and re-assembling them on this side of customs. But the EPA regulations also covered motor vehicle engines, so to import a car piece by piece required dismantling the car far too much to be practical in most cases.

That's not to say it didn't happen. The author encountered one case of a Citroën 2CV that had been completely dismantled and shipped into the country in crates labeled as French champagne. That particular case was successful but just as many were not. However, in most cases it was far too labor intensive to be profitable so it didn't become a big part of the importers' business.

Once the appropriate boxes were checked, the car still could not be released by customs until the owner put up a bond at least equal to the value of the car. Depending on the port, that figure could go up considerably. Naturally, that commitment alone could be prohibitive, particularly with the more exotic examples where the value of the car was similar to the value of a home. Insurance companies might be engaged for this if the owner could offer collateral of some kind, but either way, just putting up bond for the car was expensive enough to keep those short of ready cash out of the game for a while. The bond would later be released when customs officials received letters from the DOT and the EPA confirming that they were satisfied that the car was now in compliance with rules. As the importation of gray market cars became more and more popular, bonding companies emerged to fill the market need and a car owner or importer need only forfeit a percentage of the cars value to have a bond posted.

After the car was "bonded in" and released to the owner or agent, it was their responsibility to perform or contract the necessary modifications to bring the car into compliance with the laws applicable at the time the car was built, or if some modifications weren't necessary, they had to prove that those particular parts were in compliance. In the early days of the 1970s, satisfying the requirements of box three might be little more than a case of filling out the right forms or making minor changes such as adding seat belt mounts and installing U.S.–style sealed–beam headlights. If there was a similar model car sold in the states by the manufacturer, the cars were often the same in many respects and where differences did exist it was sometimes possible to borrow parts from the U.S. model. But with each passing year, more and more pages were added to the rules and the job of converting a car to drive in the U.S. was becoming more difficult and expensive. The years of 1973 and '74 brought the low-speed impact crash resistance specifications that required a car be able to endure a 5 MPH frontal impact and a 2½ MPH rear bump without damage. (It started with 10 and 5 MPH but the DOT backed off on that shortly after the rule was implemented.) And side impact rules went into effect indicating a maximum amount of intrusion when the door was hit from the side which required reinforcement of the door structure. In 1974 cars built specifically for the U.S. market took on a carnival bumper-car kind of look as engineers experimented with ways to meet the standards. The ungainly appearance of the federal model cars only added to the desirability of the European models with their comparatively sleek nose and tail treatments.

The bumper and side protection regulations were of course those that everyone remembers, but there was a plethora of other rules, each of which had to be dealt with. There was a requirement that the glass in the car be of a certain type and sport a label to prove it. Dashboard ideograms were regulated and various warning lights and buzzers had to be installed. The DOT was very specific about type, size, shape, color and location of every light on the outside of the car. Reflective materials couldn't be used on any part of the interior of the car in the driver's field of view. The list went on and on.

Satisfying the DOT of course was only half the battle. With the implementation of the 1975 specifications, bringing a car into line with EPA regulations was considered the most difficult and expensive part of the importation

3. The First Compliance Shops 37

process. If the car was not one already certified by a manufacturer, after modification it would have to be tested by an EPA approved laboratory to demonstrate compliance. Testing alone cost in the neighborhood of $1,000 whether the car passed or not. Even the major manufacturers considered the 1975 regulations to be too difficult and expensive to pass, so an importer who agreed to do the deed knew he might have a difficult job ahead.

When the agent or private owner cleared the first hurdles thrown up by Customs, if they weren't going to do the work themselves like Mr. Webb did with his Morgan, they had to find someone to do the actual modifications. In many cases individuals contacted mechanics who found the work an interesting departure from a steady diet of maintenance and repairs though they often regretted the commitment when they realized the complexity of some parts of the job. Often contractors would find themselves spending hours on the telephone with representatives of the various government agencies trying to get clarification of the often-nebulous requirements set up in the forms. Reacting to the increasing number of applications, and the amount of time the office spent discussing procedures with one-time importers, the DOT published a pamphlet containing necessary instructions for filling out the appropriate forms and for putting together the documentation verifying the work that was done.

Crash compliance could be a huge issue. In most cases somebody would have to crash a nearly complete car into a wall at the Transportation Research Center or some other facility to enable the NHTSA to decide whether the dummies inside were killed too badly. In many cases it only took one or two crashes to do the job, then everyone else with a similar model could use the data, but nobody really wanted to be the first to sacrifice a perfectly good car on the altar of highway safety. Fortunately for the independent importers, if they could prove that their car was similar or identical in the critical areas to a model that had already been tested and approved, it would be accepted. Photographs, engineering drawings, or a statement from the manufacturer were usually accepted as such proof. Once an example had been crashed by somebody (usually the manufacturer) and the data from the crash was submitted to the DOT, that data was available to everyone through the Freedom of Information Act, through which any government paperwork that was not classified became available to anyone for the asking. It's easy to imagine how well that went over with the manufacturers when the data that they acquired by crashing their own cars and then used on their applications for DOT approval became available for anyone. Nevertheless, it was there for the asking and gave the independent operators a good starting point for planning their modifications.

Any modification performed had to be documented by a photograph showing the parts installed on the car and accompanied by a plaque indicating the serial number of the car. A complete application packet to the DOT might contain 50 photographs of various components such as seat belt anchorages, labels on window glass, dashboard markings etc. Additionally, if the car in question could not be fitted with bumpers and door side reinforcements from an approved car, then the packet also had to include an engineer's report showing that the modifications done would be able to endure the DOT's low speed impact requirements. In a rare concession to the importers, the DOT agreed to accept the engineer's report as proof of compliance rather than submitting each car to an impact test. Likewise, the packet of documents submitted to the EPA contained photographs of equipment installed in addition to documents showing lab test results.

The statutes that spelled out the details in an application to the DOT and EPA for approval pointed out that both agencies reserved the option of inspecting the car in question. Indeed, according to the fine print, an owner of gray market import could conceivably be visited by government representatives at any time and asked to submit their car for inspection or testing. At first, during the second half of the 1970s, the number of independently imported automobiles was small—less than a 1500 per year—and the occasional spot inspection was not unheard of. In fact, it could seem that U.S. Customs would go well out of their way to prove that they were ready to enforce the letter of the law. Steve Barney, who had been dabbling in Ferraris for years before he opened his dealership in 1978, spoke of his experience importing a pair of 275 GTB 4s. He said that the cars were virtually identical, the serial numbers only being a few digits apart, but one car had a build date in December of 1967 and the other was completed in January of 1968. Two customs agents showed up one day at the home of a family member where the January 1968 car was parked in a garage and confiscated it, leaving the car that was built only a couple of weeks earlier alone. When he tried to recover the car, he was told it would have to be brought into compliance with the 1968 emissions regulations.

The regs for a 1968 car were not that tough; many cars could get past the specs with little modification other than a positive crankcase vent system. But the short-stroke V12 of the Ferrari was a little on the extreme side and the exhaust hydrocarbons were far too high for the newly environmentally conscious Americans. The car would have to be modified if Barney wanted to keep it.

There were only a few individuals doing emissions conversion work at the time and those who were had made their market in just this sort of case: individuals who had run afoul of the regulators either by accident or design and needed some emergency work to keep their cars. Barney was able to line up a well-known Ferrari technician, Alfredo Caiti, to do the necessary work. Using the tried-and-true technology of the domestic car manufacturers, Caiti was able to render the Ferrari legal with the installation of an air pump and air-injection plumbing, but between the seizure, the paperwork, and the compliance modifications, it was nearly a year before Barney was able to get his car back.[5]

DOT and the EPA were occasionally tweaking their requirements as they tried to anticipate the needs of the markets, and there were a small number of venues available to perform the required emissions test. But this was not enough to inspire more than a little interest in independently importing cars in volume because, as the people who tried it soon found, it was a tedious and expensive process. The profit margin for that kind of work remained elusive and uncertain because of the amount of highly skilled labor required and the need for expensive research and testing. Examples like Webb's Morgan mentioned earlier, even though they may represent a successful conversion, served as evidence that there was little or no profit to be seen spending more than the retail price of a car to make it legal for import, except where the cars were extraordinarily expensive to begin with. It was of course the Italian makers Ferrari and Lamborghini who made the cars that got the first gray-market shops off the ground.

Ferrari's presence in the U.S. was small at the time and Lamborghini's was even smaller. Neither company made nor sold more than a thousand cars per year, and both had been stepping in and out of the U.S. market depending on their current status with the regulators. Enzo Ferrari's chief focus was on racing cars, and he really didn't want to be bothered with the passenger car market or the regulations necessary for selling them overseas. They applied for and received small volume exemptions with the DOT that allowed them to continue selling cars, but these were temporary measures that didn't really constitute a business plan.

In 1975, Ferrari showed that in spite of rumors to the contrary they did indeed intend to continue in the American market by introducing the 308 GTB. The 308 was intended to be Ferrari's world market car and had many of the new and upcoming safety standards designed into the body. The front and rear of the body had strong mounting points for shock-absorbing bumpers, and in anticipation of roll-over standards, the convertible versions that came in the following year had a strong rear section supporting a removable, targa-style roof. The small three-liter V8 engine was mounted sideways directly behind the cabin, like the set-up in the Dino series that the 308 replaced. The engine was equipped with a now familiar air pump (in fact, the emission control components came from Ford) and all the other necessary bits to bring it into line with U.S. regulations.

The 308 was underwhelming to Ferrari enthusiasts in the U.S., particularly because its introduction was shortly followed by the far more exciting 512 BB (Boxer Berlinetta). Commonly called the Boxer, in reference to the shape of the car's horizontally opposed flat twelve engine, the 512 set a new standard among Italian exotics. Its body shape, particularly the nose, resembled the styling of the 308 but slightly larger and longer behind the doors. With 360 horsepower and a claimed top speed of 180 MPH, the 512 far outperformed its more available little brother, but Ferrari did not announce that they planned to offer a version of the car for the American market, and that sin of omission threw more fuel on the fire that had already been started among the independent importers.

Lamborghini was another small-volume maker of high-performance sports cars, but one that had teetered on the edge of bankruptcy practically from birth. Founded by Ferruccio Lamborghini, a successful farm equipment manufacturer, *Automobili Lamborghini S.p.A.* produced only hand-made high-performance road cars for the ultra-rich auto enthusiast. Legend has it Lamborghini himself, dissatisfied with a Ferrari he had purchased and further annoyed at Ferrari's unwillingness to discuss it with him, started up his own sports-car manufacturer. Unlike their chief rival, Lamborghini did not have a presence in motor racing and depended solely on the sales of their sports cars for revenue. Lamborghini's designs were bold and unconventional and had a very narrow appeal. The cars sold because there was no shortage of rich Europeans who could throw down the cash for such a prestigious ride. Their facilities were small, and their supply chain and financing often erratic, so sometimes they could produce only a handful of cars in a year. For that reason, research and development required to build a car for America was, for Lamborghini, prohibitively expensive; so they could only maintain an erratic presence in the U.S. as they struggled to continuously update their cars and engines while applying for extensions and temporary exemptions with the EPA and the DOT to meet constantly changing federal regulations. Eventually, with the introduction of the Countach, they appeared to give up on the Americans for the time being and, like Ferrari with the Boxer, announced no plans to make a North American version.

But wealthy American car enthusiasts were not going to be content to look at the Lamborghini Countach and Ferrari's newly minted 512 BB in pictures and be told that they couldn't own one. Though federalizing these cars would be an extraordinarily complicated and expensive job requiring specialized skills and engineering know-how, where these cars were concerned cost was not really an issue; so it turned out there were a few enterprising Americans willing to tackle the job the manufacturers had decided was too tough.

Relief for hungry Ferrari buyers was offered by Richard "Dick" Fritz, one of the true pioneers of the independent importers. While attending

Clarkston University in New York, Fritz got to know Luigi Chinetti, Jr., the son of Luigi Chinetti, chief of Ferrari North America's eastern arm. He worked occasionally on the pit crew when Ferrari raced at the nearby tracks at Watkin's Glenn and Lime Rock, and when he graduated from college in 1962, he took a job as manager at the Chinetti's Ferrari dealership. During the early years, the Ferrari business wasn't as strong as it later became; sometimes the dealership even had trouble making payroll, and the failure of Ferrari to build a U.S. version of any of the V12 cars wasn't helping. Fritz saw the opportunity that appeared when Ferrari stopped importing their V12 cars, and when the Boxer came out for the European market but not the Americas, he had the connections, audacity and know-how to try to accomplish what the factory could or would not. In 1976, with Luigi Chinetti's blessing, he founded Amerispec, for the purpose of modifying the Ferrari 512 for use on the streets of the USA. His market was ready-made as wealthy Ferrari enthusiasts had found the performance of the 308 disappointing and were ready to pony up whatever it took to get a "proper" twelve-cylinder Ferrari in their driveway.[6] Fritz's modifications to the 512 were thorough and reliable and his cars earned a good reputation, cultivated and well maintained by close association with the automotive press. He and his cars frequently appeared in *Car and Driver* and *Road & Track*, where he was hailed as the miracle man who had saved the V12 Ferraris from perpetual exile.

The cars cost as much as a nice house. An original 512 in European factory trim could be purchased for $38,000. Unfortunately, it couldn't be driven anywhere on U.S. roads in that form. An American car enthusiast who wanted to put a flat-twelve in their garage was going to have to pony up more than half that again. An ad placed by Amerispec in the 1978 *New York Times* offered a new 512 for sale in full legal U.S. trim for $59,000. While that was a staggering amount of money to pay for any car in 1978 it was a figure that made it well worth the while for Fritz to perform the major modifications needed to pass the cars and wasn't out of reach of many U.S. drivers. With that kind of mark-up, Fritz was able to make a comfortable business specializing in converting 512s. He later branched out into other types of Ferraris and later, launched a high-performance arm of his business, Ameritec, which specialized in equipping already-legal 308s with turbocharger systems.

Dick Fritz and Amerispec became practically synonymous with Ferrari in subsequent years. Dealers who wanted to offer more than the V8s Ferrari had federalized were buying cars in Europe and shipping them to Fritz for federalization. Steve Barney, who moved the occasional Boxer through the gray market channels, engaged the services of Amerispec regularly. When Barney bought his first Boxer, Fritz was not yet in the conversion business so he had the compliance work done by another of the early players in the conversion business, Jas Rarewala. Barney was unhappy with the performance of the car when it was completed and said the car never worked right until all the add-on controls were removed. Subsequent Boxers that Barney bought he had done by Fritz and said that all of those cars performed well right out of the box.

Once Fritz had ironed out his methods, his shop started cranking out street legal Boxers at a steady pace so that by June of 1981 he was responsible for 50 cars having hit the American roads. His cars had earned a reputation for being reliable and fully legal, though the bumpers that he fabricated were necessarily ugly and many of the end users replaced them with original equipment as soon as, or even before, the cars were delivered. Considering there were less than a thousand 512s built in that period of time, he accounted for a considerable chunk of Ferrari's business. To be sure, Fritz and Amerispec were not the only channel through which one could locate and purchase a Boxer ready for the U.S. roads. There was significant competition on the west coast and in the port cities of Texas. But Fritz's consistency and reliability and the fact that he was able to obtain small volume certifications for several models of Boxer made him the number one name for importing twelve-cylinder Ferraris.

In Newport Beach, California, Albert Mardikian, a Syrian born engineer educated in America, was beginning to do EPA and DOT modifications. He had a customizing shop, Trend Imports, where he did upgrades and one-off body conversions, primarily on Italian exotic cars; so it was only natural he should move into the conversion business. In 1978, he made a name in *Road & Track* when he took a job federalizing a Ferrari Boxer for Michael Pokony and Werner Schoch. Pokony and Schoch, two of the West Coast pioneers of the gray market, were a pair of Porsche dealers who made it their business to locate exotic and unusual cars and import them to the States. They would contract the work they couldn't handle themselves and Mardikian and Co. got the job of developing the emission control system and the impact absorbing bumpers the car needed to satisfy the feds. The job on the Boxer took eight months, but the finished product satisfied the powers that be and got great reviews from the writers at *R&T*.[7] When the gray market started its boom in 1980, Mardikian's business was well established as a converter and positioned to boom with it. Mardikian was later immortalized as the symbol of the automotive gray market when he served as the model for the character Charlie Babbit in the 1988 movie *Rainman*. Tom Cruise plays the fast-talking gray market car dealer who, while arguing with a customs official about importing four Lamborghinis, is heard to say: "The whole world is choking on smog and they're going to correct the situation by keeping my four cars off the road?" Mardikian kept a high profile, and the story of his company served well to represent the story of the whole gray market in cars.

Jasjit (Jas) Rarewala was to become another big player in the conversion business. An Indian immigrant when he came to the U.S. to study industrial design, he went to work for Alfredo Caiti at Modena Sports Cars in Spring Valley, NY. At that time Caiti was the east coast importer for Lamborghini. Of course, Lamborghini was having some difficulty in the U.S. The cars that they were selling were mostly brought in under temporary exemptions. Rarewala was first involved in designing a DOT compliant 5 MPH bumper for the Urraco P250, a V8 powered counterpoint to Ferrari's 308. While working in Spring Valley he met Dan Morgan and together they Founded American Specialty Corp,[8] a business built around independent importers and small-volume car manufacturers who were daunted by the complexity of U.S. law and regulations and needed help with the process. Their company earned notoriety in the automotive press by being among the first to import a Countach into the U.S. in 1975 and continued to show up in the pages of automotive journals for years after. In addition to helping individuals import cars, they assisted the manufacturers in obtaining the certifications, exemptions, and credentials necessary to sell cars in the U.S.

Morgan saw opportunity among the small volume makers of what he called the "boutique cars"—cars like the Iso Rivolta Lele. The Iso Rivolta was a Bertone designed 2+2 fitted with a 351 Ford V8. Morgan and his company re-designed the interior of the car in accordance with American safety rules, removing protruding corners and sharp items that were outlawed by the NHTSA. With American Specialty's modifications, Iso Rivolta was able to market their hand-made sports cars in the U.S. without having to hire the know-how or devote a workshop to the project.

The technical arm of American Specialty was a shop called Automotive Compliance Center (ACC). ACC was a proper conversion shop, devoted to engineering and performing the modifications necessary to bring cars into compliance with the U.S. laws. As the other half of a business devoted to importation of non-compliant cars, ACC would enjoy a steady stream of customers whose needs could not be satisfied just by providing documents and filling out forms. They would take on the task of strengthening bodywork for front and side impact protection, installing U.S. government approved lighting, and engine and fuel system modifications to meet the needs of the EPA. For a cool five to ten thousand dollars, or even more depending on the extent of the modifications required, American Specialty and ACC could deliver a car fully approved and ready for the U.S. roads, or even re-sale if that was the plan.[9]

And re-sale often was the plan. The original gray market exotics were rare and exclusive and when they were offered for sale, would often inspire bidding wars among buyers. A wealthy sports car enthusiast might be persuaded to spend 75,000 on a car that cost 50,000 at the source, if he didn't have to be involved with the hassles and delays of buying a car overseas and contracting the work required. More and more gray market dealers were emerging to fill the growing (but still quite small) market for exotic European sports cars. Often financed with an investor's money, dealers would tour Europe looking for examples of Ferraris, Maseratis, Lamborghinis, Porsche Turbos and big engine Mercedes to bring back, modify, certify, and place in a good home.

The smaller manufacturers didn't see this kind of activity as a threat; rather it was an enhancement of their market, though in some cases they may not have admitted it. Lamborghini couldn't quite make 100 cars in a year, but even squeezing out such a small volume, their cars were often considered "over the top" by many European buyers and they desperately needed access to the U.S. market. Initially the Lamborghini factory was not interested in doing the development work for federalizing their cars; they wanted to leave it up to their distributors. So if someone in the U.S. was willing and able to complete the work of federalizing their cars, it was that many more cars they could sell provided they could build them. There were only a handful of companies bringing in the occasional Countach. Trend Imports owned by Al Mardikian in California was one other example, and Mardikian was claiming that his specially built engines made more power in U.S. trim than the factory European version. But for a time, Lamborghini found themselves looking to Rarewala to come up with an acceptable version of their supercar to market in the States. Rarewala and his conversions would go on to play a short but significant part in Lamborghini's market. Likewise for Ferrari and their V12s. They had developed the 308 with the American market in mind and that was the car that their dealers got, but it was the only one that was available through official channels. In order to sell their latest car, the 512BB, in America, Ferrari unofficially aligned themselves with conversion shops on the East and West coasts. It was often a wink and nod kind of relationship. Factory dealers publicly appeared to regard the gray market importers with a kind of condescending tolerance, but in private they found them to be quite necessary. Both companies enjoyed cozy relationships with the gray market importers of their choice, sometimes even to the point of sharing technology, as the gray marketers enabled them to sell all models of their cars in the States while they worked on plans to build their own U.S. versions.

Morgan automobiles, the English maker mentioned earlier also developed a working relationship with a conversion shop, though they took a more unorthodox approach. Bill Fink, owner of Isis Imports of San Francisco, wanted to sell new Morgans and set up shop to do just that. He had little trouble making the necessary modifications to satisfy the DOT. But to satisfy the EPA, instead of modifying the Morgan to comply with the ever-changing standards for gasoline engines, he completely sidestepped the issue by converting the cars to propane power. Not only were his cars legal for the U.S. roads, but he claimed increased horsepower and improvement in the car's cold weather behavior.

Fink travelled to England and converted a couple of cars there to convince Peter Morgan that his method was worth their endorsement. Morgan was sufficiently impressed that he agreed to cooperate, and the arrangements were made to ship cars to Isis without a fuel system, so they came in under the *incomplete* category. The conversion to propane involved placement of an appropriate fuel tank with the fill valve in the center of the spare tire. The intake manifold was replaced with an Offenhauser aftermarket piece and an Impco propane carburetor. The parts cost to Isis was probably less than the cost of one EPA test procedure, and because the cars were not gasoline or diesel powered, they didn't have to be tested at all. In 1977 Fink announced that he was planning to import about two dozen cars per year. The 8-cylinder cars were priced at $14,500 and the four-cylinder cars at $10,500. There was a six-month waiting period for anyone wanting to order one.[10] Conversion to propane fuel might have been impractical for a typical passenger car. But for an exclusive sports car that only came out on sunny days for fun outings, the lack of infrastructure was not considered by Fink to be a problem.

Much to the chagrin of the various U.S. agencies involved, the direct import and conversion business showed nothing but growth during the late seventies and early eighties. The importers themselves attained a kind of cult hero status in the automotive press, as they were the ones who faced down the regulators and made it possible to buy and drive cars that were otherwise prohibited. That they were looked down on by the "legitimate" automotive industry made it that much the better. The bad boys of the sports car market used their reputation to the fullest and for a time, as far as the buyers were concerned, they could do no wrong. Bolstered by excited automotive press announcements like "Finally! The (your dream car here) is available in America!" independent importers were experiencing exponential increases in orders, and many responded by rapidly expanding their businesses.

Mardikian's Trend Imports, for example, had only been a going concern for a few months before experiencing rapid growth. His location near Los Angeles gave him access to a market full of well-heeled car enthusiasts who hesitated little over dropping $75,000 on a car, as well as upper middle-class buyers who liked the idea of saving money on a new Mercedes. His rapid growth led the local business publications to treat him like some kind of prodigy, publishing articles about his rapid rise accompanied by pictures of him standing next to a Ferrari or Lamborghini. Though the exotic cars always made good press, Mardikian was quick to take advantage of the shift in the market from the ultra-expensive exotic sports cars to the high volume that could be enjoyed with the big German sedans. Within a year, his shop grew from a handful of technicians federalizing two to three cars a week to about 50 employees converting 15 to 20. At that time, before competition drove the prices down, an EPA/DOT conversion and test on a standard Mercedes-Benz might run about $5,000–$7,000, so a shop completing 20 conversions in a week could be grossing over one hundred thousand dollars. Growth like that went on to inspire more and more people to move their business into the gray market hoping to get a big piece of the action while they could.

4

Making Them Pass

Building a car to satisfy Congress was not an easy job, as evidenced by the number of car makers who simply chose to opt out rather than undertake the complexity of making their cars safe and clean enough for the newly socially conscious Americans. For those makers who had been struggling in the American market to begin with, the investment required looked like too much of a gamble. Much of the technology, if not necessarily new, was untried and the makers were often frustrated in their attempts to predict what they would have to spend, and how long it would take to get each year's model ready for the market. So on top of—and sometimes instead of—research and development, they spent millions on lawyers and lobbyists to try and get the laws rolled back at every opportunity.

The DOT requirements, while they added cost to the cars, didn't really push the envelope of technology. Many of the requirements involved such minor things as specific lighting and dashboard labeling. Some were a simple rounding of the edges and corners of interior components to make them less injurious to a body that might find itself hurled against them. Other safety features, like collapsible steering columns and dual circuit brake systems, were known quantities and were easily built into a car once the initial development work had been done. Bumper standards, though, were considered something of a nuisance. In their first issuance the requirement was that the bumpers be able to withstand a 10 MPH front and a 5 MPH rear impact without functional damage. Efforts on the part of the American automakers were successful at least in that case and the standard was almost immediately cut in half (5 MPH front and 2½ MPH rear protection). It wasn't that the makers couldn't build front and rear bumpers to take the punishment, but more a matter of not making the nose and tail of the car look like a piece of construction equipment. In most cases the bumpers turned out to be heavy aluminum structures with some sort of shock-absorber mounting to soak up the energy of a low-speed collision and there wasn't an easy way to make that look good. Additionally, the bumper specs had uniform height requirements, which further reduced the stylists' options. The 1974 cars were probably the worst looking cars of the decade. In many cases, if the bumpers looked like they were added on at the last minute, it's because they were. The whole of the automotive industry had been watching the U.S. makers' attempts to roll back the legislation and held off on re-designing their cars in hopes that they wouldn't have to. By the time it became clear that the cars were going to have to comply, the options left to them were aesthetically narrow. Subsequent model years got a little better as the designers had the time and learned to more gracefully fold impact-absorbing bumpers into the body lines.

One of the biggest problems with the DOT regulations for small manufacturers, and especially for converters, was that satisfying the DOT could mean sacrificing a few copies of a car for crash testing. The NHTSA guys at the research lab would load the cars up with anthropomorphic dummies and, using an air-powered catapult similar to the device used for launching jets off of an aircraft carrier, crash them into a barrier at various speeds to see just how much damage they could do. The specifications for crash testing were not concrete, but the testing studied details like intrusion of exterior car body parts into the passenger compartment and the condition of test dummies. If the researchers saw obvious flaws that could result in more severe injuries, changes were recommended, and the manufacturer would do what they could to remedy the safety problems. The changes might not actually be required if the problems weren't clearly in violation of the requirements. But if the cars went into production and were sold in the states with crash safety issues, they carried the stigma of a bad rating from the NHTSA.

The bumper and side impact tests were less subjective: Testers would strike the car in front, rear and on the sides with a pendulum or other movable object equal in weight to an average car. Damage inflicted to the front and rear of the car by the object was evaluated and penetration into the sides of the car was measured to see if it held up to the standards. It was an expensive process involving the destruction of many complete cars, but for a builder of tens or even hundreds of thousands of cars, it became just a part of the cost of doing business.

After some negotiation, in most cases, the independent importers were not required to crash test. DOT required instead that documentation be submitted to prove that a car being considered for clearance was identical or even just similar enough to a model that had been crash tested before, usually by the manufacturer. In some cases, pages from a parts manual showing that a car shared certain critical parts with an approved model were enough to win approval. For example, compliance for the Ferrari 288 GTO, a very low-production GT not intended for sale in the States that changed hands for as much as a million dollars per unit, was demonstrated using crash test data for Ferrari's world market car, the 308, which shared a number of body components. In most cases, data on an approved model was not hard to come by because most of the developed countries in the important world auto markets had begun to require a certain amount of crash testing from car makers.

Side impact and bumper impact standards were unique to the U.S. for a time, so there wasn't always a certified equivalent car for the importers to compare to. Sometimes importers would attach bumpers and other parts from unrelated but certified car models, resulting in some ugly combinations. Try imagining a Lamborghini Countach with a Chevrolet Celebrity rear bumper for example. But if the converter was interested keeping a reputation for quality work, the shops found it necessary to install auxiliary bracing inside existing bumpers and bodywork designed to resist impact. Though many of these structures were untested, the DOT again threw them a bone and permitted them to submit engineer's reports on their modifications to prove that they would stand up to the test and therefore they were not required to do destructive testing. In most cases, the reports simply described the strength of the reinforcing structure and fell short of describing the material of the car to which the bumpers were attached.

Installation of Chevrolet Celebrity rear bumper on a 1985 Countach. Brackets were welded to the car's frame, but the rest of the installation was bolted on so, it could be easily removed by the final owner (private collection).

One of the real strokes of genius to emerge from the gray market shops was the "telescoping door beam." The side impact standards handed down by the DOT covered several pages of text, and had been revised many times, but boiled down to an easily understood formula: The side doors were required to have a crush strength of twice the vehicle weight or 7,000 lbs, whichever was less. In the lab it was tested by running a weighted cart into the side of the car.

Building a car door to resist that kind of abuse was not difficult. Most auto makers did it by welding a corrugated steel reinforcement to the inside of the door's exterior skin. But duplicating this structure in the conversion shop would have involved completely dismantling the door and then re-painting it after the welding had been done. Although it was likely that many standard car doors from companies in Europe would have passed the test even without the installation of the reinforcement just the presence of the window regulator assembly in the door was almost enough to keep the weight outside the car. But proving the strength of such a complicated structure on paper was difficult. Describing the deformation of a simple piece of a tubular steel alloy, however, was not. Using basic calculus, it was a project that could be completed by any competent mechanical engineering student, so conversion shop operators (just who was the first has been impossible to determine) used two pieces of tubular alloy steel, one telescoping inside the other. The resulting two-piece reinforcement could be collapsed to fit inside the small interior openings in a car door, and then extended the length of the door and fastened at the ends by welding or by bolted brackets. The engineer's calculations showed that beam alone could withstand deformation enough to pass the DOT test, so by adding the beam to any door, the door was rendered compliant.

The engineering reports for door beams and bumper braces were probably the most plagiarized pieces of paperwork in the industry for a time, as hundreds of small-time operators took to selling twenty dollars' worth of alloy steel or even mild steel tubing as "DOT approved door bars and bumper braces complete with engineer's reports" to would-be independent importers for a few hundred dollars.

DOT compliance also meant replacing the variable European headlights with fixed U.S.–style lights. European cars were often equipped with headlights that could be adjusted manually by the driver at the dashboard. The DOT didn't trust drivers to do a good job of that, so the control had to be deactivated and the headlights themselves had to be replaced with the various types of sealed-beam headlights that were on the DOT's approved list. Brake systems that were not up to U.S. standards had to be altered, though this was usually unnecessary as most of the world had adopted the dual hydraulic circuit standard. A collapsible steering column was another

4. Making Them Pass

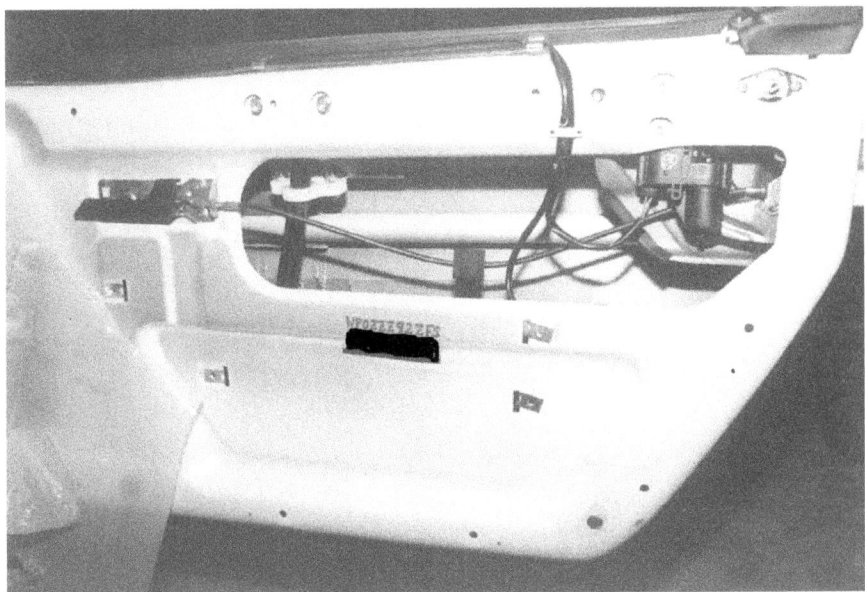

Porsche 911 showing the telescoping door reinforcement necessary to meet DOT standards (author's photograph).

standard in which the rest of the world had caught up with the U.S. But there were many very small issues such as dashboard labels, door key and seat belt buzzers, and rear door locks that required minor modifications; and each modification had to be accompanied by photographs and documents before a car was said to be safe to drive on American roads.

The DOT compliance project was time consuming, requiring a great deal of paperwork, and was often expensive, but in most cases, it was a barrier that could eventually be overcome. For an operator with experience, it was largely a matter of making sure all the paperwork was done correctly. EPA compliance, however, was less of a sure thing. The manufacturers themselves had enough trouble bringing their cars into line; so much in fact that they continually lobbied the government to back off on the ever-tightening rules. Independent importers trying to get their cars through the test lab got a taste of what the manufacturers were up against. The science of automobile emission control was still very new.

Though engineers understood the internal combustion engine pretty well after some 60 years of producing them, until the late 1960s nobody had put much time or effort into making them cleaner. Government sponsored studies had defined just what the offensive components in auto exhaust were but didn't offer any answers about how to reduce them. They simply said that it had to be done. Of course, many automakers at first didn't believe they

Collapsible door beams are one of the more clever innovations to come out of the grey market shops. Two pieces of tubular alloy steel are fitted on one end with an attachment point and one tube is fitted into the other. The resulting bar is collapsed so that it can be inserted into the small openings on the inside of the door structure under the panel.

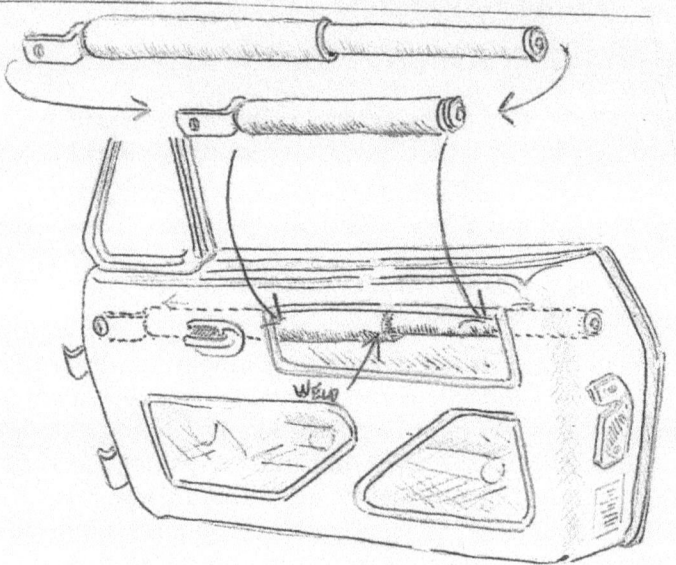

It is then extended and th ends bolted to the inside of the door. In this way the door can be rendered compliant without modifications that require welding and re-painting the door structure

Author's drawing describing the process of installing a telescoping door beam.

would really be required to meet the new standards. The relationship between government and big business had been one of pushing back and forth for decades, and tradition held that the government made rules and the industries filed complaints and lawsuits until a compromise was reached. Eventually, invoking well-worn logic about damage to the economy and loss of jobs in the automotive industry, U.S. automakers were able to convince EPA administrator to roll back the 1975 standards for one year to 1976 and then to modify them for 1977. And they continued to hold out hope that they could do it again, maybe even indefinitely. Many of the lawmakers were on their side saying that meeting the standards would be too much of a burden on the industry, and the carmakers kept getting signals from Washington that they interpreted as prelude to a softening of the EPA's position. But that softening that they expected didn't come, so they got off to a late start when it finally became clear that emission standards were really going to stay in effect.

The emission standards as originally written didn't hold up long, but it wasn't because the government was backing off on its position. It was because results exposed flaws in the standards and methods of testing that required a fair amount of adjustment to work in the real world. Writing the regulations continued to be a work in process. Of course, carmakers seized on these flaws as good reasons why regulation wouldn't work at all and some of their arguments even made a certain amount of sense. Initially the standards were written in terms of exhaust gas concentration. Early regulations of 275 parts per million (PPM) hydrocarbon (HC) and 1.5 percent carbon monoxide (CO) represented about a 60 percent reduction of the offensive gasses as they exited the tailpipe but didn't take into account the fact that larger engines produced more total exhaust than smaller engines. Furthermore, some of the modifications intended to reduce concentrations of the regulated gasses (retarded ignition timing was found to lower HC levels for instance) increased fuel consumption and therefore increased the total exhaust gas produced so in some cases it was actually possible for a regulated engine to produce more total pollution than an unregulated one. Some tweaking of the regulations was clearly required.

Along with the 1970 amendments to the Clean Air Act came the necessary updates to the method for measuring and testing exhaust pollution that actually took into account the amount of exhaust produced during actual driving. PPM and percent measurements gave way to measurement of the pollutant weight per mile driven in grams per mile (GPM). HC and CO concentrations were regulated but NOx (oxides of nitrogen) initially was not, the reason being that NOx was not well understood at first and was measured in the first few years for the purpose of gathering data for later standards. The measurements were derived by sampling and measuring the *quantity* and concentrations of exhaust while the car was being driven on a chassis dynamometer. The Constant Volume Sampling (CVS) test method took a number of variables into account, including ambient temperature and barometric pressure, and yielded consistent results. In 1972 the CVS method went into effect and while the test cycles were adjusted over the years, the CVS method became the standard still used by the EPA today.

After the EPA had settled on their methods, and after the various rollbacks and temporary standards had run their course, the EPA's scoreboard for automobile emission standards looked like this:

1968–69 HC: 275PPM (parts per million) CO: 1.5%; NOx: No Standard

1970–1971 HC: 4.1 Grams/mile; CO: 34 Grams/mile; NOx: no standard

1972 HC: 3.0 Grams/mile; CO: 28 Grams/mile; NOx: no standard; Evap: 2 Grams/test

1973–74 HC: 3.0 Grams/mile; CO: 28 Grams/mile; NOx: 3.1 Grams/mile; Evap: 2 Grams/test

1975 HC: 1.5 Grams/mile; CO: 15 Grams/mile; NOx: 3.1 Grams/mile; Evap: 2 Grams/test

1976 HC: 1.5 Grams/mile; CO: 15 Grams/mile; NOx: 2.0 Grams/mile; Evap: 2 Grams/test

1977 HC: 1.5 Grams/mile; CO: 15 Grams/mile; NOx: 2.0 Grams/mile; Evap: 2 Grams/test

1978–79 HC: 1.5 Grams/mile; CO: 15 Grams/mile; NOx: 2.0 Grams/mile; Evap: 6 Grams/SHED test

1980 HC: .41 Grams/mile; CO: 7 Grams/mile; NOx: 2.0 Grams/mile; Evap: 6 Grams/SHED test

1981 HC: .41 Grams/mile; CO: 3.4 Grams/mile; NOx: 1.0 Grams/mile; Evap: 6 Grams/SHED test[1]

The evaporative standard looks like it was loosened going from 1977 to 1978, but only because the method of measurement changed for that as well. Earlier tests focused on the weight of the carbon canister before and after the test, which represented only the vapor recovered during the test. In 1978 EPA went to the Sealed Housing for Evaporative Determination (SHED) test. To perform the SHED test, the car is driven into a small hermetically sealed room and parked for a period of time. The air in the room can then be sampled and the amount of fuel that evaporates off of the car calculated. Because the test is more thorough and accurate than the earlier method, the standard limit is raised.

From 1981 on, the standards remained the same until the next update that occurred through a series of Clean Air Act amendments in 1990.

Any technology that enables someone to make money has a very short trip from the R&D department to the marketplace, and the aftermarket converters wasted little time in adapting the recently developed strategies for emission reduction. Once the new cars hit the streets it was a small matter to study the emission control systems to see what could be coopted for use on other cars. There were few secrets in the emission control business, in fact, because air pollution and its effect on the automobile industry were considered to be something of a national emergency. Congress had done some customizing of patent laws to enable carmakers to employ each other's strategies without fear of litigation. Consequently, the conversion shops were also able to tackle the tailpipe emissions while working out of the same toolbox.

Among the gasses issuing from the exhaust pipe of an unregulated engine, HC (hydrocarbon) is probably the most noticeably offensive, as it has a strong odor and in high concentrations it can cause burning in the eyes and nose. HC is simply excess unburned fuel that makes it all the way through the engine during normal operation and out into the exhaust stream. Tiny amounts of fuel might accumulate on relatively cooler surfaces inside an engine and hang out in a zone where there isn't enough oxygen to burn them, before being swept out of the combustion chamber on the exhaust stroke. The HC content of a car's exhaust is little different from the evaporated fuel that is easily detected by the nose and produces an unpleasant and sometimes visible atmosphere. Consequently, it is regulated not only at the tailpipe, but in the form of fuel vapor that evaporates out of the tank while the car is parked. This form of HC is contained by the evaporative (Evap) control system.

Carbon monoxide (CO), which often accompanies high levels of HC because it too is a product of incomplete combustion, is far more dangerous, because it's not nearly as noticeable. It's invisible and odorless and is taken into the bloodstream through the lungs, where it robs red blood cells of their ability to transport oxygen to the body. In high concentrations, it can cause dizziness, sleepiness, irreversible brain damage and eventually death. Because both gasses are a result of incomplete combustion of hydrocarbon fuels, running an engine on leaner fuel/air ratios can reduce their formation inside the engine. But when engineers tried that with cars they were already making, it led immediately to performance problems; so the first few years of emission controls saw makers concentrating on cleaning up the exhaust *after* it left the engine.

Since HC and CO resulted from partial combustion, engineers tried continuing combustion and it turned out to go a long way toward reducing levels. Exhaust manifolds were made thicker and heavier to maintain heat and promote turbulence and were given the impressive sounding name of *thermal reactors*. Belt-driven air pumps and various assortments of pipes were installed to inject fresh air into the exhaust stream as it left the cylinder head, to fan the flames in the exhaust ports. Retarding the ignition timing by a few degrees sacrificed some horsepower but kicked the exhaust temperature up even higher. The resulting higher temperatures combined with the additional oxygen from the air injection pump allowed combustion of residual unburned fuel to continue for the short period between the time exhaust left the engine and entered the exhaust pipe, considerably reducing the HC and CO content of the exhaust.

Air pumps came into common usage among most of the carmakers in the early seventies and were quickly picked up by the gray market importers. Auto enthusiasts hated them, believing that the pumps robbed power, but the actual power consumption of an air pump compared to even a small engine's output was quite small. The changes that were really hurting the performance of the new cars were the leaner fuel mixtures and retarded ignition timing. But because the air pumps were large and visible, and clearly hadn't been there before, they were quickly assigned the blame for the poorer performance bad gas mileage of cars of the 1970s. In a misguided effort to improve performance and fuel economy, mechanics and car owners frequently removed the air pump systems, filling the resulting holes with pipe plugs and homemade contrivances. Their efforts did little to improve the performance of their new cars. Eventually, some mechanics realized this but continued to strip the air pump systems off of the new cars because, in fact, the most objectionable thing about pumps and thermal reactors was that they and their associated plumbing took up a lot of space and often inhibited access to other serviceable parts.

The tailpipe is not the only measurable source of hydrocarbon emission from the average car. The other source is the *evaporative* emissions. Since hydrocarbon is basically just unburned fuel, gasoline that evaporated from

The author installing an auxiliary air pump on a Countach. Because of the width of the delicate aluminum fenders, it was usually most efficient to work while sitting inside the engine compartment (private collection).

the car into the surrounding atmosphere was also taken into consideration. It can't be measured in terms of grams per mile but is measured in a separate portion of the test designed to simulate the effects of a car sitting in a sunny parking lot. Like the standards for tailpipe emissions, evaporative standards were designed to tighten up with each passing year. What started out as a requirement for controlling the evaporative leakage from the gas tank evolved into a fairly complex system designed to contain fuel vapor that came from every nook and cranny of the engine compartment and store it in a charcoal canister. Unlike the tailpipe emission controls, containing the evaporative emissions was an applied science. Engineers knew how it was done and what was likely to work, it was just a matter of installing enough of the right hardware. When the evaporative emissions specs became tight enough that the fuel vapor emitting from the carburetor became a problem, most of the manufacturers installed little automatic doors in their air cleaners to shut the top of the carburetor off from the outside air when the car wasn't running.

The air pumps and thermal reactors alongside the carbon canisters helped carmakers meet the standards up until 1974 but they could only go so far, and with the introduction of NOx standards in '73, the job of bringing the exhaust into line became far more complicated. NOx is a product of extraordinarily high combustion temperature. Nitrogen is usually inert and is not given to easy combination with oxygen, but the temperatures and pressures inside a combustion chamber are just the conditions likely to enable the reactions necessary for the formation of NOx and NOx wasn't something that could be consumed inside a thermal reactor. So the later standards required more attention be turned to cleaning up the combustion process inside the engine. In some ways, the NOx standard conflicted with the HC and CO standard in that leaner fuel mixtures used to reduce HC and CO resulted in higher combustion temperatures which produced NOx.

Another factor in NOx formation is the compression ratio. Increasing the compression ratio in an engine was a well-known trick among the performance enthusiasts for getting more power out of an engine, and hot-rodders had been machining cylinder heads and installing dome-top pistons toward that end for years. The factories were following suit and standard compression ratios had been coming up all through the 1960s, as the manufacturers tried to out-sell each other by offering more and more powerful engines. But with the higher compression ratios came higher combustion temperatures, and with that came higher NOx output. So, with the advent of NOx standards compression ratios began to fall, and the specific power output of the new engines fell even further. It wasn't a major change—usually a small modification to the shape of the piston crown was all that was required to lower compression substantially—but it had an effect on power noticeable even to inexperienced drivers.

Even with lower compression ratios, conquering NOx was still sometimes a problem. The shape of the combustion chamber had a profound effect on NOx formation. But changing that required re-designing cylinder heads and most manufacturers wanted to save costs by using the same tooling hardware for as long as they could, so many resorted to exhaust gas recirculation (EGR) systems that diluted the fresh intake charge with exhaust. Using a valve controlled by engine vacuum, EGR systems diverted a portion of the engine's exhaust back into the intake airstream at the manifold. The presence of the exhaust in the combustion chamber absorbed some of the heat of combustion and reduced the formation of NOx. Unfortunately, though, it also noticeably reduced power output. NOx production was not usually a problem during light loads or periods of idling—in most cases it was more of a problem during acceleration—so it was precisely when the driver was demanding the most power from the engine that the EGR valve was most likely to be fully open and reducing performance. A fully open EGR valve during acceleration could make a car feel weak and hesitant about accelerating and during the first few years of EGR systems being installed on cars, many car owners brought their machines into the garage for repairs only to be told that everything was working correctly. Mechanics and owners alike frequently became frustrated with the effects of the EGR system, so it was not unusual for the components to join the air pumps and thermal reactors in the scrap heap to be replaced by fabricated plugs and cover plates.

Other car builders found they could sufficiently control all three of the regulated gasses by precise metering of fuel and air entering the engine. Volkswagen, with the help of Bosch, pioneered an electronic fuel injection system in their air-cooled Type III series starting in 1968. Their system laid the groundwork for the electronic fuel injection systems Bosch would sell to high-end European builders like Mercedes and Jaguar. The new fuel systems, though they were crude compared to engine management systems that would develop in just a few years, gave the engineers a level of fuel control that was practically impossible with a carburetor. Most of the European auto makers saw fuel injection as the key to meeting the emission specs in the future. Other manufacturers, particularly the American car companies, thought developing fuel injection to be too big an investment and they continued to add one device after another to their carburetors and intake systems to try and gain enough control over their fuel systems and achieve some kind of compromise. Leaner fuel/air mixtures, lower compression ratios, milder camshaft profiles, EGR, all went into the mix, degrading a car's performance in favor of cleaner exhaust. But even with all these measures in place, the 1975 standards turned out to be a high-water mark for emission levels and the car companies (in America at least) all cried foul. It was in late 1974 after much ado that the EPA grudgingly rolled the implementation of the 1975 standards back one year, making them effective in '76 and then coming up with modified interim standards for 1977 to give the makers time to develop their new systems. Eventually the factories had to turn to what they considered drastic measures: exhaust catalysts.

Catalysts had been used to sweeten the smoke of factory chimneys for a decade before engineers started thinking about putting them in the exhaust stream of an automobile engine. It had been found that in the presence of enough heat and oxygen, platinum and palladium in the exhaust stream could cause an exothermic reaction that oxidized HC and CO into H_2O and CO_2. It was a kind of burning process, but more complicated than what took place in a thermal reactor. Automakers found that by using a catalyst in combination with an air pump and thermal reactor, they could clean up the exhaust enough that they could recover some of the performance lost in earlier years by allowing the fuel system to run slightly richer mixtures. The 1976 cars equipped with catalytic converters performed so much better than their counterparts from one or two model years before that the catalysts were considered a true breakthrough in their time.

Catalysts for converting exhaust gases were not a brand-new technology, but they were something completely different in the automotive world and were naturally controversial for a time. To begin with, they were very expensive because of the materials required. It almost seemed like some kind of divine joke that cleaning up car exhaust required passing the exhaust through a matrix containing some of the most rare and precious metals known to man. A typical catalytic converter might contain 3 to 7 grams of platinum and the earlier ones used a little more. Depending on the individual design, the cost of the precious metals could be from one fourth to one half the value of the converter. Manufacturers claimed that the use of the catalysts added about 200 dollars (in 1975) to the price of a new car.

In addition to the cost, catalysts made some people nervous because they produced a lot of heat. In fact, they produced enough heat during normal operation that they were capable of starting fires if there was grass or other combustible material under the car in contact with the exhaust system. Carelessly located catalytic converters could represent a fire hazard if they were mounted too close to flammable materials or fuel lines. Carmakers found it necessary to add heat shields and other insulation around the catalysts, and at the behest of the government they launched a campaign to educate the motoring public about the dangers associated with driving and particularly with parking catalyst equipped cars. Vehicle owner's manuals added several pages describing the hazards of hot exhaust and sun visors began sporting large warning labels explaining the hazards of parking in tall grass or similar environments.

And catalysts stank! If everything else about exhaust catalysts could be brushed off, that was one fact that didn't get past the motoring public. The smell was like rotten eggs and many drivers of new catalyst equipped cars remarked that the smell of their car was so bad that they were embarrassed if there were people around when they pulled up to park. The larger part of the problem was that the fuel sold in the 1970s had a higher sulfur content, and under the right conditions, particularly if the air/fuel mixture wasn't just right, the catalyst could cause a reaction that produced hydrogen sulfide, an offensive smelling gas that could contribute to acid rain, the latest pollution crisis of the '70s.

But the biggest obstacle to the catalytic converter's nationwide adoption was that they could be seriously degraded by the presence of lead in the exhaust, which was a common gasoline additive at the time. At the time, tetra-ethyl lead was considered an important component of a good automotive fuel. (Some drivers will remember that the high-grade fuel in the 1960s was called ethyl.) Lead in the fuel was used to help stabilize combustion and lead deposits would coat the valve seats and guides, providing a beneficial lubricating effect. So widespread use of catalytic converters was going to require not only that the oil companies develop a whole new series of lead-free motor fuels, but that the car makers alter some of their practices and develop engines that could perform *without* the benefit of lead in the fuel. Different valve, valve guide and valve seat materials would have to be developed. Compression would have to be reduced if an alternate chemical was not found with lead's knock controlling properties. The car manufacturers did not like the idea that they would be making major changes to accommodate lead free fuels. The oil companies, who had been making fuels containing various amounts of tetra-ethyl-lead for decades, would have to come up with an alternative. Nobody really wanted to spend the money that the changeup would require.

But without the addition of the catalysts to their systems, it was unlikely that most of the carmakers would be able to meet the new standards. The EPA administrator balked at the idea of rolling back the standards yet again, and manufacturers insisted that they would be out of business if they were not allowed to employ the catalysts, so everyone including the oil companies did what they had to do to keep the industry working. New lead-free fuels were developed, and a third gas pump appeared beside the regular and premium pumps at the gas station to service catalyst equipped cars. The EPA came up with a regulation placing a restrictor plate in the filler pipe and the lead-free pumps were standardized to have a smaller spout that fit in the restrictor. That way, motorists were prevented from accidentally filling their tank up with leaded fuel. In the long run, the lead issue turned out to be a positive development. Airborne lead was only just beginning to be identified as a health problem, so the need to invent lead-free fuels to preserve the catalysts actually sped up the implementation of a vitally necessary public health policy of phasing out leaded gasoline altogether.

Even with the catalysts, however, American performance cars were in a pretty dismal state as the decade of the seventies neared its end. Bumper and safety standards had added hundreds of pounds to the weight, while lower compression ratios, leaner fuel mixtures, retarded ignition timing and shorter camshaft profiles had reduced power output to the point where a car that could reach 60 MPH in ten seconds was considered fast. Even General Motors' flagship performance car, the Corvette, only produced 200 HP in factory trim. It was this state of affairs that further fueled the desire of some drivers to look elsewhere for their performance cars, further enhancing the market for the exotic performance cars available only through the independent importers.

But if automobile companies, with their vast budgets and engineering know-how, couldn't build a car that would meet the specs with acceptable performance, or in some cases couldn't produce a car that met the specs at all, how could a private converter accomplish what the builders of the cars themselves could not? The answer lay in the rules they had to play by. It turned out that a big gap had developed between what was required of the car builders and what it was necessary for the independent converters to do to market a car in the U.S.

In order to install the label of emissions compliance that the customs officials were looking for and to sell a particular model of mass-produced car in the USA, the manufacturer was required to obtain a certificate of conformity from the EPA and the DOT. Obtaining a certificate from the EPA required the maker to prove that the emission control system was reliable and that the car would continue to be in compliance after 50,000 miles of driving. It's well understood that automobile engines and related systems deteriorate over the time and miles and emissions necessarily increase, so they wanted to be somehow assured that a car that met the standards when it was new would not deteriorate so much that it couldn't pass the test after 5 years or 50,000 miles of driving, which was considered the useful life of a car at the time. (Today the standard has been increased to 10 years and 100,000 miles.) Originally, the prescribed way to prove this was to test the car and drive it on a closed course for 50,000 miles, with subsequent re-tests during the process. There are test tracks at some of the larger transportation labs for just that purpose and many college students and other low wage employees as well as technicians working for a little extra cash spent their off days simply driving round and round the long oval courses accumulating the required mileage. The applicant (car maker) was allowed to perform routine maintenance on the car during the test period, but if any problem occurred during the 50,000 miles that affected the tailpipe emissions, the car failed and there would be no certificate. Any subsequent attempt would require that accumulation of mileage start over. Even if the car accumulated the required miles and passed the test at the end, if the EPA decided that any part of the emission control system didn't seem like it would be durable enough, they reserved the authority to reject the certificate until changes were made. Once a carmaker had a certificate, they were allowed to sell the certified car without submitting each unit for testing. The design had proven its durability, so it was accepted by the EPA that subsequent copies would also be in conformity. Random assembly line tests were required, and the EPA performed what they called "selective enforcement" in which they might at any time select a sample batch of cars from the manufacturer and subject them to testing, but the larger part of the production run was spared the expense of individual testing.

For relatively small sports car companies like Ferrari or Lamborghini, the requirements for a certificate were in some cases more than they could bear. While they may even have had the wherewithal to crash a few cars into a wall to satisfy the DOT, the 50,000–mile endurance test sometimes just proved to be too much. It wasn't so much the idea of wearing out a car on the EPA's test track that discouraged them as the fact that their high-strung engines frequently couldn't go 50,000 miles without repairs. Like race cars, sports car engines and drive trains were built to be lightweight, powerful, and to perform well but life expectancy and reliability were secondary. Often the engines needed to be tuned or tweaked at short intervals. Sparkplugs fouled at low engine speeds and needed to be changed often. Multiple carburetors required frequent re-balancing, and some Lamborghinis had a reputation for overheating and head gasket failures around 30,000 miles. For cars like that, the chances of making it through the EPA's endurance test were slim to none.

Even if the car made it through the 50,000 miles, the catalysts likely would not. Catalytic converters operate at internal temperatures around 1,300 degrees, even higher when severely loaded. At temperatures slightly above that, the precious metal coating begins to evaporate off the ceramic substrate and catalyst performance rapidly deteriorates. If the engine misfires, or if the fuel air mixture is not adjusted properly, the catalyst will rapidly overheat. Even under ideal conditions, as mileage accumulates, the catalyst's efficiency drops to the point where it might be no more effective in cleaning up the exhaust than an expensive muffler, so passing the emissions test after the endurance run looked nearly impossible.

The conversion shops, however, if they were working under the "modify and test" rules, had no such endurance test to contend with. The EPA rules provided for the "convert and test" category for individually imported cars, in which each car would be tested in an EPA approved lab; and even if it barely made the numbers, it was usually cleared by the EPA if it was passed by the lab. On paper, the EPA reserved the option of requiring a re-test at a later date; but that was an option they didn't have the money or manpower to enforce, so it was rarely done. The conversion shop technicians knew that it was unlikely that their modifications would have to perform the test more than once, so tricks could be employed that would increase the performance of the catalysts at the expense of longevity.

One such trick involved the placement of the catalyst. Exhaust catalysts did not begin to function until they reached a temperature over 600 degrees. At that point—the "firing off" point, in the jargon of the conversion technicians—the catalyzed reaction would begin, and the concentrations of illegal gasses would fall off dramatically. In the test lab, with the gas analyzers running and the car being driven on the dyno, it was a magical moment, usually between 30 seconds and a minute, when the three needles of the chart recorders would disengage from their maximum pegs and drop precipitously toward the zero line. Once the catalysts had done this trick, in order for the car to pass, the HC, CO and NOx needles had to stay near the zero line with just the occasional spike showing on the chart, usually corresponding with an acceleration of the car on the dyno.

The federal test procedure required that the exhaust be sampled from the moment of start-up, so it was essential that the catalysts "fire off" as quickly as possible. If there was a problem with cleaning up the exhaust quickly, the technicians could mount the catalyst as close to the exhaust manifold as possible, to take all advantage of exhaust heat as it came out of the engine. This was not considered a risky practice but car manufacturers, constrained by the durability requirements, built their catalyst containers out of materials similar to the heavier exhaust manifolds, if they had to be mounted in such close proximity to the engine components. Conversion technicians would often weld the same sheet metal catalysts that they used further downstream high up in the system, where they could heat up quickly; sometimes in the engine compartment, close to the steel brake and fuel lines. The catalytic reaction produced heat of its own, so once the catalyst was in operation, the temperature of the stainless-steel container would often rise high enough that it would have a visible glow. This glowing steel "can" mounted so high up in the engine compartment naturally was something of a fire hazard; and even if it didn't ignite anything, the excessive heat would not only seriously degrade surrounding components, it was also damaging to the catalyst itself. In the extreme cases represented by the short stroke V12 engines of the Italians, the catalysts might be so heavily loaded and made to run so hot that they would be practically useless after just one test procedure, and a car that had passed the test once might not even pass a re-test done immediately afterward.

So the key to the conversion business was that the standard for a "modify and test" car was not nearly as tough as the standards placed on the car makers. Manufacturers pursuing a certificate not only had to pass the test more than once, they also had to multiply their results by an EPA "durability factor" that had been derived from past performance of cars driven for the prescribed 50,000 miles. For the conversion shops, the standards were straight off the chart, and unconstrained by the need for durability, conversion technicians could build their system like a hand grenade—designed to work well, but only once. They had most of the same tools and technology available to them off the shelf that the manufacturers had, and with years of experimentation they learned which factory emission control components were the most effective for the cost. But often they didn't worry about how their system or its surrounding components would hold up under use. Well informed car owners sometimes knew this, and frequently, once they had obtained the letters of release from EPA and DOT and pocketed their bond from Customs, they contracted their family mechanic to remove the modifications and return the car to its original condition. Sometimes, with a nudge and a wink, the conversion shops themselves could be persuaded to perform this same service. This fact wasn't lost on the manufacturers, and they continued to raise the issue with the EPA but, for a few years anyway, the rules for box three on the customs form remained unchanged and the converters were allowed to continue to ply their trade.

While the rules for the convert and test clause may not have been as demanding as the requirements for a manufacturer's certificate, it was still not an easy test to pass or to perform. Testing the exhaust just once, in a fashion to satisfy the EPA, was a complicated and expensive affair and it had taken the EPA themselves several years to figure out how they were going to do it. But by 1974 they had settled on the process and the various test labs were expected to religiously adhere to the procedure, spelled out over about 50 pages in the Federal Register. If the car passed, the data and the test files were sent, along with a package of photographs of the modifications performed and other mountains of paperwork, to the Mobile Sources department in the EPA for approval. If everything was up to their scrutiny, a release letter went from the EPA to the appropriate customs office where the car came in instructing them that as far as they were concerned, the car was fit to drive; the bond could be released, and a title could be issued.

In the late '70s and early '80s, an EPA test procedure could be performed by an approved lab for $1,000–$2,000 per car depending on the lab. Naturally, for a manufacturer who was hoping to sell 100,000 cars or more for $10,000 each, it didn't make any sense to test each copy, even if it did, pre-conditioning and testing could take as much as 24 hours. A mass-produced car would likely spend more time in the test lab than it did on the assembly line, so if a company wanted to sell a quantity of cars in the States, it made sense to jump through the hoops necessary to obtain a certificate. But for a builder who was only looking at selling a handful of cars for 60 to 70 thousand dollars each, case by case testing could conceivably make sense, particularly if the durability requirement need not otherwise be met. It was this little niche of the rules that made case by case compliance feasible and inspired cooperation between the Italian sports car makers, and the "gray marketers" and for them, the conversion shops were able to provide channels they would otherwise not have had to the U.S. markets.

5

The Stoichiometric Closed Loop Electronic Feedback Controlled Breakthrough

Now that a few compliance shops had gotten off the ground, and there was a steady trickle of exotic European machinery coming across the border with conditional papers, the technicians charged with getting the cars past the authorities found they had to pit their know-how against the progressively tightening emissions regulations. The DOT requirements had for the most part leveled off and changes from model year to model year by 1980 were minor. For a time, the DOT waffled back and forth over the bumper specifications. In fact, beginning in 1982 the front bumper standard was eased yet again to 2½ MPH. But safety compliance overall was fairly routine, except when the manufacturers made body changes. Continuing to satisfy the EPA, however, was shooting at a moving target. An annual tightening of emissions standards had been written into law, right up to 1981. After the 1981 model year change, the emissions standards would remain the same until the next Clean Air Act revision in 1990, but the last leap from 1980 to 1981 was set to be a big one. The federal limits would be practically cut in half, and methods and devices that were sufficient up until then wouldn't have a chance of working by themselves.

The regulations had continued to reduce the allowed levels of HC and CO and more recently of NOx, and the problem there was that these were not compatible goals. Measures taken to reduce the former invariably ended up producing more of the latter and vice-versa. It wasn't just a puzzle for the converters, it was a serious challenge for the automakers themselves. While the domestic carmakers were lagging in solving the problem and continually lobbying for a roll-back in the standards, carmakers outside the U.S. were quietly making significant developments. In 1977 Volvo showed the world how it could be done.

5. The Stoichiometric Feedback Controlled Breakthrough

Ironically, Volvo's breakthrough came using an old piece of Ford technology: the three-way catalyst. In the late 1960s, Ford researchers had identified elements that could promote a reaction that could simultaneously oxidize HC and CO and reduce NOx, leaving exhaust containing primarily CO_2, nitrogen, and water. The catch was that the reaction would only occur under very specific conditions. The air-fuel mix going into the engine had to be almost exactly at the stoichiometric point of 14.6 to one by weight for everything to work. A stoichiometric mixture is one in which the quantities of reactants are exactly right for complete conversion of everything. A perfect stoichiometric ratio of hydrocarbon fuel and oxygen would leave, after combustion, nothing but CO_2 and water. There are many other components in gasoline and in air, but the theory is good, and the mix is right when the 14.6/1 ratio is maintained. When the mixture was at this "sweet spot," the three-way catalyst did its job remarkably well and the larger part of all three of the offensive gasses was converted. But if the mixture varied by two percent or more to either side of stoichiometric, efficiency fell off drastically: too rich and the NOx stayed low but the HC and CO would take off. Too lean and the NOx content would shoot up. Therein lay the rub: an automobile engine, operating at a wide range of speeds and under a wide range of loads, had widely varying fuel requirements; and in their early experiments, Ford engineers found that even when using fuel injection, they were not able to control their fuel systems precisely enough to take advantage of the three-way catalyst's properties. While they hadn't completely given up on the three-way cat, the technology had been shelved when Volvo picked it up and looked it over.

Volvo found the key in an old piece of aerospace technology developed by Westinghouse in the early 1960s. Westinghouse had been working on fuel cells for the space program and experimented for a time with a solid electrolyte material made from zirconium dioxide (zirconia). They found that, when heated, the tiny tubes of zirconia had the property of allowing the passage of oxygen ions while blocking ions of other gasses. The material they made didn't work out for fuel cells, but in the right context it turned out to be a remarkably sensitive and reliable detector of oxygen.

In the early seventies Bosch and Bendix, a builder of fuel injection systems, were experimenting with sensors made from zirconia in the exhaust stream of gasoline engines. When at operating temperature of about 1200 degrees Fahrenheit, the thermocouple sensors they made would produce about a volt when there was little or no oxygen in the exhaust. At any fuel mix even slightly leaner than the ideal stoichiometric ratio, there would be enough residual oxygen in the exhaust to cause the sensor voltage to drop off sharply. Conveniently, the voltage drop would take place at exactly the oxygen content that worked best with the three-way catalyst. If this property could by the somehow be used to control the fuel mixture, the new three-way catalysts could be useful.

Engineers for most of the major automotive companies were well aware of the research and the possibilities that it implied, but at the time the challenge of building a system that could employ the technology to practical effect was a big step up from the research lab. Bosch, however, while not a car maker, had been building electronic fuel injection systems for European production cars since 1966. So it was natural that they took the lead on integrating the oxygen sensors into their systems. At first, they married the sensors to their L Jetronic system that was already in widespread use by Volvo and Saab, as well as Volkswagen and Mercedes. L Jetronic injection employed electrically operated needle valve type fuel injectors that had fuel pumped to them at a relatively constant pressure. The amount of fuel sprayed into the airstream depended on the amount of time the injector valve was opened. Different fuel mixtures appropriate for operating conditions were achieved by using fairly crude microcomputers to control the injection time. Injection times on an engine using the L Jetronic system might vary from about 1 millisecond at idle to 5 milliseconds under acceleration, and any amount of time in between depending on operating conditions. To make a rough determination of how much fuel was required, the L Jetronic system used a movable flap in a pipe that measured the amount of air the engine was drawing. Other sensors that measured engine and air temperature and throttle position were used to further refine fuel requirements, and Bosch used the oxygen sensor to fine tune the injection time the computer generated. The oxygen sensors were installed so that about ¾ inch of the sensor protruded into the exhaust header pipe or the exhaust manifold, where the engine exhaust would bring it up to operating temperature. The 0–1 volt signal it produced could be read by the engine's electronic control unit and used to modulate the injection time by fractions of milliseconds. An engine equipped this way could continuously monitor its own exhaust and make the minute corrections necessary to keep the fuel mixture in the very narrow range required by the catalyst.

Work went on for some time with the L Jet system, but microcomputers were only in their infancy at the time, and the goal of achieving the necessary precision of mixture control with a system that had not been originally designed for it was seeming elusive. So Volvo turned their attention to a new system Bosch was working on at the time: the *continuous injection system* or the K Jetronic. The K Jetronic system was initially an elegantly simple mechanical injection system that employed no electronic controls at all. Fuel was continuously sprayed into the airstream of the intake and the amount of fuel sprayed was governed by the amount of air drawn into the running engine. Like the L Jet system, air intake was measured by the

5. The Stoichiometric Feedback Controlled Breakthrough   69

movement of an aluminum plate in the airstream, but rather than sending an electronic signal, the plate moved a spool valve in a "fuel distributor" that directly regulated fuel flow to the injector nozzles. To modulate the fuel mixture for cold start and warm-up periods, Bosch used the fuel to produce a variable hydraulic pressure that offered resistance to the movement of the metering plate, slowly raising the "control" pressure as the engine warmed up. This gave the system the initial enrichment it needed to run well cold, then gradually leaned the fuel mixture as the engine approached operating temperature.

Since the engine had no electronic controls the signal from the oxygen sensor could not be used to directly influence the fuel mixture. Bosch solved the problem by building a simple digital circuit that generated a regular 12 volt on-off pulse and modulated the duration of the pulse according to the signal from the oxygen sensor. They used the pulse to drive one of their electronic injectors. The end of the injector, instead of being mounted in the airstream, was fitted at the nozzle end with a fuel return line so that the fuel that passed through the injector simply went back to the tank. This layout used the fuel injector as a pressure bleed and effectively made the pressure side of the injector into an electronically controlled modulator with a very quick response time. They re-named the injector a "frequency valve" and connected it to the part of the system that controlled fuel feed to the injectors. In that position Bosch could use the frequency valve to finely tune the fuel delivery according to the electrical signal from the oxygen sensor.

The method of adjusting the fuel system while driving according to the oxygen content of the exhaust was called electronic feedback control and it was remarkably successful both in providing the catalyst with the exhaust mix that it liked, and in maintaining good drivability. In engineering shorthand, it became known as *lambda-sonde*, lambda being the Greek letter used to express air/fuel ratio in engineering calculations, and *sonde* the German word for sensor. When an engine was operating this way and the mixture was in balance, the fuel system would be continuously shifting back and forth from a few percent rich to a few percent lean about two to four times a second. At this time, the engine was said to be running in closed loop. The fine adjustments made by the feedback system were usually small enough and quick enough to be barely noticeable by the driver.

The improved efficiency of fuel injection over carburetion, coupled with the precise fuel control made possible by the closed loop system and running into a three-way catalyst, turned out to be the breakthrough technology that engineers in the emissions business had been hoping for since the whole emissions control thing got started. A car running in closed loop used less fuel, produced less pollution, and made more usable power all at the same time. Cars equipped with a lambda-sonde system could often pass the new exhaust standards without the use of an air pump, thermal reactor, or exhaust gas recirculation, so in many cases the builders were able to dispense with these heavy and expensive mechanical devices. As an added benefit, the Bosch fuel injection systems that were employing the technology also made a car that was easier to start at any temperature, and easier to drive under any conditions. It took Volvo a few years to work out the details; they had started in 1972 and it wasn't until 1977 that they had a car in production using the new system. But the results spoke for themselves. Volvo had proven that with the right technology, the toughest emission standards yet recommended by the EPA could be met and even surpassed using closed loop systems.

Why did it take Volvo, a small car company with a barely noticeable presence in the U.S. to bring this research to fruition? It was precisely because of who they were that they made it happen. Being a small company outside the U.S., the management at Volvo didn't understand political maneuvering and could see no future in trying to exercise influence over the U.S. government the way the domestic companies did. Instead, they thought it would be more useful to spend their time and money actually trying to meet the upcoming standards. Another foreign car company, Honda, had the same philosophy, and they concentrated on the physical design of an engine that produced less pollution rather than trying to clean up exhaust after it left the engine. Honda was successful with their new CVCC (compound vortex controlled combustion) engines and even met the 1980 standards without a catalytic converter. But Honda's technology would not play a role in the gray market because it was designed into the internal configuration of the engine itself and therefore could not be retrofitted to other cars.

Seeing Volvo's success, the other automakers quickly started working on lambda-sonde systems of their own, and more and more lambda sensor equipped cars were showing up in the market by 1980. But the system Volvo and Bosch developed had the biggest implications for the gray marketeers. The basic K-Jetronic fuel system without lambda control developed by Bosch became very popular among European manufacturers for its low cost and relative simplicity. It came into common use with the 1980s by Mercedes, BMW, Volkswagen, Porsche-Audi, as well as Ferrari. The development work done for Volvo had actually been a sort of retrofit that had adapted the lambda technology to an existing fuel system. By adding an oxygen sensor and a frequency valve, with a relatively simple electronic circuit to control them, Bosch turned a simple mechanical fuel system into a feedback system. With a feedback system, a three-way catalyst could be employed. By that way of thinking, any car with Bosch K Jetronic fuel injection could be retrofitted with the same parts and brought into line with the

5. The Stoichiometric Feedback Controlled Breakthrough

latest emission standards. If Bosch could do it, there was no reason that the aftermarket couldn't do the same.[1]

With the shift from the 1980 to the 1981 emission standards, carburetors practically disappeared from the U.S. automotive market. The leap from 7 grams of CO and 2 grams of NOx to 3.4 grams of CO and 1.0 grams NOx cut the permitted level of the gasses in half and was just too big a jump to accomplish with a carburetor. Not to mention that tightening *evaporative* emission standards were making the use of carburetors impractical. Coincidentally, with the notable exception of the Lamborghinis, most of the cars that were considered desirable among the gray market buyers were now fitted with Bosch fuel injection systems at the factory. In most cases of the most sought-after European model cars, the fuel systems differed from the systems on cars built for the states only in that they didn't have the lambda controls. Converters quickly figured out that even though the fuel distributors on the non-Lambda systems didn't have the appropriate drillings for connecting the frequency valve, they could install a frequency valve in-line with the control pressure regulator (the device chiefly responsible for cold running fuel enrichment) and achieve nearly as much control as with the factory set-up. The response time was a little bit slower than the Bosch factory systems, so the small mixture adjustments done by the system were more noticeable in the performance of the car. But in most cases the control was adequate, and the add-on systems worked pretty well. The electronic controllers built by Bosch for the Lambda-controlled cars could be purchased at any parts department and didn't necessarily have to be built for the car being converted, so the converters shopped Bosch parts books and usually chose the simplest and least expensive controllers. The different controllers available had different features and capabilities, but mostly the converters were interested only in reading the oxygen sensor and driving the frequency valve. In the case of most Mercedes, there was a lambda controlled counterpart to many of their cars and conversion might mean installing a few parts available right from the dealer's parts department. Other popular cars, like the early BMW 325 and the Ferrari Boxer, had K Jetronic fuel systems but no Lambda-style counterparts, so they would be converted often using the hardware designed for the Mercedes.

At this point the electronics geeks got involved. Over the counter the Bosch Lambda controllers were a high-ticket item, costing over $300 retail. But the important circuits inside were pretty basic. A voltage comparator, an integrator and a driver could be made up with a handful of simple components purchased for less than ten dollars at an electronics supply store. With a custom-made printed circuit board (also an inexpensive item) they could be slapped together in an hour by a high school kid with a soldering pencil and mounted in a cheap plastic box the size of a cigarette case. If the boxes were sold to converters for $100, the converter would save substantially over buying the Bosch parts and the maker had a tidy margin of about $75 per unit.

It was opportunities like this that made the conversion business so big for so many players. Automotive technicians could understand the mechanical installations well enough. They could study the mechanical emission control systems on production cars and make simplified, but functional copies of them. But the electronic controllers were regarded as black boxes filled with mystery and the mechanics usually didn't have the technical know-how to design a logic circuit of the type that would appear quite simple to an electronics technician. For the electronics guys, it was a simple matter to study the circuits in the controllers, trim off the fat and the unnecessary features, and build a much less expensive (and often less reliable) circuit of their own. With a margin like the one that was possible with these controllers, the sale of a just a thousand "lambda boxes" could net $75,000. Not bad for a back-room operation.

A big player in the aftermarket lambda controller was a company based in California that called themselves DC Johnson. Getting started around 1982, they built an ultra-simple controller, put it in a Radio Shack project box and marketed it for about $120. It was crude, and only moderately reliable, but it worked. It could read an oxygen sensor and drive a frequency valve very much like the Bosch equipment. Unlike the Bosch equipment, it had a couple of fine adjustment points which the conversion techs liked. The boxes were not as stable as their Bosch counterparts, and the adjustment points made it possible for the techs to compensate for that, but the units often required frequent tinkering to keep them working well.

Unreliable though they were, the "Johnson boxes" turned out to be a low-cost alternative to the Bosch controllers. And they became very popular among the converters. Of course, their simplicity and low manufacturing cost were too obvious, and it wasn't long before countless copies were turning up, some of them indistinguishable from the original. If duplicating the circuitry in a Bosch factory control unit was simple, copying the copies that Johnson was marketing was child's play. The technology had pretty much become public domain, and anybody studied in basic electronics could get into the act. By 1984 there were enough players in the conversion business to absorb the knock-off products of dozens of different makers. Some of them were better than others. Some had their own innovations and features, but most of them were the same circuit, maybe in a different looking box.

Nevertheless, the term "Johnson box" became part of the converters' lexicon and was used to refer to practically any aftermarket Lambda control box.

Bosch however was prolific at building different types of fuel injection systems, and the European car makers employed them all. Microelectronics technology was advancing quickly during the 1980s and as they were able to squeeze more and more computing power into the controllers, with the advances Bosch injection systems became more and more sophisticated. The chief rival for the K Jetronic system, the L Jetronic that had been the original subject of Lambda system research, was still around and by employing recently developed computer technology, Bosch had been able to build an L Jet system that could successfully employ lambda control. The manufacturers liked the L Jet system because being fully electronic, it offered more precise fuel control. The new series of L Jet systems became popular with BMW and Porsche after 1980 and were closely followed by the use of the Motronic systems which integrated fuel injection with ignition control.

The L Jet system presented a new challenge for the aftermarket electronics guys that was a little tougher than the K Jet. While in the early stages, Bosch had found it difficult to integrate a Lambda control into the L Jet system, with the snowballing advances in microelectronics that were occurring at the time, they eventually developed a reliable way to use the oxygen sensor signal to modulate the injector pulse within the controller circuitry. But the aftermarket guys could find no easy way to tap in and modulate the system like they did with the K Jet. They found their answer in the various sensor inputs.

The coolant temperature sensor was primarily responsible for allowing an engine to run well with the engine cold or hot and in all kinds of weather. It was simply a temperature sensitive resistor that diverted a portion of a 0–5-volt signal to ground and the computer used the voltage at the sensor to trim the mix. The controller could vary injection time as much as 400 percent, according to the value of the temperature sensor, so it was a bit heavy handed (lambda systems require less than 25 percent modulation). But very small changes in the temp sensor voltage resulted in mixture changes that could be modulated well enough to achieve closed loop control. The Johnson company initially built an adaptor box that could be installed in line to their original box that took the pulsing signal of the first box and converted it into a variable resistance intended to be put in series with the temp sensor—basically a digital to analog conversion. Later they integrated the adaptor into the first circuit, combined it into one box and sold it as a different type of controller. The system was clumsy and slow, but under the right conditions it could achieve *just* enough lambda control to get an L Jet equipped car through the test.

Because the Johnson boxes were only just adequate, particularly for cars equipped with systems other than the K Jet, the field was wide open for any other electronics hobbyist or engineer to try their hand at lambda control. One engineer who was inspired to take a crack at it was Mike Valentine. Aside from being an electrical engineer, Valentine was a car nut with a particular affinity for German cars. The piece that got him involved in the gray market car business was a BMW 745i that he saw at a shop in Cincinnati. A large four-door sedan equipped with a 3.5–liter turbocharged engine, it was BMW's flagship car in Europe. But they didn't make it available in the U.S. because, like the 500 Mercedes, its fuel consumption was high enough to skew their CAFE rating. ("Corporate Average Fuel Economy" standards meant to improve fuel economy had been implemented following the Arab Oil Embargo.) An outstanding performer in its time, it used the relatively new Bosch Motronic engine control system which integrated fuel control with ignition and idle speed control. It was also an uncommon car among the gray market importers because no one had yet developed a good Lambda control to work with the Motronics.

Valentine wanted the car badly and the importer said he would get the car to him as soon as the EPA and DOT conversions were completed. But he shortly found that they couldn't get the car through the federal test using the available technology. They were using the Johnson box and its adaptor but it was a clumsy arrangement and there just wasn't enough control to satisfy the catalyst. After weeks and weeks of delays and excuses, mostly about the failure of the control systems to get a handle on the emissions, he

The BMW 745 was a turbocharged version of the 3.5 liter 735 and was unavailable in the U.S. except through gray market channels (private collection).

5. The Stoichiometric Feedback Controlled Breakthrough

decided that in order to own the car of his dreams, he would have to invent something that would get the car out of the test lab and into his driveway. Visiting the lab while the car was on the dyno, he learned enough about the process to make a plan.

Valentine was not an automotive technician. He admitted that what he knew about cars he got from reading car magazines. But once he understood the nature of the problem, he could look at it as an electronic control issue and that put it into his home field. In an article published by *Car and Driver* in 1984, he gave an easy to understand account of how he worked out the problem:

> On the backs of radios and stuff you've seen the warning *no user serviceable parts inside*. That means you don't need to know. Bosch is like this. You're not supposed to pry the top off of the air flow meter. There are even paint seals on all the screws just to make sure you understand. But I did it anyway. Inside there's a flap in the airstream, pivoting on a shaft. It's held shut by a cuckoo clock spring. When the air comes in it blows open the flap, kinda like a screen door with no latch. The harder it blows, the harder the door goes out against the closing spring. On the shaft is a potentiometer, looks like a volume control on a radio. As soon as any electronics buff sees this it's AHA! Now I know where the signal comes from! It's like an air-volume knob. The more air coming through, the louder it turns up the knob ... that's easy.
>
> So I was poking around in the engine compartment with my oscilloscope. I would hook up an injector wire then play around with the throttle and see what happed to the pulse width. I had the oxygen sensor in the exhaust by then, so I was watching the output too, just to see where the mixture was. I was doing various things just to see what would happen. I tried opening the air flow flap to make it think more air was coming in and the pulse got longer, just like you would think. Then it immediately got shorter again. What's this? So I held it the other way and the pulse got shorter, then it fattened back out. It was fighting me, trying to get back to where it thought it was. Something was wrong. The air-flow meter would logically be the first link in the chain that controls fuel mixture, just like a simple eyewitness report to the brain. The only link in the chain I could take for granted. But now it seemed to have a mind of its own, which meant all my assumptions were wrong.

It was in this moment of frustration that Valentine realized that among other tasks the "brain" was responsible for maintaining a steady idle speed. When he manually leaned the mixture, the engine idle slowed down just enough to cause the brain to respond and fatten the mixture back up in order to bring up the idle speed. Likewise, when he went the other way and richened the mixture, the brain would compensate in the other direction. His assumptions were not wrong, he just hadn't taken all the variables into consideration. The Johnson box was trying to control the fuel mixture via the temperature sensor, but he decided that the air-flow meter would be the key—the point where he could introduce a bogus signal that would make the brain produce the EPA fuel mixture rather than the German market mixture.

Bosch wasn't giving up the plans for their brain, so Valentine had to work out the details of the system himself. Much of his research took place on the road, driving the car with a number of instruments and experimental gear wired into the control circuits. He called this setup his "kamakazi dyno" because of the things that would happen in traffic while he had his head down watching the meters. It was a dangerous practice, but not uncommon among gray market technicians who didn't want to pay $250 per hour of dyno time.

> Once I knew how everything worked, I could design a circuit that could put my biases into the reference signal going to the airflow meter. BMW wanted fuel economy, so that's how the brain thinks. I said uh-uh, we're going to get stoichiometric 'cause that's what the catalyst wants. And we're going to accept any fuel economy we get.

Valentine's standards were higher than the average shop building products for sale to converters.

> The design standard I was aiming for was "this car is for me" so I was going to put enough circuits into the box so that it drives right. I really beat the project to death, engineering wise. My shop has a drive-in door, so I've got EPA-style starting temperatures in the morning of about 68 degrees. So, every morning I'd start the thing up just to see what would happen. Before the oxygen sensor comes up to temperature you might just as well have a piece of glass down there for all it does, so the box has a little compensator, it compensates for hot starts, too.[2]

Valentine's box worked well enough to get the car through the test on the first try with a good margin. He went on to make and sell copies and also made versions to work with other BMW models as well as the Porsche 911 and 928, but he didn't get rich off of his product like so many other gray market operators. His boxes sold for about four times what other controllers were selling for, so they were popular only among the more quality oriented converters. Likewise, there were plenty of technicians who might not have been capable of the development work but were perfectly able to open up the box and do enough reverse engineering to build one of their own. After getting his reward in the 745 BMW that inspired the project, he eventually dropped out of the gray market business, going on to develop and market a well-respected radar detector.

With Johnson and Valentine and countless other small operations in the business of emission controls, EPA conversion went from halls of the research and development to off the shelf technology in a matter of a few short years. Not all the products worked well, some didn't even work at all, but simply making the claim and pricing the products low enough was usually sufficient to generate sales. Johnson kept marketing their same basic system with new adaptors to cover new models as they came out and they worked backwards as well, trying to provide for the growing market of used cars. One of their adaptors consisted of a lambda-controlled air bleed valve to be plugged into the intake manifold of a carbureted engine: a device that may have worked in theory, but in practice was likely only to cause a technician to run up huge bills for dyno time and failed tests. Fortunately for the black box builders, gray market conversion was a gambler's game, so there was little if any repercussion for selling a device that couldn't get a car through the test. Emission testing was a complicated process, and any number of other factors could easily contribute to a car's not successfully navigating the federal test procedure. This left the window wide open for any number of snake oil salesmen who had a product to market as an emission control device.

6

The Boom

Up to 1979, gray market imports were just a small blip in the government radar. To be sure, their numbers had been steadily increasing as more conversion shops emerged to get a piece of the exotic car pie. But in a country of 200 million where cars were imported through normal channels by the hundreds of thousands, 1500 gray market imports in a year might not be enough to attract any attention at all. But for the EPA they were something of a nuisance.

Government wheels generally turn slowly, so it should be no surprise that EPA was not quick to react to the number of applications for clearance coming in from gray market importers. In the interest of fairness to individuals, the laws had been changed in 1972, making available the option of altering a non-compliant car to fit the rules. But nobody had anticipated there would be much action in that department, and there really wasn't any provision made in any office or budget for processing applications. The EPA just didn't want to be bothered. The administration had simply never dreamed of the number of independent imports that would be requesting entry under the "modify and test" rules on the customs form.

But while companies like Amerispec and ACI might at first have brought in just a handful of cars each year, word had gotten out that there was a legal path to owning European dream cars in the States via conversion shops. EPA personnel were spending far more time reviewing applications and answering questions about procedures and requirements than they wanted to, and things only seemed to be getting worse. So as early as 1977, they began considering another rule change they hoped would relieve some of the pressure.

For EPA, the first step in changing the laws was publishing a "Notice of Proposed Rule Making," in the Federal Register. The Federal Register is the public document where the government continuously publishes all of their decisions, and where the EPA, NHTSA, or any other rulemaking agency would publish a summation of what they intended to do and invite all interested parties to comment in writing on the changes. If there was enough interest, they would hold one or more public hearings where individuals were invited to speak before a panel about why they may or may not like the proposed rules and offer suggestions for modifying them. So when they announced in June of 1977 that, among other things, they were considering abolishing the modify and test clauses from the rules, it raised a few eyebrows. The question didn't reach the public hearing stage, however, until July of 1980 and by then it had been kicked around the desks at EPA enough that it had indeed taken a completely different form. On one hand, the EPA proposed to eliminate the options for importers entirely and on the other they were ready to throw up their hands and permit anybody who had not imported a car since 1970 one opportunity to bring in the car of their dreams without having to modify it to meet regulations. They cited several reasons that revolved around the hardship the modify and test rules were causing for U.S. citizens buying cars abroad, including persons who had been working and living overseas and wanted to return home with a car they bought while out of the country. In their rules proposal they spelled out some of the hardships that they had seen brought upon the heads of the citizenry over the last eight years.

The modify clause of the customs form stipulated that the non-compliant car be altered to make it identical to a vehicle that had a certificate of conformity. Their remarks, in lawyer-speak, told of the unintended effects of that rule.

> This option has the potential to mislead importers into believing that modification is an easy option requiring only a few minor adjustments to their foreign vehicles to make them identical to U.S. certified models. As Federal emission standards become stricter, it becomes more difficult and highly impractical to attempt to convert an uncontrolled vehicle to be identical to a controlled vehicle. For example, many later model year vehicles modification requires total engine replacement to bring the cars into conformity.... In addition, because manufacturers cannot be required to inform EPA or the individual importer of the modifications necessary to bring a particular vehicle into conformity, importers often cannot obtain the information necessary to bring their vehicles into compliance. Without such information, importers are required to test the vehicles.... Otherwise, they are subject to the loss of their bond and the assessment of civil penalties under the act.[1]

They went on to take a shot at unscrupulous foreign car salesmen in typical government understatement.

> Foreign salesmen sometimes take advantage of the availability of this option when selling foreign models to U.S. citizens, since they have no incentive to inform the purchasers of the expense involved in attempting to import their vehicles into the U.S. As long as the vehicle is able to be imported in some way, U.S. citizens will continue to be deceived as to the hardships involved.[2]

In plain English, this meant that foreign used car salesmen were delighted to see American car buyers come onto the lot. They would explain to the buyer that they could indeed import their car to the United States because it was virtually identical to the U.S. version. All it needed was a few minor adjustments. They showed them the right boxes to check on the customs form and told them to have a nice day. Sometimes it wasn't until the car arrived at a U.S. port that the owner became painfully aware of the true expense of getting their car out from under Customs' scrutiny and onto public highways. By that time the car had been paid for and shipped overseas ... there was no way to turn back that didn't involve forfeiting thousands of dollars.

Regarding the modify and test provision, the EPA again cited the enormous expense of testing a car, the uncertainty of the results and the fact that some of the labs were not following procedures, while acknowledging there was a new market emerging over which they had little control.

> Another problem is created by the availability of this option to importers other than individuals importing vehicles for their own use. Many importers for resale are importing non-conforming vehicles with the object of performing their own modifications, testing the vehicles, and selling them. Because this option imposes less rigorous testing requirements than does EPA's certification program for auto manufacturers, this practice undermines the certification requirement of the Clean Air Act, and arouses protest from the factory licensed distributors for manufacturers participating in the certification program.[3]

But having cited all these facts, the EPA's announcement finally got down to the real reason they were considering changing the rules: "The burden imposed on the EPA and Customs in administering both modification and testing options is substantial."[4] They were admitting that they were overwhelmed by the new "gray market," and hoped they could make it go away with a few rule changes. Or failing that, perhaps they could just wash their administrative hands of the whole affair. First, they intended to eliminate the modify and test clauses entirely, allowing only cars that had a certificate of conformity to enter the U.S. Second, they were willing to offer an exemption for each individual to import one car for their personal use without having to comply with EPA standards at all.

Using importation figures from the past, they suggested that maybe what car enthusiast had been saying all along was true: that in the big picture, the effect on overall air quality of some 1500 outlaw cars per year wasn't going to amount to much. Maybe if they let wealthy car nuts bring in one Ferrari or Lamborghini each, then the problem would go away, and they could get back to the more important work of protecting the environment.

When the EPA announced they were considering this compromise, it was not, as might be expected, met with cheers from the American car enthusiast community. The announcement took place in the Federal

Register, where it was buried among hundreds of thousands of pages of small print, where it would be seen only by people who were looking for it. The announcement was of a hearing: on November 3, 1980, a workshop would be held in D.C. and "interested parties" were invited to attend and speak their mind as to the proposed changes in the gray market import rules. EPA officials proposed to listen to what they had to say then skulk back to their Washington cubicles and decide what to do.[5]

As it turned out, car enthusiasts—the people for whom these rule changes were clearly intended—were not well represented. Of the 11 persons who chose to testify, only one spoke in favor of the changes. William Long of the Alfa Romeo Owners Club spoke in favor of the new rules. Another individual seemed interested only in ensuring that the EPA should continue to offer the already existing exemption for race cars. The rest wanted the EPA to maintain the status quo.

Those who took notice of the rules and took the trouble to go to Washington and make their case against the one-time exemption were not green-minded environmentalists, though they might have tried to appear to be. They were businessmen. The first of them to speak were representatives of the American International Automobile Dealers Association. They spoke on behalf of the "legitimate" (read factory authorized) car dealers they thought would be hurt by the proposal, pointing out that cars sold in the authorized dealerships of Porsche, Mercedes, Ferrari, Lancia, BMW, Jaguar, Alfa, Maserati, etc., would be replaced by cars directly imported by individuals, estimating future numbers of 100,000 cars per year. Of course, they finished by reminding officials of the many thousands of people who were employed by those dealer networks whose very livelihood would be threatened.

Volkswagen of America was next, represented by Phillip Hutchinson, who suggested that as much as half of all Porsche sales in the country would be siphoned off by individuals bringing in European models, in effect admitting that Porsches sold in the U.S. were not as desirable as those sold in Europe. He noted that there would be a big market for the Porsche Turbo and the Volkswagen Beetle, neither of which was imported to the U.S. at the time through the dealer network. But he didn't offer any explanation as to why the company wasn't catering to what they perceived to be such a strong demand by offering their own U.S. legal versions of the cars.

Gary Rodriguez, the representative of Ferrari North America, said that Ferrari dealerships would cease to exist if the new rule change went through. Ferrari was still dragging its feet with respect to federalizing their V12 cars, leaving only the V8s for the American dealers to sell. Apparently, they were afraid their customers would all rush off to Europe and buy Boxers rather than the 308s then offered in the dealer network. There was probably an element of truth in that, since Ferrari buyers often didn't suffer the same economic constraints as the average car buyer. And while Ferrari itself was already enjoying some sales through the gray market—sales they would not have made otherwise—as long as the company did not offer a certified version of the V12, the North American division had some legitimate concerns about sales to be lost to the European dealers. Rodriguez wanted to see a total ban on importing cars that didn't get their EPA Certificate the hard way with *no* exceptions or exemptions. He stated, "There currently are dozens of items Americans cannot import into this country. We do not believe adding an additional item to this list will cause a great problem for consumers in this country."[6]

While Ferrari might not have benefited from a total ban on uncertified cars, their U.S. dealer network would have. Those dealerships that sold only the cars provided them by Ferrari would like to have seen the gray market imports taken off the table. Likewise, the Porsche dealers wanted very much not to have to compete with their own company in the independent imports. The compliance shops that had emerged during the late seventies naturally wanted things to stay exactly as they were, allowing the conditional importation and modification of non-compliant cars. Owners of two such shops, Dick Fritz of Amerispec and Al Mardikian of Trend Imports, appeared that day to state their case. That their concern was for their own financial self-interest was clear and quite understandable, but they still appeared to feel the need to pretend that they were motivated by a more altruistic concern for the public health.

Albert Mardikian, introducing himself as the president and chief engineer of Trend Imports, opened his comments eloquently expressing those concerns.

"First, I'm against this act proposed by your department for various reasons. But the most important reasons which have concerned me are the health of the American public, especially in California, my state, which the air pollution with all the modified vehicles in the country; it's tremendous. If you will pass this act, it will be a lot more worse than what we got now" [sic]. He went on to express concerns about the economic impact of the changes: "We're going to have a lot of unemployment again. I mean, I have fifteen people, you know, are going to be unemployed."

Mardikian and other conversion shop owners knew well what they stood to lose if the rule changes went through as written; everything he had gained when the 1972 amendments to the Clean Air Act were passed to begin with. The emergence and growth of the gray market shops went a long way to demonstrate the truth in the seemingly cynical remarks of Nobel laureate economist Milton Friedman, when he said that the largest benefactor of government regulation is always the industry being regulated. While the manufacturers cried foul with each new law, they did find a way to use the laws to narrow down their playing field by making sure that only the most profitable car models were available in the largest automobile market in the world, America. The conversion shops were in business because the Clean Air Act opened up a market niche where they could thrive. And while the business owners themselves may or may not have cared a bit about the state of the atmosphere, they seemed to think the best way forward was to keep the legislation as it stood and continue business as usual while representing themselves as environmentalists.

Dick Fritz of Amerispec was less flagrant than Mardikian, but he chose the same platform. Fritz had found good business in federalizing Ferrari Boxers and would rarely even bother with other types of cars. The rules as they stood worked for him, and the proposed changes could have put him and all the other conversion shops out of business. In alluding to the environmental impact of non-compliant cars, he suggested that the complicated and expensive process of privately importing a gray market car was a valuable "deterrent." "Yes, it's a bureaucratic hassle for the EPA but the payoff is that it keeps these imports down to a trickle. With the new rule it was our thought that the 1400 or 1500 [per year] vehicles that are now trickling in would very quickly jump to 20,000 or even more." Alfredo Caiti of Automotive Compliance Center Inc. suggested that things would go much further and that the figures on independently imported cars could go into the hundreds of thousands.[7]

Armed with the information from these testimonies and stacks of written comments submitted by other interested parties, EPA officials returned to their offices to try and figure out what to do next. Ultimately, they decided to put off the decision, but in the meantime, they came up with a compromise. They announced in a November 1981 press release that conditional importation of cars pending modification and testing would be allowed to continue. Additionally, they would exercise a one-time exemption for individuals wanting to import a non-compliant car, but the car had to be five years old or more. They were hoping this compromise would achieve their original goal of reducing the number of applications they had to process, remove the potential threat to the new car dealers, all while maintaining the flow of business for the conversion shops and import car sellers.

If the EPA administrator had called up the folks at the DOT and asked them if they thought the new rules change was a good idea, he probably would have heard some unprofessional language. They had been warned by the testimony of a large, pent-up market for European cars, and might have been able to anticipate the boom in imports that would result, but by the time the government agencies realized how quickly their free-enterprising citizens were reacting to such a money making opportunity, the snowball was already rolling down the hill.

The EPA's rules were built around the big picture: the overall quality of the air we breathe. It's true that in the grand scheme of things the admission of a few "dirty" cars was not going to set things back too far, so they could consider such a compromise without seriously affecting the success of their program. But officials at the NHTSA felt that they had to look at things differently: the rules were considered an issue of the safety of the occupants of each individual car, and relaxing the rules supposedly put individuals at risk. Allowing a waiver of the rules was not on their agenda. So, while the EPA was able to get a lot of paperwork off of their desk (temporarily) with the rule change, the DOT still had to process a packet for each and every car, including the ones that came with the increase in import traffic that the rule change brought.

The one-time exemption included a requirement that the car not be re-sold by the importer, but that stipulation was largely ignored. Once customs officials received the letters of approval from the EPA and the DOT, the car was issued a title in the state of residence of the owner and from that point on it was difficult to track. During the 1980s the state and federal governments were only just transitioning from paper to digital records and what computerized records they had were not very sophisticated; they didn't have the computer power to keep track of every car that crossed international borders once it was out of Customs' hands. The importers knew this and felt little inhibition about selling cars brought in and cleared under the new rules.

It took a couple of years for the impact of the one-time exemption to spread to the lower middle-class shoppers, but it did get there, and it had a profound effect on the used car market in Germany. Naturally, young men in the military stationed in Germany were thrilled at the idea of bringing home a used Porsche or BMW at the end of their tour, and some of the converters and dealers even advertised in publications popular with the military. They provided an eager market for the "Honest Hans" used car dealers that infest free-market economies throughout the world. The boom in gray-market tourism was the best thing that ever happened to used car dealers in Germany. Every used car dealer has a "low end" inventory that they have to dispose of one way or another. Whether by accident or design, they will accumulate tired old trade-ins that have to be moved out into the market. They might be cleaned up and sold on a low-priced retail lot or they might be sold at auction to other dealers or individual buyers looking for a bargain. But they tend to be a perpetual problem because it's hard to get them to go away for good. Germany's climate is rough on an automobile, much like the American Northeast, so rust is a serious problem in their used car market. A car body that is perforated with rust can be cosmetically fixed with fillers and paint, but like cancer, the rust will continue and will pop out of the fresh paint, usually within months. Cheap body repairs and paint jobs show their true colors quickly, and the unhappy buyer comes back in a few months with the car looking for some kind of satisfaction. Low-budget temporary repairs might fail shortly after a car reaches the home of its new owner, like a knocking engine that might be temporarily quieted with some kind of ultra-thick oil additive, but the damage is still there and it doesn't take long for it to become apparent again.

Like the man in *The Grapes of Wrath* passing off jalopies by putting sawdust in the gearboxes, many used car dealers had a bag of tricks for disguising mechanical noises—tricks designed to get the car off the lot. But sooner or later, they know they are likely to be held accountable for deceptive practices. The dealer may or may not find himself obligated to make restitution, but either way it's a nuisance to deal with an unhappy buyer and nobody wants to spend any more time in such negotiations than they have to. But if the car has been put on a ship and sent to America, the seller has little worry that he will have to face the buyer ever again. So the American gray market provided the ultimate solution: sell your losers to the Americans.

Even as the EPA and DOT were trying to figure out how they could best get out of having to process all the paperwork associated with direct imports from Europe, another branch of the U.S. government, the military publication *European Stars and Stripes*, was throwing fuel on the fire. In the winter of 1984, they began a series of articles on the automotive gray market and continued to do updates and re-visit the scene with subsequent issues throughout the 1980s. They offered the opinion that the industry was born with the beginning of the one-time EPA waiver, as it provided a chance for service personnel to bring home the used BMW, Mercedes or Porsche that they had been enjoying driving while they were stationed in Germany. They did not initially recommend GI's taking on the expense of trying to accomplish an EPA conversion but allowed that converting and shipping home their EPA exempt klunker might represent big savings or even a money-making proposition for them. For information, they went to the owner of a conversion shop in Germany conveniently located near a U.S. military base.

John Gordon specialized in Porsche conversions. At the time, Gordon's business was federalizing 10 Porsches a month. He stressed to his customers that it was far more economical to do the conversion work in Europe because, like car prices, parts prices were substantially lower than they were in the U.S. Gordon himself charged about $1,000 to convert a pre–1974 911, and twice that to convert a car made after 1974, when the bumper rules went into effect. At the same time, other firms were charging anywhere from $2,000 to $3,000 for a DOT only conversion.

Subsequent issues of *European Stars and Stripes* went on to cover the gray market at length, ensuring that every GI who read the paper was likely to entertain thoughts of importing a car of their own. Later installments published lists of cars that were the easiest to find and the least expensive to convert, and lists of workshops anxious to do the necessary work. Like most of the importers, they later backed off of the position that performing an EPA conversion was too much trouble or too expensive, as more and more shops were performing that work and the price of a total conversion was coming down. Later issues offered counterpoints and caveats, including a horror story of a man, Larry Roberts, who imported a 1982 Mercedes 280 and never got to drive it. Roberts' story was just one example of gray market experiences that became far too common.

Robert's car needed compliance work for both the DOT *and* EPA because the car didn't qualify for the one-time exemption; but he still felt that he could get a bargain because of the relatively low price of the car. He had the conversion work done while the car was still in Germany and had the car shipped to the States, believing everything was taken care of. When the car crossed customs, he was initially surprised to find that he still had to post a bond equal to the value of the car. That was his first big stumbling block. His next big disappointment came when he was informed that the paperwork submitted by the conversion shop had not been approved by the respective agencies. The EPA required that the car be tested, and it failed the test. He had a consultant inspect the DOT work and was told that the work was not properly done, so he had to engage shops to again perform the modifications he had already paid for in Europe, costing him $2,600 for EPA work and testing and $2,000 for DOT compliance. So, while engaged in long distance legal battles with the first European shop, Roberts' advice to *Stars and Stripes* readers was to get the work done stateside, or just to avoid gray market cars altogether.[8]

In spite of these and other warnings, many American service personnel were still excited at the prospect of bringing home a Mercedes or Porsche that they otherwise would not have been able to afford, so the used car dealers in Europe lined their pockets with American dollars and unloaded their junk on naïve American soldiers, as well as the budget conscious tourists. On the other end, the technicians in the American conversion shops sometimes had a headache trying to weld bumper reinforcements to rusty attachment points, or their lighting modifications became more complicated as they tried to fit new parts to damaged goods. But the cars continued to move through and often ended up parked and decaying in the back yards of their disgruntled new owners.

Of course, the EPA's rule change was not aimed at car dealers or brokers. But most new legislation has unforeseen consequences and as it turned out, the EPA's attempt to relieve some of the pressure brought on by the growing number of independent car imports had exactly the opposite effect than they had intended. Many gray market dealers actually got their start in the conversion business by exploiting the new exemption. Would-be importers knew that an EPA conversion was often prohibitively expensive and required a certain amount of know-how. The prospect of importing a car that for some reason or another might not ever pass the federal test procedure could make importing a European car the automotive equivalent of investing in an oil well only to come up with a dry hole. But on the other hand, by 1980 DOT compliance had pretty much been developed into an applied science and importers could even purchase ready made parts and pre-prepared forms from other operators to make things go smoothly. If a dealer or broker had been considering direct imports but was unsure about making the investment to convert a European car, the new rule was enough to encourage them to get started in what appeared to be a lucrative and fast-growing market.

The fact that the one-time exemption was aimed at individuals certainly didn't mean a dealer couldn't import a volume of cars; it only meant that each car had to have a different owner on the paperwork when it came into customs. A car dealer could act as a broker and sell the cars while they were still in Europe, insuring that each car crossed the border under a different name. Or a dealer who wanted to bring in a handful of cars with the intent of re-selling them down the road needed only to see that, in the eyes of the customs agents, each car would at least appear to belong to someone else. For that it was only necessary for the importer to associate each car with the name and social security number of an individual that they could be relatively certain would never attempt to import a car under the exemption at a later time. Wives, ex-wives, estranged husbands, ancient grandparents, distant relatives, and toddlers frequently went on record as having purchased a European car, with or even without their knowledge. Again, it was the increasing volume of paperwork involved in importing cars that prevented customs from scrutinizing applications; and once the dealers began to realize they could get away with it they started looking in stranger places for identities to assign to used cars. Cars were purchased and imported by dead persons and there were rumors of homeless persons having given up their social security number in exchange for a small cash payment, never learning that they were, for a short time, the owner of record of an expensive European luxury car.

For many small importers, these first steps into the gray market were enough to get them hooked. Selling European imports was good business and getting better, and while they were running out of ideas for importing cars under the individual exemptions, they began to look hungrily at the newer cars and the developing market for them. Many decided it was time to get into the conversion business proper and they set about learning how to modify cars to satisfy the EPA. Some took the job on themselves, even more contracted the work to the existing conversion shops, adding further to the snowballing business that they were already enjoying.

7

More Fuel on the Fire

It's almost spooky to ponder the number of factors that came to be the perfect economic storm that fueled the boom in the automotive gray market. While the dismal state of the American performance car was increasing interest in European cars, a new upper middle class was emerging in America, and they were flexing their economic muscle. Dubbed "yuppies" by the financial media—an acronym for young, upwardly-mobile professionals—they were well-educated careerist in their twenties and thirties. If they were married it was usually to another professional and they often put off having children until their later years; so their combined household income and cash-on-hand was unusually high. They were interested in many of the exciting, expensive things life had to offer, including travel and high-performance cars, and as a class their combined buying power could move mountains.

While the yuppies and their ilk were thriving, the U.S. economy writ large was in about the same shape as the American performance automobile. Unrelenting inflation had been confounding U.S. presidents throughout the decade of the 1970s. Nixon actually tried implementing a wage and price freeze. It failed. His successor, Gerald Ford, tried to tame it with a naïve plan that attempted to tap the power of the American consciousness. Invoking his new slogan, "Whip Inflation Now," his administration pushed campaign-style WIN buttons, hoping the collective will of the citizenry would cause the changes the markets needed. It failed, too. Ford's successor, President Carter, sacrificed his own political future by appointing Paul Volker as chairman of the Federal Reserve.

Volker and his fellow bankers theorized that they could slow inflation by slowing the flow of money to the banks. So in steady increments, the Fed raised the interest rate to the banks to unprecedented levels. It was extremely unpopular to everyone except people who had lots of cash on hand. If you had to borrow, you were badly screwed. Home mortgage rates climbed to over 18 percent. But conversely if you had money to invest, you could do very well. Money market funds were paying extraordinary rates and even conventional CDs were showing better returns than investments that were normally considered high yield. One of the results of these high returns was that American dollars in American banks became very attractive to foreign investors with other currencies. The international value of the dollar climbed steadily for several years, particularly against the German mark. During the late 1970s, rates moved from less than 2 marks per dollar to a peak of 3.4 marks per dollar in 1985, which increased buying power for an American travelling in Germany by more than 40 percent.

American yuppies who had lots of dollars and liked travel, investing, shopping, and luxury cars went to West Germany for their vacations. They exchanged their dollars at a rate that padded their pockets well with marks and went looking for a car to buy. They might choose to take advantage of their newly minted one-time exemption and buy a used car. Or, now that the conversion shops were more visible and were dealing with more conventional cars, they might choose a new Mercedes, BMW or Porsche and have the entire DOT and EPA conversion done when the car was shipped back to the U.S. In either case, the volume of independent imports was increasing drastically in the eighties. Sometimes they simply brought their cars home to drive. Just as often, they sold them in the U.S. and pocketed a handsome profit. Occasionally, they would enjoy the process so much that they would go back to Europe and do the whole thing again.

Buying a gray market car had started out as a complicated and expensive adventure for hard-core auto enthusiast but was rapidly becoming a trendy indulgence. Articles about saving money by buying cars overseas began appearing in publications like *Forbes* and *Business Week*, and soon the news was spreading to lifestyle and tourist magazines. Even summertime newspaper inserts dedicated to promoting vacation spots sported articles that described how you could save enough money buying a car overseas to finance your European vacation. Hundreds of American tourists became small-time dealers as they dabbled in the car business, taking semi-annual European vacations and bringing home a car with each trip. The articles in the travel magazines turned out to be true; there was a great deal of money to be made just by traveling to Germany and back. The exchange rate was so lopsided that even the most inept amateur car dealer could make *some* money and persons who knew something about moving automotive stock could make much more. Anybody with enough loose cash to buy a car could buy a German car, ship it home, contract the conversion and sell the car to an eager buyer who had also been reading the travel magazines but didn't want to take a gray-market bargain excursion themselves. One regular traveler admitted to the author that when he was getting nearly four marks for a dollar, he and his partner converted all their cash into marks, sewed it into the linings of their jackets and crossed the

7. More Fuel on the Fire

border with 250,000 marks each, in anticipation of returning to Germany later to buy more cars.

While the performance car crowd continued to import and modify cars that were small and fast and priced like a fine home, the yuppies and their friends were showing more interest in more practical rolling stock. Most of the models made by Mercedes and BMW for export to the U.S. were also available in a European version that differed from the U.S. version in only a few minor details. While most of the safety features were intact, and for all practical purposes the European versions were every bit as safe in a crash as their U.S. counterparts, some of the European bumpers were not as strong and consequently didn't have that bull-nosed look to them that the U.S. models were famous for. For many, this made the car more attractive. The U.S. version of the Mercedes SL series, for example, had a front bumper protrusion wide enough for a large man to stand on. Additionally, the necessary headlight change for the SLs had an awkward appearance. The European headlights had the turn signals integrated under a common lens, but there was no place for the turn signals on the U.S.-style sealed beam headlights, so they were mounted hanging beneath the bumper like accessory driving lights. Some shops, in the course of making the required changes, simply mounted U.S. version equipment; others made less obvious modifications that retained the more trim and attractive European look.

Like the DOT conversions, EPA conversions on many of the more common imports had moved into the realm of applied science. So, while startup gray market dealers may not have wanted to tackle emissions work at first, EPA conversions were becoming a practice not limited to the exotic imports. Federalizing popular passenger cars quickly became just as popular a vocation. Conveniently, as of 1981, the maximum emissions levels were frozen, so the bar stopped rising with each passing year. The converters didn't have to keep changing their systems to keep up with the regulations so it became feasible to develop a working system that could be used for more than one model year. After the pioneer work was done by the factories and the original converters, the mystery of modifying a car to pass the federal test procedure was gone and the job of installing the emissions equipment often was delegated to semi-skilled labor. Small shops set up practical assembly lines to attach the necessary equipment and the car was shipped off to a testing facility. There at the lab someone from the staff of the conversion shop, who usually had a little more know-how than the rest, would make the final adjustments to "dial in" the car and it would be submitted for testing. By this process the ever-increasing number of volume conversion shops could maximize their production and therefore flood the EPA with applications for approval just as they did the DOT.

The difference in emission equipment was not as obvious, and in some cases, there was very little difference at all. Germany had been kicking around the idea of exhaust emission controls for a while and in the eighties encouraged car buyers to purchase catalyst equipped models by offering a tax break. But whether the car was equipped from the factory with emission controls or not, if it didn't have the sticker declaring that it met the American specifications, it still had to be modified and tested via the conversion shops. Cars like these were usually pretty easy for the converters to deal with because the German catalyst equipped cars also had most of the other equipment required to pass the test. If it didn't, the conversion shop could simply copy the technology of the factory's U.S. version though generally using less expensive aftermarket (read inferior) parts. Either way, for an experienced converter, moving a Mercedes or BMW that had a U.S. approved counterpart through the emissions conversion process amounted to pretty good money. An average EPA conversion on a 500 SEL Mercedes, for example, might involve $500 worth of parts (less if the converter was buying in quantity) and could be performed by an experienced crew of two in a few hours.

As the number of gray market operators went up, of course the price of conversions went down. By 1985, most of the major operators were charging about $5,000 for a complete EPA and DOT conversion. On the surface, they would split the price right down the middle, charging about the same of an EPA or a DOT conversion. But if a customer wanted just one or the other, the price would inevitably go up. The margin was much better in the safety conversion because there wasn't the expense of a lab test, so most shops that were really moving large numbers of cars were doing the EPA work for less, largely so they could do the much more profitable DOT work.

European retail prices on the most popular passenger cars turned out to be thousands of dollars less than their counterparts in the American dealers' showrooms. Some of the difference could be accounted for in the additional technology present in a car certified for U.S. sale. Some of the difference could be chalked up to the exchange rate of dollars to marks. Yet thousands of dollars in price difference could not be accounted for and the manufacturers and dealers were often not willing to discuss it. When the gray market was at its peak in 1985, a top-of-the-line Mercedes that sold in the U.S. for $52,000 could be had in Germany for $27,000. The buyer could ship the car for under a thousand, gave the conversion work done for about $5,000 and still save $19,000 off the price of the same car at the dealer. If a car dealer were to do the same thing, and many did, they could mark the car up by $10,000 and still sell the car for thousands less than the authorized dealer's price. The only thing the buying public had to say about it was "Bring us more!"

7. More Fuel on the Fire

Besides the obvious attraction of the lower price, taking European delivery on a Benz or BMW meant that there were more options and features available. BMW and Mercedes had long used the formula of building just a few different bodies and fitting them with a wide variety of powertrains, but they didn't offer all of the combinations to the U.S. market. Mercedes' venerable little 240D diesel, a small-bodied passenger sedan that was painfully slow but very economical, could be bought in Europe equipped with a manual transmission but was only available to Americans with an automatic. Or the same body with a 2.3-liter gasoline engine, and also available with a manual transmission, was sold as the 230 sedan, a much quicker car but indistinguishable from the 240D on the outside. Mercedes did not offer either version in the U.S. because they didn't really reflect the high-priced luxury car image that they wanted to promote to American buyers.

At the other end of the price range, the big-bodied 500S Mercedes sedans equipped with the 5-liter V8 option could be purchased only in Europe. Larger engines were unavailable in the U.S. because of political fallout from the Saudi Arabian oil embargo of 1973.

Because of U.S. support for Israel during a short war between them and Egypt, several Arab countries had temporarily stopped the export of crude oil to the States. Persons old enough to have been of driving age during the gray market days of the 1980s will remember how, in 1973, U.S. gas prices doubled practically overnight and the country was made painfully aware of how vulnerable they were to interruptions in the foreign oil supply. Mile-long lines developed at gas stations and station owners were putting limits on how much gas an individual could buy. Of course, there was rampant speculation about whether the shortage was real or contrived, but real or not, the effect on drivers was very real and made all of America more aware of how much fuel their cars were using. In a token effort to appear to be doing something about the problem, Congress passed the Energy Policy and Conservation Act of 1975, which included a feature called the CAFE standard. The letters stood for Corporate Average Fuel Economy. The new standard set maximum fuel consumption figures applied as an average for all the cars sold by any given car company. Beginning in 1980, the average fuel consumption for the entire range of cars had to be 20 MPG or above. The standard increased in increments each year until it reached 27.5 MPG for 1985. Failure to meet the minimum standards meant the company would have to pay a hefty "gas guzzler" tax that could amount to over a thousand dollars per car. By not importing the cars that had the largest and thirstiest engines, European automakers could keep the average fuel consumption figures of their fleet of imports down and avoid having to add the tax to the cost for their cars. That thinking seemed to work in the Mercedes and BMW boardrooms. But in the American car market, the demand for the larger, more powerful engines was very strong, in spite of poor gas mileage or any additional tax that came with it.

Ironically, there were also safety features available in the European versions that could not be had at the U.S. dealers. While the DOT was worrying about bumper height standards and headlight specifications, the Germans had been busy developing sophisticated safety systems for their cars, such as airbags and antilock braking systems. Antilock braking (ABS) and supplemental restraint systems (SRS), commonly known as airbags, appeared on Mercedes and BMWs in Europe in 1980 but didn't become available on U.S. version cars until Mercedes offered the 500SEC to the American market in 1983. ABS and SRS were yet two more spin-offs of the microcomputing boom. ABS systems employed speed sensors on all four wheels, which fed into a braking computer that could calculate the relative speed of the wheels and modulate the brake system pressure to any wheel that was nearing lock-up. This could prevent wheel lock during panic stops, enabling the driver to retain traction and some control. Airbags were another system that took advantage of the new computer speeds. Crash sensors distributed throughout the car fed into a computer that could determine if the car were in a life-threatening crash and instantly deploy explosively inflatable airbags to cushion the occupant's impact.

Probably the first such example of how the gray market was going to change the landscape of the automotive market, the 500SEC was a two-door coupe version of the big 500 sedan and had been a popular model with gray market importers. Mercedes finally got the hint and offered their own U.S. version to the buying public in 1983, along with all its appropriate bells and whistles. While ABS and air bags have been standard in the U.S. for decades, their popularity with gray market buyers demonstrated the American appetite for these features when they were new and relatively untried. There was some early reluctance at Mercedes, perhaps fueled by America's abundance of ambulance chasing lawyers, to offer these types of active safety systems to the Americans. Only after the independent importers demonstrated the demand for these features did they start to equip cars destined for America with the new systems.

With everybody getting in on the act, the numbers of gray market imports rose rapidly. While the 1980 figures of 1500 independent imports were almost enough to overwhelm the agencies in Washington, nothing could have prepared them for the numbers coming their way. The year 1982 saw 5,500 gray market cars, in 1983 the number was 12,800, and in 1984 it was 34,900. The DOT and the EPA were completely overwhelmed with applications with no end in sight and no plan for dealing with more to come. Unlike a private business, a government agency cannot expand quickly to respond to a rapidly growing demand for its services. Projections have to be made, budgets must be proposed, and changes approved by Congress. A sudden spike in demand has to be studied and evaluated before any changes can be made, and by the time there was any additional staff available, the agencies were already way behind so the application packets at both agencies languished in boxes that were stacked up in vacant rooms and hallways from the floor to the ceiling.

According to a DOT official who was there at the time, attempting to review the packets was bad enough. A DOT packet might contain as many as 50 photographs, engineering reports and pages of supporting paperwork. But on top of that, they had to spend most of the day fielding phone calls from car owners wanting to know what the status of their application was, so there was even less time to spend actually reviewing the material. In self-defense, they modified the DOT compliance form, reducing it from 8 pages to 1—not so much to make it easier for the applicant as to reduce the amount of material DOT staff had to process. To deal with the phone calls from car owners wondering why their car had not yet been cleared, they put together a form letter that might contain any one of about 20 standard responses describing why a particular car might not have cleared. Anyone who called the DOT trying to see about their car was told that it would be looked into, and they received one of those letters in response. Long delays in government approval became the norm in the business, even to the point where the government agencies themselves became impatient with each other.

During the peak of the confusion, around 1985 the DOT took six bureaucrats away from their desks and put them in a room with thousands of application packets, sorted according to the company that performed the conversions. Their instructions were to review a randomly selected packet from a company and, if it was in order, to approve the entire stack of pending applications from that company. In this fashion they disposed of tens of thousands of packets in a matter of about a week. Whether this event was supposed to have been kept quiet at the time is anybody's guess, but rumors did get out among the converters that the DOT had "flushed" about 40,000 packets and issued release letters without even looking at the applications. Converters were only further encouraged by this and many of the conversion shops became even sloppier and more careless about the materials they sent into the government agencies.[1]

Some businesses went from being conversion shops to "picture shops." Having performed enough conversions on conventional cars like the MB 500 or the BMW 325, they had files full of photos and pre-filled-out forms for all the work that had been done. Eventually they stopped performing the modifications at all and simply altered the forms and pictures to show the serial number and dates of the new applicant. Engineering reports were included, but they might or might not have any basis in reality. They might simply be complicated looking drawings accompanied by figures that couldn't be interpreted by your average office worker. The DOT did employ some engineers, but nobody had the time to review even a small sample of the packets that were coming in the mail every day. Often the engineering reports submitted were all identical, even if they weren't appropriate for the type of car on the application. Like the copied photos of the pipeline welds in *The China Syndrome*, they served their purpose simply by taking up space in the file.

In spite of the overwhelming number of files, not every car was approved, but they might as well have been because the government lacked the capacity to catch up with a car after a certain amount of time. Since three agencies, the DOT, the EPA, and Customs, were involved with each car, they usually weren't on the same page together and had little patience with one another when it came to accommodating each other's delays in processing. At one time, the DOT had accumulated rejections on about several thousand vehicles, and they instructed the various customs agencies to recover the cars. Each of the customs offices has their own policies for dealing with tardy release papers. Unlike the earlier days, where they had the time and money to send agents out looking for non-compliant cars and confiscating them, in many cases they simply gave up. They kept a file open on a car for six months in case they wanted to review the dutiable value of a car. If, for example, a buyer brought in a 400i Ferrari and declared it to be a $15,000 car, they kept the file active long enough to be sure that any changes could be made to correct that figure. But after six months without action, Customs disposed of the file—in their jargon, "liquidated the entry"—released the bond and the car was gone. So if the car had been out of customs for six months waiting for release from the DOT, it simply fell off their radar and they had no interest in enforcing it. There were a few seizures and deportations taking place, but in many cases, the cars had already been resold, sometimes several times, and were virtually untraceable. So if the DOT delay in processing caught up with the customs period on the file, the car would likely not be recovered.

The EPA had things a little bit easier than the DOT when it came to reviewing applications because they could base their approval on the data from the lab tests that were submitted with the packets. While the converter had to submit photos of the modifications and papers describing the emission systems installed, it was the lab results that told the rest of the story, and when a car passed its lab test, issuance of a release from the EPA was considered to be just a matter of time. In theory, EPA officials scrutinizing the application could reject the car because they might look at the photos and decide that the equipment wasn't properly installed, but that rarely

7. More Fuel on the Fire

happened. Like the DOT, they simply didn't have the time or the manpower to properly study the submitted paperwork. Of course, there were delays due to the large and ever-increasing volume of applications, but the pass/fail gate wasn't so much at the EPA Mobile Enforcement Division as it was at the test lab. If the car didn't pass the test, the paperwork was never submitted, so if the paperwork reached the EPA, it was considered a done deal and a car that left the lab with a diploma was considered fair game for dealers and buyers.

It was at this point in the life of the car that things really started to get out of hand. Because of the delays that were occurring at the EPA and DOT, dealers and individuals alike ran out of patience and started selling their cars even before the releases were issued from the respective agencies. Those who had been in business for a while knew how the process worked and, with confidence that the releases would be forthcoming, decided they couldn't be expected to sit on these cars indefinitely, waiting for the respective government agencies to catch up on their paperwork. So they sold the cars to other waiting dealers and individuals with the assurance that the paperwork was in the mail. Once this became an accepted line, it was common for individuals to buy gray market cars from each other with the exchange of a check and a handshake, no title in sight. Worse yet, the cars in question would sometimes be sold repeatedly by various self-appointed middlemen before the paperwork ever caught up with them; that is, assuming it ever actually did.

One effect of this casual attitude toward paperwork was to open up a window for moving stolen cars. If one were to judge by the amount of anti-theft equipment installed on new cars in Europe, particularly in Germany, theft of luxury cars was even more of a problem in Europe than it was in the United States. Germany in particular had far more complicated rules regarding titles and documentation, to the point that even minor changes to the car, such as installation of a non-stock set of wheels, had to be noted on the car's paperwork. Now that there was a steady stream of new, high-priced luxury cars going into the ports via individual importers and shipping out across the ocean, car thieves and the people who bought from them could send their products overseas to be lost in the vast car markets of America. Because of the back-up at the DOT and the EPA on processing packets, there were already vast numbers of cars on the streets whose release forms and title could be described as "pending." So a buyer could be induced to hand over the funds and feel no real concern when, instead of signing over a title, the seller would ask for their address and tell them that the paperwork for the car would come to them in the mail in a couple of weeks. To be fair, quite often this kind of transaction went off with little or no trouble. But if a buyer waited patiently for their paperwork to come in the mail and it didn't, by the time they decided that there must be some kind of problem, the seller could have long since disappeared.

8

In the Workshop

Talk of emission control conversion, DOT compliance modification and automotive test labs conjured up images of guys in white coats with multiple engineering degrees and pocket protectors, carrying around clipboards full of undecipherable documents. It may have looked that way from a distance. Indeed, many conversion shops had their technicians don lab coats for publicity photos. But the real world in a conversion shop could go anywhere from that extreme to the other logical end. The small output shops, some of which specialized in doing only one type of car, might look and function much like any garage operation. Many began as repair shops and picked up gray market work as a lucrative sideline. But during the boom, the successful large volume operations would necessarily take on an assembly line, factory like character.

For an entry-level gray market shop, performing their first conversions was necessarily a challenge. The modifications all had to be custom engineered, and the paperwork involved was a bureaucrat's nightmare, but the challenges weren't insurmountable. While the DOT may have considered independent imports a nuisance, they maintained that they had an obligation to help anyone who asked to negotiate the process. They even published a pamphlet on the subject to save their office some telephone time. Persons new in the conversion business, particularly those experimenting with their own one-time exemption, had *lots* of questions and the people at DOT hoped that by shipping out advisory materials, they could head off some of the more common ones.

At first the EPA wasn't nearly as helpful to independents as the DOT was. The rules were published there in the federal register (never mind that the rule book just for emissions testing was 60 pages long) and there were only a few labs that could be contracted for the testing, but the actual modifications were anybody's guess. Many cars, especially those which had a corresponding U.S. model, could be modified to be identical to a certified model, and in that way be rendered compliant; but in that case it had to be made *completely* identical, which meant buying all the factory equipment through the dealer's parts network and paying the factory recommended prices. Working that way, the expense of modifying a car was usually so high that it negated any financial advantage gained by directly importing the car to begin with. It certainly cut into the profit in any case. While that didn't stop some people from trying, and the guys at the dealer parts counter were baffled at first when people started making special orders for parts that had been largely ignored in the past, direct importers who had decided to go the convert it yourself route but were looking for a better margin could opt for the *modify and test* clause. It was potentially more profitable, since many of the small details of the factory systems could be ignored and expensive OE parts could be substituted with less expensive, generic pieces. But it did involve an expensive test without guaranteed results, and who knew just what hardware would be required. How much of the factory installed equipment was really necessary just to pass the test? What were the options? Surely there must be a less expensive way to meet the specs without buying these stainless steel and platinum catalysts from the dealer's parts departments at or near retail prices. With that in mind, the importers turned to the only available resource for combining innovation with off the shelf technology: their local auto mechanics.

From about 1980 on, mechanics in European car specialty shops found themselves being approached more and more frequently by people interested in emissions conversions, people who had heard of Dick Fritz and his Ferraris or Trend Imports and ACI on the West Coast but didn't want to lay out tens of thousands of dollars. At first many such approaches were quickly brushed off, but some technicians found the idea intriguing and opted for the challenge. The idea of modifying a high-performance car to meet the emissions regulations was counter-intuitive for most mechanics. In those days, emission controls were still considered a nuisance and many mechanics' approaches to them was to strip all the surplus parts off and plug the holes that were left behind. An engine compartment stripped just so was easier to work in and had a clean and logical appearance mechanics found appealing.

They removed catalytic converters because they were considered to be too restrictive in the exhaust. On new cars they were often replaced with conventional mufflers, even before the paint had burned off of the exhaust system. Air pumps didn't affect the way a car ran but were considered a nuisance because they took up so much space, so they hit the scrap heap. Tubular exhaust headers were much more elegant than cast iron thermal reactors, and EGR systems, the source of many drivability problems, were frequently removed and replaced with flat metal plates. Oxygen sensors and their associated electronic controls were a new development and little understood; when mechanics were pressured to quickly fix an engine that was running a lean surge, the solution was often to unplug the oxygen sensor and turn the fuel mixture up rich.

If a mechanic in the past had spent any time doing any serious modifications to a car, those modifications were bent toward increasing power and performance and consequently, emissions. Higher compression, longer camshaft dwell duration, and more mixture delivery … the favorite tricks of the hot-rodders that made cars more fun to drive all resulted in higher concentrations of the legally offensive gasses. The idea of making modifications to achieve the opposite result appalled many a typical mechanic.

But for others it presented an appealing challenge. Performing a successful emission conversion was not just a moneymaking proposition money, it was a puzzle to be solved, a test of a mechanic's mastery of the technology in which he or she was immersed. To bring a car into compliance without using the factory recommended parts required a thorough knowledge of all the engine's systems *and* perfect control of them. It meant learning the details of parts the average mechanic couldn't have been bothered with, and working with equipment heretofore only available to engineers in research and development. It could also mean working with automobiles that were enjoyed only by the very wealthy. For some, the idea was irresistible.

For those who took the challenge on, it became baptism by fire. While factory sponsored training for mechanics working in the dealerships covered the operation of the emerging emission control systems, technicians in the independent shops had had a sort of hit-and-miss exposure to anti-pollution equipment. A production-oriented environment usually led mechanics to learn as much as, and no more than, they needed to know about a component to solve a particular drivability problem. But when the repair went into extra hours, the most expedient approach might often prove to be finding a way to bypass the offending component and configure the car to work without it. In many cases, the car owners themselves became unwitting accomplices; a trusted mechanic who had been servicing their cars for years or might solve drivability problems by removing emission control hardware without even telling the owner what they had done. Few drivers who raised the hood knew that anything was missing and those who did usually didn't care. It wasn't until the mid–1980s that many states other than California required any kind of emission inspection, so the equipment was considered an unnecessary nuisance and consequently there just weren't that many mechanics well enough acquainted with the theory of emission controls to fully explain how they worked, let alone design a system that put them to practical use, so modifying a car to meet the regulations meant a crash course in automotive emissions equipment.

8. In the Workshop

Of course, anyone who had been working in the business for a few years had seen the changes as they came down the line. Air pumps and thermal reactors had been around for years; EGR systems started showing up in 1973 with the beginning of NOx regulation; catalysts were in wide use by '76; and most repair shops had a pile of the aforementioned items in the back of the shop they had been stripping off cars for years. The irony was not lost on the mechanics, as they rummaged through the piles of discarded emission controls in search of something they could adapt to cleaning up the exhaust of someone's new European import. If they didn't have the parts on hand, their first trip was to the salvage yard to try to find something they could make work.

Owners of salvage yards had not yet caught on to the emerging new uses for these pieces, so they initially welcomed the chance to sell off what they considered to be useless parts, while privately wondering what anybody could want with them. Suddenly, people were buying bits of hardware that for years the shop owners had been selling to scrap metal companies by the pound. But the salvagers eventually caught on and belatedly raised their prices on emission-related items. But by then the converters who had experienced some success had made some money, and now actually had an operating budget. Faced with the higher prices in the junkyards, they turned to new equipment. Additionally, ever-tightening regulations meant that more effective products than the junkyard converters were needed.

It was during the early eighties, when the dollar first started its steep climb on the foreign exchange, that things really started to happen. Mercedes had inadvertently thrown some gas on the fire by not making their 5-liter V8s available in the U.S. At the same time, they were offering new safety options on the European versions—antilock braking and driver's side air bags—that they did not make available to the U.S. buyers. Likewise, BMW kept the six-cylinder 325 and the big 745 Turbo on their side of the ocean; so a second wave of import conversion shops—those devoted to the more popular German models—sprang up and quickly focused on the big Benzes and BMWs.

Fortunately for the converters, the Mercedes were not difficult to bring into line. They only produced a few body styles and versions of all of them were approved for sale in the U.S. in some form or another, so most of the safety features required by the DOT were already there. In most cases it was just a case of proving their existence with photographs and records. Many of the DOT requirements, like lap and shoulder belts, collapsible steering columns and dual braking systems, were just good sense and quickly found their way into "world market" cars like the W123 and W126 body style cars that Mercedes was building during the '80s. Bumper and door reinforcement and headlight replacement were usually the biggest issues—the ones requiring some assembly—and the remaining details simply involved changing a few dashboard labels and installing some relays and buzzers. The requirements included a buzzer to remind drivers that the key was still in the switch when the door was open, a buzzer and light to remind the driver to fasten their seatbelt, and a safety relay to ensure that the power windows wouldn't work when the key was withdrawn from the switch, presumably to keep children playing in an unattended car from running a power window up on their necks. Among technicians installing these parts, the trio came to be known as the annoyance package, as few customers really appreciated having these features installed on their cars.

Once a converter had successfully certified a type of car with the DOT and had become familiar with the process, they could use what they'd learned to turn towards mass production. Some of the pioneering converters had gone to the trouble of inventing bumper reinforcements and having them evaluated by engineers. Usually, they supplemented their conversion income by selling brackets and braces to other converters who worked a little lower on the food chain, and found it more expedient to buy their modifications ready-made. For the more run-of-the-mill conversions—popular German passenger sedans and such—a look in the back of an issue of *Autoweek* revealed that much of the needed hardware for the impact resistance part of the job was available from those shops that had successfully engineered the necessary bumper and door changes. Hardware for sale often came complete with substantiating paperwork, and purchasers usually had welding and metalworking equipment of their own, so they quickly copied what they purchased, Xeroxed the documentation and never bought the hardware again. It was of no great concern to the company they bought the braces from—that was the way *they* got *their* start.

Using pre-purchased accessories, it took little more skill than the ability to turn a wrench and a screwdriver to complete a certifiable DOT conversion. By breaking the operation down into its basic parts, a kind of an assembly line could be set up and it was only necessary to train a few people to repeatedly perform a few simple tasks. This meant that an ambitious shop owner could draw from a broad and inexpensive labor pool; and they did indeed.

The U.S. economy had been in one of its periodic downturns during the late seventies and early eighties and, as usual, every factory town was afflicted by layoffs. Government efforts to put people back to work included economic incentives to hire laid-off personnel, and the gray market entrepreneurs were happy to accommodate. One shop in coastal North Carolina was staffed largely by ex-workers from a recently closed boiler factory, while another shop further inland worked with staff recently laid off by a chicken processing plant. While they liked to keep that information private (dressing the workers in lab coats could be helpful in this case), the facts were not lost on members of the motoring press who took the trouble to find out. A *Motor Trend* article published in 1986, when gray market cars were quickly losing some of their charm, referred to cases of "cars that don't run right and never will because they were converted by a guy who was a pool maintenance man six weeks earlier."[1] In their defense, this didn't mean that the workers were necessarily incompetent—boiler plant workers, for instance, were largely highly qualified welders—but it did mean that the workers often had little understanding of the end result of the work that they were doing, or for that matter any of the legal implications. This was often another advantage for the shop owner who might like to play a little fast and loose with the rules. If he came into the workshop and instructed the exhaust guy to cut out and replace the catalyst that he had installed only a week before, it was better for everyone if the worker didn't know the implications of such an act. Likewise, if a welder was instructed to install bracing in a bumper that didn't follow the engineer's drawings, he usually didn't ask any questions; he just went to work.

While the government had their own ideas about process, the workers in the shops usually had a more practical attitude, and this sometimes meant protocol would have to be sacrificed. Even when all the mechanical work was done by the book and all the requirements were met, the requirements for completion of the paperwork sometimes led to absurd practices in order to go through all the motions. Completing all of the photographic material frequently turned into a problem that could only be solved with a little deceptive practice. Digital photography and Photoshop were still about a decade from the retail market in the 1980s, so each set of pictures had to be done on film and then processed. The gray market was actually a launching pad for a number of instant photo process shops that sprang up around the conversion shops, but even with the one-day turnaround the corner kiosks offered, sometimes photos got lost or didn't come out for one reason or another. In a large volume shop, there was enough work to keep one person busy full-time just taking and sorting photographs. If a car went out the door and it later turned out that there were photos missing, something had to be done to complete the packet. If the car owner lived nearby, it could be a matter of re-visiting the same car and re-shooting the photos. But, as was more often the case, if the car had been picked up and transported cross-country before the missing pictures were noticed, something else had to be done.

In the case of the more common cars, it was often a matter of shooting a duplicate set of pictures from another car in the shop. Sometimes, if a converter was doing a number of the same type of car, applying assembly line practice to the photo-documentation meant that a worker would shoot pictures of the same part over and over again with different ID plates appearing in each photo. It didn't necessarily mean that the modifications weren't done to each individual car, but it still constituted submitting false information and was frowned on by officials. For the workers, it was just a more convenient way of filling out all the packets.

There was talk of a shop that was busted because they had done that very thing. They submitted photo packets for what was supposed to be a whole series of cars, but the person who reviewed the packet noticed that in the door beam photos for each car, there was a cigarette butt on the floor in exactly the same location. Since the pictures were supposed to represent different cars over a period of time, it seemed unlikely to the reviewer that they would have gone so long without sweeping the floor, so he flagged the packets for further study. It stood to reason the people reviewing the packets would find such lack of attention to detail insulting and would derive some satisfaction from taking those operators down. The more alert technicians took the trouble to change the angle and lighting of their duplicate photos.

Sometimes pictures were missing that might not be easy to replace. When this happened to one shop photographer in a high-volume East Coast business, he was told by the management it would be up to him to replace the missing photos—and they didn't care or want to know how he did it. The missing photos were of the side markers installed on the front of a Ferrari 328. The car had gone to its final owner before the absence of pictures was discovered. There was another 328 in the shop at the time, but it was red and the car in question was blue. His solution was to put some sticky putty on the back of a side marker lens, set up the photo ID board for the car and drive to a Ferrari dealer in a neighboring city. He walked around the showroom and the front lot until he felt like he was unseen, stuck the lens on a similar Ferrari and took two quick pictures. The results were odd, because his photos showed an aftermarket marker right next to a factory marker, but the photos made it past scrutiny.

While such scenarios may have occurred over and over during the boom years, the earlier work of the conversion shops was more likely to hold up under close inspection. While the volume was still low and the business was still in its infancy, DOT was scrutinizing application packets, and the labs were still testing cars by the book. Converters were importing and selling more and more cars, but it was a cumbersome process, and they were always looking for ways to streamline the process. They had not yet learned what they might or might not get away with and the guys who could study the book and jump through the hoops were the ones in the best position to come out ahead.

There were plenty of operators on both coasts that did just that to improve their volume, and some truly mastered the process and were able

8. In the Workshop

to turn gray market conversion into a kind of assembly-line manufacturing business. Bill Rogers of Village Imports was one such example. Rogers teamed up with Al Bloodworth, the owner of a BMW specialty shop, to perform some of his first conversions. Bloodworth had already gotten his feet wet doing conversions on a pair of BMW 325s at the behest of a customer. He saw the potential in the conversion business and did a careful study of the EPA's rules. In there he found a shortcut that a small volume manufacturer could use to obtain a certificate of compliance for a car. It involved performing what amounted to an abbreviated version of the EPA's durability test.

Obtaining a certificate from the EPA for a major car manufacturer involved using up a number of cars on the test track, and the accumulation of tens of thousands of miles. The EPA wanted makers to demonstrate that whatever systems they used could stand up to 50,000 miles of normal driving, and in order to satisfy them, the makers had to actually run several cars the whole distance, testing them at appropriate intervals. It was fully expected that the exhaust would become dirtier over time, as the engine and emission control systems wore out, and EPA used the results of the tests to calculate a "durability factor" to gauge how the toxic content of the exhaust would increase over time.

A small-volume manufacturer (producing 10,000 cars a year or fewer) played by a different set of rules. And the legal definition of a manufacturer could be interpreted to mean that a company that modified cars could qualify. For them, obtaining a certificate involved only one test car and 4,000 miles of driving. The amount of mileage required was based on what EPA considered to be the point where the emission controls became stabilized. They acknowledged that catalysts and other systems worked best when brand new, and their effectiveness went downhill from there; but there was a point, relative to what many car owners considered to be the "break in" period, where deterioration leveled off and the emissions could be expected to remain relatively stable for a time. The EPA then extrapolated a durability factor from a variety of test data. After the required miles, the tailpipe results of the test car, multiplied by that factor, still had to come in under the specifications for that year. The durability factor might be different for each measured gas. It might be something like 1.1 for CO content, but 1.2 for NOx, representing the fact that different systems might deteriorate at different rates. Whatever it turned out to be, the maker who passed the test by the necessary margin and obtained a certificate could equip his cars with the system that had been approved, and not have to test every copy to get EPA clearance.

He focused first on the big Benz that Mercedes had opted not to offer in America in favor of keeping their CAFE figures up—the 500 SEL. By obtaining a certificate, he could not only convert and sell the car without the expense and uncertainty of testing, but he could sell his conversion "kit" to other conversion shops. They could install his kit and, instead of testing, simply have their installation inspected by a representative of Rogers's company. Because the 500SEL was the heaviest of the body styles that carried the 5-liter V8 engine, the other cars that shared the drivetrain—the 500SE, a slightly shorter version of the SEL; and the 500SL, a two-seat open roadster—were also covered by the certificate, so the market potential for the kit was enormous.

His first certificate was obtained using the tried-and-true old technology that the American car companies had worn out during the 1970s. It worked, probably because the Mercedes V8 started out as a pretty efficient powerplant and had cleaner exhaust than the American V8s to begin with. His conversion consisted of a General Motors air pump, two oxidizing pre-catalysts mounted immediately behind the exhaust manifolds and two three-way (oxidizing and reducing) catalysts mounted under the car on either side of the transmission. The evaporative system he lifted from the production models that Mercedes was already importing. The catalysts produced a tremendous amount of heat, but they were located and shielded in a fashion that the EPA considered safe and functional. Primarily because of the heat, they successfully consumed and converted enough of the offending gasses that Rogers's car exceeded the specs by a sufficient amount that he was granted a certificate. With the success of the first certificate, he launched an effort to certify systems for the most popular European imports. With Bloodworth doing the development work, they obtained certificates on several lines of Mercedes gasoline and diesel engines, as well as a cross section of BMW models, using only one catalyst and the more sophisticated closed loop technology. In later years, when his first certificate was old news, he would jokingly refer to the first version as the old "build a fire system."

The "cert kit" was a great example of the right idea at the right time. Thanks to the imbalance of the dollar against the mark, dealers traveling to Germany were flush with cash to buy cars. The technology for getting past the EPA, a big stumbling block for some importers, was for sale in the cert packages being marketed by Rogers and other operators who also exploited the small-volume rules. Typically, the components for a kit might have cost about $700–$1,000 and were marketed for as much as a thousand dollars or more above cost. That gave the seller a tidy margin, and though the markup represented the actual cost of an EPA test procedure, using the pre-approved kit saved the installer the hassle of transporting the car to a lab and eliminated the uncertainty of testing. Using the kits also meant that the necessary skill level and therefore the labor costs for the technicians installing them would be lower. The installation process was basically a bolt-on procedure and workers didn't really need to understand the subtlety of the devices they installed. Since the catch was that it was necessary for an employee of the company holding the certificate to inspect and approve the installation, converters would buy the kits, install them on several cars, and the company would send a representative out to inspect and sign off on a batch of cars. Inspecting the kits, which often meant flying around the country and being entertained like a rock star by various shop owners, was a burden born cheerfully by the shop foreman.

The success of the early kits inspired Rogers and others in the field to branch out to other types of cars and newer technology. The lambda-controlled fuel injection systems were hitting the market and the "build a fire" system quickly became outdated. Since Bosche's Lambda control system, using a frequency valve on the popular K Jetronic fuel system, was essentially a retrofit to begin with, it was an easy matter to adapt the technology to the European version cars using just a few simple components. Using the Lambda system, it was possible to eliminate the air pump and to use only one catalyst. Again, the system was tested for the cert in the heaviest model car (the big SEL sedan in the Mercedes case) and it was assumed by the EPA that the same equipment installed on the same engine in the lighter body cars would perform just as well. In that way, a certificate based on the Mercedes 500SEL enabled the holder to sell the same kit for the whole series of cars that used the same 5-liter V8.

The converters later went on to apply the same technology to the 3.8-liter V8, which was also offered in four bodies, and the 2.8-liter six cylinder, which was offered in three. While development costs for a certificate were substantial, by developing only three kits—for the 500SEL, the 380 and the 280—the builder was able to market an emissions kit for eleven different models. Of those eleven, only the 380s were available through normal retail channels. The 500 and the 280 could only be had through the gray market.

The big V8s were not that difficult to clean up using the available technology, and many other independent importers were able to obtain small-volume certificates for conversion, which made them very popular. But attempts by importers to certify the Mercedes 280 series—the same body series car using a dual overhead cam inline six-cylinder engine—using the same oxygen sensor/Lambda box/frequency valve system frequently came up short. While it was possible to get the cars through on a case by case convert and test, the cold start period was just too dirty for technicians to achieve the more stringent numbers required for a certificate. Some builders were able to pull it off by adding an air pump and thermal reactor but at least one maker found another method to clean up the 280.

They found a source for small pre-catalysts ... tubular in shape and about the size of a can of frozen orange juice concentrate. The technicians cut the exhaust head-pipes and installed the "juice can cats" right up to the exhaust manifold and welded the pipes up around them. The small cats could warm up very quickly because of their proximity to the maximum exhaust heat, and convert a large part of the HC before it even reached the main catalyst. This gave them the edge they needed to get the car through the cold start portion of the test and get the numbers needed for a certificate. The pre-cats in the exhaust header were never mentioned in the paperwork for the certificate and they were not visible to EPA engineers or anyone doing an under-hood inspection, so they were never listed as part of the equipment in the kit. Technicians knew pre-cats couldn't possibly last long in that position and would eventually overheat, break up, travel down the exhaust system and potentially block up the main converter. They also knew that the EPA engineers, if they knew about them, would arrive at the same conclusion. So, they kept their existence a secret and crossed their fingers that they would last through the duration of the 4000–mile cert testing cycle so that they would be awarded a small volume certificate for the SE, the SEL and the convertible SL—three very popular cars in the Mercedes 280 series.[2]

The EPA, DOT and conversion shops alike realized this was a business where the money that could be made was directly proportional to what you could get away with, but there was little the government could do to keep a lid on it. Budgets were always tight, manpower was always short, and the technicians could be pretty darned clever. In the case of a small-volume certification, it would seem that there was little or nothing to be gained by deception, but a shop that was trying for a cert would naturally try to make their package as inexpensive as possible, for one thing to get an edge on the competition, or if there wasn't any competition (if no one else had a small volume cert for a certain type of car), then certifying it with as little equipment as possible went to increase the profit margin in sale of the kits. If a technician could secret an additional piece of equipment onto the test car to help the car through the tests and not include it on the paperwork, then the kits need only include the components that EPA knew were there. This worked as long as nobody ever tested the cars modified using the cert kits. If the EPA were ever to take a batch of cars and test them, the whole plan would fall apart; the importers preferred to hope that wouldn't happen.

Cost of modification and testing was not the only field of competition. The performance of modified cars was every bit as important as cost. After all, customers were looking to the European imports for superior driving performance over American made cars, but also over other cars made for the import market. Once a car had been dialed lean enough to have a chance at the test, it might drive as though it had a much smaller and weaker engine than was actually the case. Usually, the answer technicians fell back on was to restore the car's fuel system to the original settings before delivery to the customer. Since clean exhaust and good performance tended to be mutually exclusive, technicians whose job it was to get the car past the tests successfully and to perform well were not always above resorting to deception when nothing else would do the trick. The idea of making a car that was just clean enough to pass the tests, only when it needed to be, was intriguing.

By 1985, most automobile engines employed some type of computer to control the fuel delivery and sometimes the ignition timing. How well the car performed or how clean it was at the tailpipe was determined by the computer's pre-set programming. If a computer could be designed to run in a "performance" mode under normal conditions and shift into a "low emission" mode under test conditions, then the maker could achieve the impossible goal of meeting the emission requirements, while still outperforming any competition during regular driving. This holy grail of auto emission conversion was the topic of many barroom discussions among conversion techs.

The author met one engineer who had worked for several major manufacturers and went into the gray market conversion business to supplement his retirement. In a conversation in 1986, he stated that the previous year, while working on a project at the EPA test lab in Ann Arbor, he learned that Bosch had built and programmed an engine control unit that "knew" when it was being tested. They didn't make any secret of it, he said. They just did it to prove the point that with the sophisticated electronic controls now available to automakers the test could be easily circumvented. That it could be done with the right computer equipment came as no great surprise, but he went on to say that a team working for American Motors had achieved that same goal with the simple installation of a hood switch (EPA always tested cars on the dyno with the hood open). There was no evidence that anybody had been successful with this ploy ... until recently.

In November of 2015, it came out that Volkswagen had done just that. An environmental group attempting to verify mileage figures on VW's most popular diesel cars noticed that the cars were not meeting emission standards under normal use. But when the cars were tested under the EPA's protocol, they passed as they should. As it turned out, the computers on the cars had been programmed to detect when they were running the EPA's test procedure. This was possible because the EPA's test was uniform to a fault. The car would be started cold, allowed to idle for 15 seconds, shifted into a forward gear, allowed to idle for 10 more seconds, then accelerated precisely the same amount on every test. It only took a properly programmed computer with a throttle switch, transmission switch, and accelerator and speed sensors 30 seconds to figure out it was being tested and slip into more conservative behavior. Any converter in 1985 would have been thrilled to get a dozen cars in with such a system. Volkswagen, it seems, did it with hundreds of thousands.

The emission scandal at Volkswagen resulted in short prison terms for a handful of executives and engineers, and billions of dollars in fines for the Volkswagen company. Some diesel buying customers were given the option of having their cars bought back, or cash compensation for having their trust violated. Volkswagen stock took a big hit but eventually the dust settled, and things went back to business as usual.

But except for that one glaring example, there was probably far less cheating among those companies who were pursuing certificates than there was among the *modify and test* crowd. The cars that saw the inside of the EPA's own lab at Ann Arbor actually had to pass the scrutiny of the engineers there. Those cars that were modified and tested at a private lab only had to work well enough to get their papers and leave. The work didn't have to look good or stand up long and quite often didn't. Some of the quality of the modifications certainly wasn't up to the standards of workmanship that might be expected on a luxury import. The installers justified their shabby work by assuming that all their modifications would be removed once the car reached its final owner. In many cases it was a self-fulfilling prophesy.

Peter Krause, who had built a small business servicing Ferraris and other Italian exotics, remarked about his first encounter with gray market imports. In 1980 he saw a big jump in business as the Research Triangle area he called home became popular among actors and other wealthy car enthusiasts, many of whom had come into the area to experience the health benefits of a trendy new "experimental rice diet" that was being administered by a local doctor. He allowed that, at first, he didn't realize where the boom in European Ferraris was coming from. Wherever it was, he was not impressed by the work of the converters: "All these cars were showing up at the shop with catalysts just barely hanging on with what looked like bubble gum and bailing wire." His natural inclination was to repair them by replacing the sewn-on catalysts with the factory exhausts. "After a while I realized that what I was doing might get me in trouble so I started sending the cars down to a local exhaust shop to have the work done. It wasn't long before they got wise and stopped doing it for me."[3]

As time went by and no repercussions came from "unconverting" dozens of Ferraris and other gray market imports, most car buyers, mechanics, and particularly the conversion shops themselves developed a fairly casual attitude about undoing recent modifications. Once the car had passed the lab and the EPA had issued a release, it was often considered a green light to strip the car of emissions equipment and restore it to its original condition. Most often this part of the job was left to the final owner. Sometimes it happened the first time they took their car to their regular mechanic. If the modifications were a detriment to the performance of the car, and they often were, the mechanic would nonchalantly remove the offending pieces and replace them with something that worked better. Some converters would quietly make arrangements with the owner to restore the car to original condition. The EPA and the DOT regulations said that the parts removed during the conversion process had to be exported or destroyed, but those rules were largely ignored and the agencies didn't ask for any proof. Either way, there was always somebody willing to take money to undo what the car owner had earlier paid thousands of dollars to have done. Sometimes they achieved their desired end by simply adjusting the fuel mixture to a point where the car performed well, and the emission controls were useless. At other times the car owner would insist that the car be completely stripped of the conversion hardware and restored to European trim.

Sometimes the modifications were made without anybody asking. Technicians charged with the task of doing whatever it took to get a car through the lab test would naturally develop preferences for equipment that performed best. For example, the most effective catalysts on the market were the BMW factory equipment for their large six-cylinder cars. But the price of a BMW cat was about $800 compared to about $200 for an aftermarket replacement that wasn't quite as effective and didn't light up as quickly. One technician with a major East Coast shop sometimes found himself pressured by management to pass a series of cars on a budget and said he had a favorite BMW catalyst that he used repeatedly.

> They wouldn't let us buy a BMW cat for every car that we tested, but the generic cats weren't good enough to get some of the cars through the test. So, if I knew I was going to have trouble, we installed the BMW cat for the dial-in and test, then after the car passed, we took it back off and replaced it with a generic. The same thing was true with the *Valentine* box. We had one of those Lambda controllers developed by Mike Valentine, it was the only thing that would get a 745 [BMW] through the test. But it was real expensive and they never made very many of them so it was hard to get; so I'd put it on a car for the test, then replace it with a *Johnson* box once the car came back from the lab. The *Johnson* box was on the paperwork and photos so as far as the EPA knew, the Johnson boxes worked, and they did on some cars, but you couldn't reliably pass a 745 on one. I drew a little picture of a car on the side of the box for each time it passed a test. I may have put 4 cars through on that one box.[4]

In extreme cases, it was essential that the catalysts or other components be removed simply for safety's sake. One converter who worked for a time with Lamborghinis that repeatedly failed emissions testing found he had to resort to desperate measures. In an attempt to get the car through the cold start portion of the test, he added more and more pre-catalysts to the system, to the point there was no more room for them in the engine compartment. The lab techs who worked with his cars joked that he should try hooking up a trailer piled with catalysts to the back of the car. The load on the pre-cats was so great during the test that they overheated very quickly, and the outer containers began to glow cherry red. Undaunted, he continued to work with the cars until this happened during an actual test and because of proximity to the rubber motor mounts, the mounts caught fire near the end of the test. At that point, the numbers on the car were looking good and the car had already failed several previous attempts. So rather than aborting the test, a lab technician put the fire out with a CO_2 extinguisher while the driver continued to operate the car on the dyno and completed the test. The car was given a passing grade and eventually cleared by the EPA.

Stories like this were not unusual. They were good comic material for the people on the inside of the trade and became horror stories for those on the outside. A small number of gray market conversions, Italian exotics and German passenger cars alike, made their local headlines when they burst into flames and were reduced to ashes, compliments of their aftermarket emission control systems. So, in some cases, removal of the systems became, for the technician, a case of choosing the lesser of two evils: commit an illegal act or take the chance of someone being hurt in a fire.

It was easy for a technician to rationalize their transgressions. Substitution, for instance of a less effective part for one that had performed well during the test, became a "service parts replacement." Everyone that was knowingly involved with the illegal activity of unconverting cars had their own personal reasons why what they did was excusable. If they didn't, they preferred not to think about it and preferred to ignore all the footnotes on government forms about falsifying information, $10,000 fines and prison time. But after hours, when the beer started flowing in the bars frequented by the conversion shop technicians, they freely bragged about how many federal laws they'd violated that day, like Wild West outlaws comparing the bounties on their own heads.

9

The Independent Labs

Testing a car's exhaust was an operation that could be done only in a facility specifically designed for the purpose. The regulations for testing labs covered about a hundred pages in the Federal Register and Code of Federal Regulations and were written in legalese and engineer-speak—interpreting them was not for the easily frustrated. Of course, the major automakers who could afford it built their own test cells, which were equipped with a chassis dynamometer and a system for sampling and analyzing exhaust gas for research and development. But outside of the EPA's own test lab in Ann Arbor, Michigan, there were originally few such venues where space was available for independent importers and conversion shops. One such operation was the Transportation Research Center in Ohio.

The TRC grew up in Ohio as a facility used by the major American carmakers. Among the test labs, they were one of the first and best equipped. Their facility, besides emissions testing cells, also has a 7.5–mile test track, a crash testing lab, an off-road endurance testing course and anything else an auto researcher might need. They probably never anticipated the business of the independent importer-converter crowd, but they were ready to accommodate them. Labs like the TRC had a good working relationship with the EPA and had been evaluated by them to determine whether they performed the federal test procedure to their satisfaction. With the agency's approval, they could perform testing of individual cars for the individual converters, but this was not their primary function. They were first and foremost, facilities for research and development mostly used by motor vehicle manufacturers and renting small blocks of test cell time to independents was not really part of their business model. More typically, they would lease large blocks of time to the foreign automakers which they used for dialing in their test cars before submitting them for testing to the EPA. A frequent visitor to the TRC remarked that Honda Motor Company leased a test cell there for 24 hours a day, seven days a week. The engineers worked in three shifts and were very secretive about their work, even to the point of covering up the engines with their lab coats whenever someone outside their organization would approach. The Honda people did earn his respect, however. Referring to the chart recorders monitoring the cars' exhaust, he said, "Those guys never did anything but draw flat lines."

Automotive test labs also might sell R&D time to the maker of an auto accessory to determine its effect on engine performance. Measuring the emissions of propane powered vehicles for indoor use such as forklift trucks could be a regular part of their business, or they might host a research team for a study. But the gray market conversion shops were a new breed.

The converters were often on a tight budget and test cell time was expensive and hard to get, so they would work fast, sometimes trying to use an hour of dyno time to check and dial in two or more cars, a task that kept the lab technicians moving fast. The labs and the technicians could cope with this, but what they weren't ready for was the steadily increasing number of persons wanting an hour of dyno time and a test. As the dockets filled up with independents and the parking lots filled up with one-car trailers and pickup trucks, the waiting lists grew and some individuals saw an opportunity for developing lab facilities designed with the gray marketer in mind.

The required equipment list was long, and the parts were expensive. To begin with, the facility had to be climate controlled, to the extent that a car in the lab for testing had to stay within a specified temperature range for the duration of the test. That meant that the building had to be large enough to store several cars and the HVAC system had to be powerful enough to control the environment even on a hot summer day with several cars running indoors. For evaporative emission testing, there also had to be room enough for at least one "shed," a hermetically sealed room large enough to contain a car and equipped with a system for heating the fuel tanks and sampling and analyzing the air inside.

The test cell itself held a chassis dynamometer, a set of rollers in the floor connected to a series of flywheels for a car to run on while remaining stationary. The dyno had to have sufficient inertial weight capacity to handle the largest automobiles and possibly light trucks. The test cell held a variety of large capacity fans that were directed onto the car during testing and EPA regulations even went so far as to specify the capacity of the fans. There was a dilution tunnel, a stainless-steel pipe about 12 inches in diameter and 20 feet long, peppered with instruments and sensors through which ambient air was pumped via a blower. The blower was of a positive displacement type, rated to move a specific quantity of air for each revolution of the shaft. The number of revolutions of the pump shaft was recorded to enable the technicians to know exactly how much air had moved through the dilution tunnel during the testing period. The test car's exhaust would basically be vacuumed out into the dilution tunnel, where it was mixed with the known quantity of air in the tunnel. From that mixture samples were taken at various times during the test and held for later analysis.

Equipment for analyzing the gas had to be of the type specified in the regulations and it tended towards being temperamental and unreliable and needed frequent service, particularly the NOx analyzers. The dilution tunnel itself was equipped with instruments to measure air density, temperature, humidity and pressure and all the instruments had to be tested and calibrated according to a schedule dictated by the EPA, so on top of being expensive to buy, the lab equipment was also complicated and labor intensive to service and had to be operated by trained personnel. It wasn't necessary for everyone in the lab to know everything, but there had to be somebody on hand for each working shift who thoroughly understood the instruments and their maintenance, as well as all the details of the federal test procedure.

The Test

After the conversion technician had dialed the car in and was satisfied (or at least hopeful) the car could pass the test, the car was impounded by the lab for twelve hours. Access to the car was permitted only to lab personnel. At the end of the impound period, the car would have all its fuel drained and be refueled 40 percent full with indoline, which was a 100 octane unleaded fuel with no additives. A temperature sensor would be installed in the fuel tank and heating blankets attached to the tank. At this point the fuel had to be at a temperature of 60 degrees or below. The car was then was parked in a hermetically sealed room—the "shed." Sealing the car in the shed made it possible to capture any fuel vapors that came off the car during the test period. For the first part of the evaporative test, the heating blankets were used to heat the fuel to 80 degrees over a two-hour period, to simulate the effects of the car sitting in a sunny parking lot. A sample would then be taken from the air in the shed and its HC (hydrocarbon) concentration, compared to the volume of air in the shed. The result would express in grams how much fuel had evaporated from the car in the two-hour period. After 1981, the evaporative standard amounted to no more than 6 grams of fuel escaping into the air over the entire four hours the car spent in the shed: two hours before the dyno test and two hours after.

After the initial two hours in the shed, the car would be pushed onto the dynamometer. A combination of weighted flywheels was engaged to the rollers to simulate the mass of the car being tested. Procedure dictated that the dyno test had to be performed within two hours of the shed test.

During the dyno part of the test, three exhaust samples would be taken that were a constant percentage of the total exhaust and were saved in inflatable plastic bags. Beginning from cold, the car would be started and allowed to idle for ten or fifteen seconds, then shifted into gear and allowed to idle for another short period before being driven up to speed. The car's operator would "drive" the car according to a rolling speed graph while a pen that indicated the dyno roller speed would trace a line on the chart recorder to demonstrate that the car had duplicated the accelerations and decelerations on the graph. To have valid results, the speed of the test car could not vary more than ten percent from the graph.

The dyno section of the test lasted about 45 minutes. The first sample (the cold bag) took about 3 ½ minutes and represented the exhaust at cold start and warm-up. A bad cold start-up or slow warm-up could easily produce enough HC, which was mainly raw, un-burnt fuel, to blow the entire test and often did. The second bag, which duplicated the effects of driving through town with many stops and starts, was usually the easiest section on which to get good results, because most cars were pretty clean after they warmed up, though NOx (nitric oxide) was sometimes a problem. After completion of the second bag, the car was shut off and allowed to heat soak for ten minutes. Then it would be restarted and sampled through a repetition of the first part of the driving cycle (the "hot bag"). The "bags" or samples would then be analyzed for hydrocarbons (HC), carbon monoxide (CO), carbon dioxide (CO_2), and nitric oxide (NOx), and the samples averaged and compared to the distance driven which was measured in rolls of the dyno. The result would be expressed in grams per mile. CO_2 was not a regulated gas, but by sampling the CO_2 the lab could use the data to generate a theoretical fuel mileage figure.

After finishing the dyno test, it was back into the sealed room for the "hot shed." Again, the car was cloistered for two hours, but this time the fuel was not heated. As the car cooled in the shed, any hydrocarbon that evaporated was contained and measured. This often turned out to be a particularly difficult period because while a good functional evaporative system may have been pretty easy to retrofit, any small fuel or oil leaks that the car had were enough to fail the test, or "blow the shed." Once the car had done its time and the air sample was taken, the test was complete. All the results were compiled and if the car failed any part of the test, the cold shed, the dyno test, or the hot shed, the entire test was considered a failure. Government regulations dictated that a retest could not be performed in sections but that the whole test had to be performed no matter which part of the test the car failed. The test criteria also specified certain time and temperature limits that had to be maintained in the lab or the test had to be aborted. If for example the test was successfully completed and the temperature recording in the test lab went above 80 degrees at any time during the test, or if too much time lapsed from one part of the test to the next, all the test data was supposed to be discarded and the car would have to be retested.

The test results were analyzed by computer, the computers of the time were comparatively primitive but the analysis was basically a number crunching process that took into account the number of times the dyno rollers turned during the test, gas concentrations of the various samples, the volume and density of the exhaust from the car, the volume, density, relative humidity, and temperature of the air that moved through the dilution tunnel as well as the ambient air in the test cell. Concentrations of CO, HC, NOx and CO_2 were also sampled from the ambient air for comparison to the exhaust samples. All of these factors were plugged in (usually manually by a lab technician) and the computer program spat out the results in an easy-to-read grams per mile figure. If the car passed the test, even just barely, the lab submitted the paperwork to the EPA recommending that the car be cleared. If the car failed, it was back to the workshop for the car and the technicians.

Naturally, converters who worked in volume were eager to have a lab open within range of their shop. Not only were approved test facilities scarce in number, but they were also scattered around the country, mostly occurring near major centers of industrial activity such as the northeast or in the auto producing states. For the gray market shops scattered around the country, a trip to the lab may have involved trailering a car for 500 miles or more for a one-hour dial-in session on the dyno, followed by a test. And that was if things went well. If a converter put a car on the dyno and for some reason found it wouldn't dial in, the car had to be taken back to the workshop for repairs or further modification. That kind of bottleneck seriously cut into production, so any converter who did more than a few EPA conversions wanted their own lab. If not one of their own, then one that was convenient to their location.

Building a lab was far more complicated than opening a store or a restaurant, but the good news was that there were an ever-increasing number of importers and converters out there who were eager to line up for a thousand dollars a pop to get their cars tested. The test process itself, not including the impound time, could take five to eight hours, with two hours of shed testing at the beginning and end; so a minimal lab equipped with a shed and dyno, if operated 24 hours a day, could test about 18 cars per week, generating $72,000 per month. Adding another shed could increase the number of tests a lab could perform without increasing personnel.

But they couldn't run continuously. Periodic instrument maintenance was one of many required parts of the procedure and required regular stoppages for calibration that took many hours. The gas analyzers themselves were a major expense in setting up a lab, but a lab equipped with redundant instruments could stagger their use, enabling them to test continuously—a capability worth $20,000 or more per week in revenue. Of course, the customers had to be able to lease dyno time for dialing in their test cars, but even at $100 per hour, dyno time was not as lucrative as testing time. It was necessary though; customers had to be able to dial their cars in before they would allow them to be tested, so a well-planned lab might have an additional test cell for customer use during the day and turn it towards testing during the night increasing the revenue stream even further.

A test lab owned by the owner of a conversion shop or gray market dealer would not be certified by the EPA. But this didn't stop some shops from setting up their own test cells. An unsanctioned test cell could still be used for testing modifications, dialing in cars, and even for performing mock tests if they wanted to go that far. An uncertified test facility could also lease dyno time to other shops to help pay the bills. In some ways, it was even preferable not to be certified because it meant not having to follow all of the more expensive regulatory procedures, as well as not doing all of the related paperwork. But for finishing the job and achieving EPA clearance, the cars still had to be transported to an EPA approved test lab and go through the paces.

The solution for the converters who wanted to test their own cars came in finding a "disinterested" party to be the official owner of the lab. While the EPA was particular about importer/converters testing their own cars, they didn't scrutinize relationships so closely that they got excited about family members or business associates owning their own lab. If a converter could find someone who was willing to sign all the papers, they and their investors could do all the legwork to build and outfit the facility and apply for EPA approval. Sometimes, the converters would approach their own customers for investment capital to open their own lab. The customers were often wealthy bankers and lawyer types who were constantly looking for new places to put their money to work, and compared to more conventional investments, it was an attractive opportunity. It could even be an especially attractive opportunity for someone who had large sums of money they couldn't or didn't want to account for. Testing cars was expensive, and a lab could easily claim to have performed more tests than they actually had. Successful tests were carefully documented with the EPA, but a failed test or time leased for dialing in a car could exist only on paper, and in that way account for a large income.

In theory, the potential return looked good: a small lab with two test cells and sheds could gross thousands of dollars a day. Of course, things rarely went smoothly enough to meet the projections, but it looked good enough on paper to attract many independent investors who, up until then had nothing to do with the automotive industry. Besides, it was a very cool thing to say at a cocktail party that you had just invested in a gray market test lab. Whether the cozy relationship between the lab owners and the converters affected test results was a source of some controversy and is of course open to anyone's speculation but labs that enjoyed that kind of relationship were often approved by the EPA.

The independent labs started popping up like weeds. They weren't as prolific as the conversion shops, but similarly, their growth was sufficient to outpace the EPA's ability to regulate them. There were potential markets everywhere for the brand-new industry, but port cities were the most popular locations as they were with the conversion shops. And as with the conversion shops, other businesses were popping up to fill every niche that arose with the proliferation of the labs. A lab owner in California, sensing opportunity, began offering training seminars for lab technicians. For $400, a would-be lab owner could send his employee to a one-week class of intensive training designed to turn any average Joe into a qualified automotive test lab technician. How well this training worked was debatable, however. One lab owner who used the service, and whose approval had later been suspended by the EPA, reported that when the EPA inspector asked his technician what was the CFM (cubic feet per minute) capacity of the fan in the front of the test cell, the technician replied, "What's a CFM?"

Conversion technicians who had been trucking their cars to places like TRC in Ohio were eager to try out any new lab that opened its doors. Even if it represented longer travel time for them, they would happily do the time in hopes that the lab would be a little more lenient on test procedure. The grapevine functioned well, much as it did in the racing world, because in many ways they were the same players. Technicians who in a simpler time used to sit at the bar talking about their performance modifications and trying to discern their colleagues' closely held secrets for making cars go faster and win races were now having the same kind of fellowship in the bars near the emission test labs. The labs were the new racetracks, a common meeting place where mechanics from hundreds of miles around would gather to put their latest innovations to the ultimate test. Some would even put small wagers on each other's cars, whether they were likely to pass this time. The opponent was the EPA, and the goal was to sneak as much past The Man as possible. The winners went home triumphant, anticipating cash rewards when the car they had just nursed through the test could move on to its patron. The losers loaded their cars onto the truck for another trip back to the workshop to agonize over the details, hoping to find the reason why they couldn't make the test.

The parallels with the racing culture went on. Professional rivals met at the test lab to dial in their cars and helped each other out with tricks of the trade, but often keeping their latest discoveries to themselves in hopes of maintaining some kind of professional advantage. The experienced operators would watch as the new kids came in and they would usually let them flounder on the dyno for a while before someone would step up and offer to help them sort things out. "Dialing a car in" for the test became an art form. Much like dialing a car in for a racetrack, it had to done on the spot and in a hurry. The equipment was already there, installed on the car, but without the finishing touches of the final adjustments, it might as well not be there for all the good that it did. To be able to work with a car for a short time and decide whether it was likely to pass the test or if it had to go home for more work took skill, intuition and experience. Operators who had practiced and perfected the process could tune a car quickly and either cull it or leave it for a successful test while others, even the technicians who installed the equipment, might struggle and run up huge bills for dyno time and not be able to make the same car pass on a bet.

The environment in the working area of an independent automotive test lab was often not like the image that is conjured up by the name. Some had the kind of high-end polish of an installation like TRC, but many of the latecomers to the emissions lab business had a more blue-collar feel to them and resembled more than anything, a garage cluttered with an unusual amount of equipment. The chassis dynamometer, a bulky piece of equipment that made turbine-like sounds when in operation, was mounted in the floor of a room at least the size of a garage. Sometimes there were multiple dynos in a room running at the same time, each one making sounds like a jet aircraft warming up. Each test cell required one or more large fans to be blowing air into the car's cooling system; the positive displacement blower in the sampling system made a roar like a freight train. When all this equipment was running at once, and it usually was, hearing anything else was practically impossible. Add to that the sound of one or more car engines running and you begin to get the idea of the continual noise level. The space itself could be a clean, well-lit new building, or it could be an old, dark warehouse on the "bad" side of town, chosen for its low overhead. The only requirement was that it be possible to maintain a certain range of temperature and humidity during the course of preparation and testing … which, on good days was going on 24-7. The EPA made no stipulations as to lighting or decor.

A dyno installation normally required digging into the floor of a building, but in one not atypical installation the renters of an old warehouse got around that by building large ramps and mounting the dyno on a raised platform about three feet above floor level. They strung a few fluorescent lamps crazily above the test station and hung the necessary electrical outlets and air lines from the ceiling around the platform where the

9. The Independent Labs   121

technicians, under a spooky pool of light, hovered over their subject like alchemists over a cauldron. Next to the dyno platform was a control booth, a hastily constructed but functionally soundproof room with a large window facing the platform. In that room lived the delicate gas analyzers and computer equipment that evaluated the data as it came in from the maelstrom outside.

The lab tech inside the control room communicated with the mechanics outside via a makeshift code that consisted of taps on the glass and a few crude hand signals. He sat in the quiet of the small office space listening to the muffled hum of the machinery just outside the glass and watched as the four needles of a chart recorder, representing the different components of the exhaust gas, moved across the width of a slowly advancing roll of paper creating a colorful drawing that looked like nothing to anyone except for those in the business. As they made small adjustments, the mechanics would bolt to the window and push their faces up to the glass, straining to see the needles of the instruments on the other side as they slowly reacted to the last changes. Once the needles started to lie flat and seemed inclined to stay there, they signaled the warehouse techies who pushed the car off of the platform toward the impound area where the car was held for later testing. Meanwhile another pair of helpers pushed the next victim up the ramp and quickly hooked it up to the instruments with well-practiced moves. Time was important and expensive, so if the mechanics went over their allotted time attempting to dial a car in, after a couple of stern warnings the lab staff unceremoniously unhooked the car and pushed it off the platform while the mechanics stood there, still holding their tools by their sides like smoking guns.

The gray market mechanics weren't the only characters to haunt the independent labs. There were other enterprises that found a need for an approved automotive test facility. Inventors of the latest gas saving devices needed a lab to give them "certified test results" that they could print on their labels in the retail stores. One story that came from a pair of sources was going around about an "independent researcher" who haunted an independent lab in Pennsylvania and called himself Dr. Laverne. Laverne, or whoever he was in his secret identity, was said to have perfected the art of filling out the right forms for getting government research grants. He would show up at the lab at unpredictable intervals accompanied by his stunningly beautiful assistant whom he called Shirley. Whenever he showed up it was with a car equipped with some odd device for which he needed before and after test results. For example, once he was said to have tested a car, then come back the next day with a pyramid strapped to the roof and tested it again. Of course there was little or no difference in the test results, and no one in the labs reported having seen his final report, but in the pure research business, it's just as important to have a report that says pyramids have no effect on automobile performance as it is to have one that proves that they do. So, Dr. Laverne would submit the results of his government funded study to the proper offices and move on to his next research project.

Of course, the labs were in business to make money, and to do that they needed a steady clientele. If a lab was the only one in a large geographical area that was not a problem, but if there were a number of labs in a radius of a few hundred miles, as there eventually were on the east and west coasts, there could be competition. The best way to address that competition was to earn a reputation as an "easy" lab. Such a reputation was a tricky commodity, it couldn't be advertised, or even talked about in some circles for obvious reasons but it had to get out there to keep the business coming in. The converters would talk about a lab's qualifications among themselves, but even they had to be careful about how far the word spread for fear of losing an advantage. Like talking too openly about a special fishing hole, spreading the word that a lab was easy might make the lab too popular with other converters and make it hard to get on the schedule. Or it might mean having a test facility with whom they had a good relationship being investigated by the Feds. The converter's relationship with the lab staff was of primary importance as there were a number of ways that the lab technicians could subtly affect test results and cultivate an easy reputation without going so far as to actually falsify data. But that option wasn't completely off the table either.

The staff in a lab usually consisted of a couple of highly trained technicians to operate and calibrate the equipment and a number of low wage hands whose job it was to push cars around from one test station to another, hook them up to the equipment, and drive the cars on the dyno during testing. "Dyno Driving" was considered a low skilled job, and it didn't pay well, but it was tricky, and some drivers had an aptitude for it while others could never "get it." In developing the dyno driving schedule, EPA engineers had hooked a speed and distance chart recorder up to one member's family car and recorded as it was driven through the course of one day's errands. The resulting chart, after some editing, became the national standard. Copies were printed out and purchased for use by the independent labs where they were mounted on another chart recorder to be placed in the view of the driver on the dynamometer. When the test was running this chart recorder drew a line representing the car's speed and the object for the driver was to match the speed of the car to the line already printed on the chart. A perfect chart had two speed graphs, almost identical, one drawn on top of another. When the test was completed, the resulting graph was among the papers submitted to the EPA to show that the car was driven through the same series of accelerations and decelerations, cruising speeds and stationary idling periods as dictated by the test schedule.

The drivers were usually teenagers or college age kids who by some family connection had lucked into a summer job that wasn't working in a fast-food chain. They shut themselves up in the cars, rolling up all the windows and running the air conditioning to shut out the noise outside. If the car had a sound system in it, they would turn it up and rock out while they took the same boring trip to nowhere. For the mechanics outside, getting their attention often involved a few hard raps on the glass to break them out of their zone.

As it turns out, there is a certain amount of skill involved in drawing a line with a pen guided by a speedometer. A car on a dyno, like a car in motion, has a certain amount of inertia to contend with, so making small corrections when the line starts to go off of the pattern is difficult. To do it well, the driver has to be able to anticipate how the car will react in advance. Trying to make rapid corrections by stepping sharply on the accelerator or the brake could cause large spikes on the graphs in the control room, as exhaust content reflected shifts in the engine's demand for power, then its return to a balanced state. With a marginal car, those spikes could be large enough to make the difference between a successful test and a trip back to the shop. So even though the test was supposed to be democratic enough that the driver would not be a factor, he was. And the better drivers found themselves being asked for at the labs.

Coaching the driver was technically not allowed, but in practice it happened all the time. There were a number of small tricks that could be employed that in of themselves accomplished little but taken together could be the difference between a pass and a fail. A car that failed one gas standard by .01 grams per mile still failed so when a converter was working with a marginal car any trick that could possibly trim off that .01 gram was employed. For example, the beginning of the test was a difficult period to clean up. The exhaust was to be sampled while the car was starting up. Then the car was allowed to idle for fifteen seconds, put in drive or first gear, allowed to idle for another ten seconds, then driven off according to the graph. There was a certain amount of error allowed on the driver's graph, so a skilled driver would stretch the limits of the graph in favor of the low side. He would allow the car to idle a little longer to warm up the catalysts slightly more before driving off and if the car had enough reserve power, he could keep the speed of his accelerations just below the graph to minimize the power drawn from the engine and therefore the production of toxic exhaust. Likewise, he could extend any idling periods throughout the test because most cars were cleanest while idling and exhaust sampled during that period would go to dilute the entire sample. The operator of the equipment could also be encouraged to be a little slow on the switch to delay sampling to the very last moment, even to the point of not beginning a sample until the car had started, thus skipping a period when a car produced a large amount of HC. Manually inputting the test data left another window open for a technician trying to squeak one through. The test charts from the samples had to be included in the packet sent to the EPA so they had to agree with the data put into the program, but there were plenty of variables that didn't need to be substantiated. Small changes in the relative humidity or the temperature could affect the final outcome by tiny amounts. Adding a few rolls of the dyno to the figures or a few hundred revolutions of the positive displacement pump could make enough difference in the case of a marginal car. The changes had to be small, so they stayed inside the margin of error allowed, but if the data added up, there was little chance that it would ever be disputed. If any of these tactics or others ever came to the attention of the feds, the lab managers could act shocked, deny culpability, and write the errors off to poorly trained technicians.

If a converter was really in good graces with a lab operator, the lab could go further and further out on a limb to produce the test results they wanted. Large amounts of data had to be submitted to the EPA for each car including the test charts from the gas analyzers and those various pieces of data had to add up, but surprisingly low-tech approaches could be used to fudge the data. But of course, plausibility was important, and notoriously dirty cars, like the Italian exotics, couldn't turn in results that looked like they came out of the tailpipe of a Honda Civic.

One lab technician remarked that he had been instructed to attach rubber bands to the needles of the chart recorders to keep them from moving too far to the high side. Like a butcher's thumb on a scale, a little bit of pressure went a long way. Early attempts to hold back the instruments looked clumsy and obviously tampered with. But after some practice, he found he could produce charts that looked like the real thing. He went on to describe his first day of employment at the lab where he was instructed to hold down one end of a roll of chart paper on a long table while his supervisor drew long shaky lines on the paper with a colored pen. At the time he had no idea what was going on, but as he became more acquainted with the procedures and equipment, he realized that he had been helping to manually forge fuel temperature charts to replace data that had been lost due to a piece of faulty equipment.

Gaining more experience in automotive testing, he became more and more acquainted with methods for forging test results. If a car came into the lab for testing and produced good results, he would stall release of the car long enough to test it again and sometimes a third time. In this way it was possible to generate packets of passing test charts and file them away for later use. It was necessary to have a good cross section of material on hand, representing every type of car, because the charts had to show results that jibed with the test subject's displacement, weight, and anticipated mileage figures. He guarded his files jealously, kept their existence to himself and didn't submit bogus data unless he considered the situation dire. It was hard to come by and couldn't just be produced on a copier or computer printer, so each stack of charts did in fact represent an actual test that had taken place, just not necessarily the test that they were submitted with. Interestingly, at least where he was concerned, whether a customer was entitled to this kind of treatment didn't have anything to do with money offered. In fact, if converters and car owners were so bold as to offer a bribe for better results, they were immediately shown the door. Only the best and most trusted clients were entitled to a packet from the files and usually they didn't even know that they had been the beneficiary of "the secret files." The best customers knew better than to ask.

It was 1984 before the EPA got around to systematically checking up on the labs. Working with the State of California through the California Air Resources Board, they selected 27 gray market cars that had been granted clearance based on test results submitted by independent labs approved by the EPA. Teams of EPA personnel re-tested them and only one passed every phase of the emissions test. In their evaluation the EPA stated that their performance reflected problems with the labs *and* the converters. They admitted that in some cases failures may have resulted from the deterioration of emission control devices that had worked well enough the first time yet could not continue to work under normal driving conditions; but in other cases, required emissions equipment was missing altogether, fueling debate over whether components had been removed or had never been installed, and the "test" was just a packet of bogus data.

There weren't enough trained inspectors to travel the country evaluating each new lab as it popped up, so the EPA started a waiting list. Of course, that didn't work out well for the owners and investors of a new lab. They had a ton of money wrapped up in construction, equipment and training and they needed to start generating cash as quickly as possible. The EPA approach to that was to offer retroactive approval. Labs were given permission to perform EPA testing on cars but the lab's approval was left pending. Cars could be tested and if they passed, they could be sold or go home to their final owners, but *final* EPA clearance was left pending approval of the lab. If, when the inspector finally made it around to check out the lab, he gave it the nod, then the approval would be retroactive to a previously set date and all the cars tested up to that date would be given final clearance. But if the lab was inspected and did not pass because of some systemic problem, be it faulty equipment or improper procedure, then the EPA would then determine how many cars they thought had been improperly tested, and they would insist that those cars be retested.

A lab that didn't get their pending approval that they had been counting on found themselves in an awkward position. First, they had to remedy fault(s) found by the EPA, then they had to track down the current owners of the cars that they had already declared clean enough for the streets and recall them. Just tracking the cars down could be a major headache, because gray market cars tended to change hands quickly and frequently. For one such lab the EPA inspectors decided that the problem with the lab had existed for several months, so they insisted the lab personnel had to locate and re-test every car that they had passed during that time. Once the cars were located, there was the problem of explaining to the car's new owner why the car had to be recalled. Naturally, this didn't always go well. The lab manager would do his best to make the process as painless as possible for the car owners even by providing transportation for any and all of the cars to be re-tested wherever they were. Two or three cars a week were showing up on the car-carrier for re-test and the word from above was that they had to be moved through with all possible speed. Fortunately, the fault found by the EPA was minor, not substantially affecting the final outcome of the test, and the cars in question were mostly ordinary German sedans and passed their re-test with little trouble, but there were a few awkward cases where the emissions equipment wasn't functioning well enough to make it through or had even been removed completely. For those cars, it often came down to a trip back to the original converter for a re-fit.

While most of the cars recovered for retesting required a fair amount of telephone time from lab personnel assuring the owners that everything was going fine and their car would be back in their garage shortly, one such instance involved by phone calls from a frightened man living in a motel. It seems he had sold the large-bodied Mercedes to a man rumored to be an organized crime figure, who didn't appreciate getting calls from the Feds, even if it was just the EPA calling about his car. The car salesman had been given an ultimatum by the gentleman and was afraid to go back to his home or even his home state until the issue with the car and the lab was resolved. Never saying on the phone just where he was, he called several times a day, each time from a different location, checking on the progress of the car until after about a week he had been assured that the car has earned its papers and was on its way back home.

Of course, the main reason for investing in a lab was to make money moving cars through to their final clearance. The reality was often less predictable. Whatever the reason, whether it was lack of know-how on the part of the customers, mechanical failures, or just bad luck, anything that jammed up the works could have cascading consequences down the line. If a car didn't earn its numbers quickly, the queue would back up and seriously affect the cash flow. It was the personnel in the labs who were usually the ones placed directly in the bottleneck, and there they found themselves under a large amount of pressure from all angles. There was the frustration of the car owners whose cars didn't pass, accompanied by the attitude of the management who were disappointed in their bottom line, and the technicians who came in with the cars who were constantly encouraging the lab techs to fudge the numbers in whatever way they could. Most of the lab techs were blue collar types who never knew what they were in for when they answered the ad that the employment agency had given them. While it may have been easy for the technicians in the workshops to divorce themselves from the legal implications of their work, the lab techs were a little closer to the front lines. Each test came with a batch of forms that had to be signed by someone and the forms had small print at the bottom reminding the signer that providing false data could land them in jail or cause them to be fined thousands of dollars, or both. Most lab workers had no interest in sticking their necks out, but being relatively low in the hierarchy, they also felt the pressure of being expendable. While it was usually OK to send the customers from the outside back to the drawing board, if the cars converted by a shop closely associated with the lab didn't pass, whatever the reason, the lab personnel often took the heat. If the boss called to complain however, he was usually careful with his wording. The phrase "pass this car or else" never actually came up. It would more likely be a subtle remark about making some changes if things didn't start going more smoothly, and a lab tech who could keep the boss off his back by being a little slow at the sampling switch would more than likely choose to cooperate.

10

The Shine Rubs Off

While the gray market importers had originally been the most exciting thing to happen in the automotive world, with all the new entries into the field and the fast fortunes being made, the polish was beginning to rub off. The press had been painting gray marketers as Robin Hood figures, reaching into the pockets of the rich automakers and passing the fruits of their shadowy dealings on to the not-so-average car buyer. The tourist magazines, business magazines, and news weeklies all were publishing stories of how much money you could save by engaging the services of a direct importer. But the honeymoon was ending. The huge increase in the market and the amount of money that could be made in a short time were attracting more unethical people to the game, and the fallout from their dealings was attracting attention. Stories of Italian exotics and German luxury sedans with no paper trail were popping up all over. In 1982, *Newsweek* wrote about a California man, George Sack, who paid $55,000 for a used Ferrari Boxer and paid a company called Ferrari Compliance Inc. $19,000 for an engine overhaul and compliance work, only to have the car die on the trip home from the workshop. "I had driven 7 miles when all of a sudden I heard this banging sound and saw smoke coming out. I pulled over and got out and saw the catalytic converters glowing a bright cherry red." The boxer's engine was ruined, and the lawyers quickly became involved.

The article went on to mention other outrages performed by the conversion shops, like disconnecting the pollution controls as soon as the car had passed the lab, or the practice of running the odometer up to 7500 miles—a curious thing for a car dealer to do, but it achieved the California definition of a used car, to get past the state law forbidding the sale of new cars that were not certified by the original manufacturer.[1]

None of these practices were news to anyone inside the gray market. But with news getting out, the automotive press became more circumspect and looked to reconsider their original appraisal of the gray market as a band of merry men pulling capers on the outskirts of the auto industry. Many of the same periodicals that had been publishing stories about how much money could be saved by buying your car from a direct importer turned around only months later with articles like "Buyer Beware," describing the regulatory pitfalls, the unscrupulous operators, lack of warranty coverage, and improperly installed components that were being encountered by more and more gray market customers.

Of course, the people responsible for policing the gray market, the EPA and the DOT, were well aware of the practices of many of the converters and labs, but for a long time they didn't have the funds to do anything about it. It wasn't until the State of California started legal maneuvers against some of the more flagrant violators that federal regulators started to get any traction.

If they were looking for a high-profile head to roll, they couldn't have found a better one than Al Mardikian. Mardikian's remarkable rise in the import business had raised a few eyebrows among officials in California early on and his business had been under some scrutiny for some time. As usual, California law read differently from federal law with respect to importing non-compliant cars for sale, and that was where the state attorney's office found their foothold. Mardikian asserted that it was just a matter of interpretation, but as Assistant State Attorney General Susan Durban interpreted it, the law stipulated that new cars not made compliant by the original manufacturer could not be certified by CARB (California Air Resources Board) and therefore were not legal to sell in the state. She had been steering an investigation into Mardikian's business practically since its founding and in December of 1981 obtained a court order forbidding him from selling converted cars in California. The rest of the direct importers were reading the news and watching the case closely as many of the other marketers of gray market conversions in California carefully steered their way around that law by selling their cars in other states. As long as the cars were titled and registered somewhere besides California, they could still be operated in California and many of the wealthy patrons of the gray market had second homes outside the state whose addresses could be employed to that end. But Mardikian scoffed at the law and according to the attorney general's office, sold his Ferraris and other exotics directly to the citizens of California.

Mardikian's fight with the state of California dragged out for several years. When the injunction forbade him from selling his cars in California, he tried calling in markers from politicians. He explained his ordeal to the Orange County Supervisor, whose campaign he had supported, and asked for help. The supervisor, who had ties to the governor's office that Mardikian hoped would earn him a break, replied that he looked into the case and told Mardikian, "These are serious problems … way beyond me."[2]

When in November of 1982, Mardikian was found in contempt of court for violating the injunction and continuing to sell his cars in California and fined $45,000, he responded by filing for bankruptcy, saying that by steering Trend Imports into federal bankruptcy court he hoped to conserve the company's financial resources while bypassing hostile California air pollution officials, and land his company in a friendlier courtroom. Mardikian insisted that the state attorney's office was on a witch hunt and that he could not get a fair hearing in California. Durban responded by saying, "I don't think he's going to do any better in Federal court. It will simply make it easier to identify his assets."[3]

The federal court had not been the only party interested in Al Mardikian's assets. Earlier that year a local news article told the story that Mardikian reported to police that upon returning home from a vacation he found that his house had been ransacked. The newspaper account of the burglary left no doubt as to just what kind of lifestyle could be earned in the automotive gray market: "Gone were 400,000 dollars-worth of Persian rugs, jewelry, antiques, silver, and crystal items." But in a curious twist, the most precious items missing were the blueprint designs for his intended foray into automobile manufacturing, his sporty custom Mardikian Car.

"It was the only copy (of the blueprint) that I had," he said.[4]

The burglary had no apparent connection to Mardikian's business affairs and was later attributed to a pair of brothers who were accused of robbing 10 homes in Mardikian's posh Spyglass Hill neighborhood during the holidays while residents were away on vacation. Details were not published as to whether Mardikian was able to recover his precious blueprints or if the loss of the papers had anything to do with the failure of the Mardikian car to ever reach production.

But for all the slings and arrows of outrageous fortune, Mardikian continued in business apparently undaunted. It seemed his projects were destined to get more and more outrageous. Among his later efforts at Mardikian Engineering was a $250,000 limousine based on a Ferrari 400i chassis. With an alleged top speed of 180 MPH and equipped with gold plated telephones, Mardikian said he had designed the car specifically for the Pope.

"I know he will buy it. I'm flying to Italy in the next few weeks to show the designs to the Vatican," he told reporters early in 1983. Officials at Ferrari of North America were unconcerned. Jack Gorrien of Ferrari's West Coast office called the car an abortion.[5]

As a legal tactic, Mardikian's move into bankruptcy backfired. While he may have done so to steer around the state attorney general, the move raised some federal eyebrows with regards to finances. By getting involved with the Federal courts, Mardikian had effectively opened Pandora's box, and in June of 1983, FBI agents armed with a search warrant came into the offices of Mardikian Engineering and seized business records. While the probe was ostensibly about bankruptcy fraud, and the records were seized to determine whether he was hiding assets, that's not where the investigation ended up. Mardikian was not formally charged until 1984, and when he was it was not with bankruptcy fraud. He was charged, along with his nephew, with filing false statements to the EPA and with mail fraud in connection with the emissions test lab operations. When the EPA tested 27 gray market cars that had been certified by test labs and found only one to be in compliance—and some without any emission controls at all—several converters were responsible. But Mardikian's head was the first to roll, probably because he was conveniently already under investigation. The EPA took another look at the packets sent in by Mardikian Engineering and by its sister company, Mardikian Automotive Research and Development and decided that they didn't add up, citing photographic discrepancies and duplicate photos.[6] Under close examination, they had decided that they were looking at photos of the same modification done on the same car and filed repeatedly with different serial numbers. They announced that they would no longer accept test packets from either lab as proof of compliance.

Mardikian and his nephew maintained their innocence right up until their trial date when they took a last-minute plea bargain. Stories in the press were of course exaggerated and estimates of the total number of non-compliant cars said to have been fraudulently imported by Mardikian et al. reached as high as 2,000. But the real number of cases that the feds were able to document was 34. When the sentencing came down, it was surprisingly light considering the time and money both state and federal authorities had been spent investigating him by over the years. Mardikian was sentenced to six months in Federal prison, and five years' probation. He was also ordered to set up a program to teach auto repair to state parolees.

This was the beginning of a "clean up your act" campaign by the EPA. They still didn't have much manpower or money for the operation, so it went slowly. CARB took the lead over the federal government in clamping down on the gray market by continuing to investigate the test labs in California. It took years but by 1987 they had revoked the certification of four labs and charged owners and staff alike with submitting false documents to a government agency. The EPA themselves had their lab inspection program in process, but rarely did they level charges. They might revoke a lab's certification temporarily, or even retroactively; however, most cases left the door open for the lab to fix their problem and continue in business. But Mardikian's example put the other operators on notice that the EPA wasn't going to continue to look the other way. The impact of Mardikian's prosecution was felt across the country, particularly among the other independent lab owners. He became a lunch table talking point among technicians who knew they might arrive at work any morning and find themselves facing government officials asking awkward questions.

Like the staff at Trend Imports, many of the shops that started out with a reputation for good quality work had allowed themselves to get sloppy. As the volume of imports had increased the conversion shops realized that their packets were not getting the scrutiny they had in the past and whether by accident or design, many had taken advantage of the loose enforcement of the rules and increased their production by taking shortcuts in both the modifications and the paperwork. Now that Mardikian had officially been busted the big question on everyone's mind was "What happens next?"

While the downfall of Mardikian Engineering and the other labs could have been a watershed moment for the gray market, the big purge everyone was waiting for never really materialized. Considering the size of the gray market and the number of violations, only a few people were charged with anything and fewer still were convicted. The shops that were left standing cautiously went about business as usual. Mardikian, who had once called himself the largest independent auto importer in the country, was on the bench for a while, which left a gap in the gray market trade that other importers were more than happy to fill. As 1985 was ending, the dollar was still very strong in Europe, there were still plenty of businesses left standing and more were always popping up to take up the slack.

11

Meanwhile, at Lamborghini

While other European automakers may have had furtive little affairs with the gray market, Lamborghini became intimately involved. When the Countach appeared as a concept car, there were no plans to make a version available in the U.S. But the gray-market converters who dabbled in Lamborghinis in the late seventies demonstrated there was a ready market for the car if someone would take the trouble. This was good news for sports car enthusiasts living in the USA but was a relatively moot point for Lamborghini because of their problems with production. About the time the gray market was becoming significant in the U.S. and Dick Fritz had imported his fiftieth Ferrari 512, getting your hands on a Countach, even in Europe, was next to impossible. In four years of production the factory had only been able to squeeze out a little over two hundred cars. Lamborghini had been encumbered with financial problems and labor disputes that seemed to have no end, and while they had in the Countach a product that seemed to have a strong demand and could probably save the company, in 1980 it looked like they might not be able to produce them much longer.

Any discussion of Lamborghini history turns up conflicting stories, and the answer to the question of who was able to federalize the first Countach depends on whom you ask. But no one will dispute that successful conversion of a Countach was a Holy Grail type of quest and the shops who worked on it found themselves pouring thousands of hours and dollars into the task. The main players usually credited for first federalizing the first Countach were two competitors: the aforementioned Al Mardikian and Mardikian Engineering on the one hand, and Jasjit Rarewala and Automotive Compliance Incorporated (ACI) on the other.[1] Mardikian completed a number of subsequent Countach conversions, and even did a custom convertible conversion on a Countach for Rod Stewart.[2] But Jas Rarewala bet the farm on the Countach and dedicated his work to obtaining federal and California certificates for the cars.

There were several issues unique to the Countach that presented special problems in completing a successful EPA or DOT conversion, and that required complicated solutions. The most visible was the bumpers. Lamborghini had crash tested a Countach and proven that the chassis of the car was strong enough to protect the passengers in a high-speed crash; in fact, even after the front barrier crash at 60 MPH, the doors of the car could still be opened. But the body work required of the conversion shops was mostly dedicated to protecting the body of the car in a low-speed impact. Even though the car was probably quite strong enough to provide side impact protection, the conversion shops were installing the ubiquitous collapsible door bars inside the doors. At least this operation satisfied the powers that be with little modification and no change in the appearance of the car. The bumpers, however, were not a problem that could be gracefully solved, since Lamborghini had not given any consideration to the U.S. market when they drew the first Countach. The nose of the car terminated at a point well below the DOT specified crash zone of 16 to 20 inches off the ground, so any U.S. legal bumper installation couldn't help but completely spoil the lines of the car. Likewise, at the rear, the sharply sloping tail presented a vulnerable expanse of thin aluminum at the height where the DOT thought a bumper should be, so the converters had no choice but to install a large foreign object on top of what had been a graceful curve in the body. They were so ugly that few people ever even saw the American versions. While most sports car enthusiasts know what a Countach looked like from the magazines and calendars, the cars that appeared in the press were usually European versions or gray-market cars that had been "unconverted." In most cases the front and rear bumper installations, if they were done at all, were devices installed over the existing bodywork without altering the underlying sheet metal so that the purchaser of the car, once he obtained his DOT release letter, could have his mechanic unbolt the offensive additions.

One innovative approach to some of the early front bumper installations done by Rarewala and later copied by others involved a wing-shaped front spoiler. It had the look of an aerodynamic device but was in fact a steel bumper placed above and slightly in front of the nose right in the car's legal impact zone. Some people liked it, but it was definitely a question of personal taste. Rarewala's later versions were adopted by the factory but were not much improved appearance wise, and involved a composite nose piece that raised the profile slightly, including the placement of twin raised rubber fists in the front nose to satisfy the height requirement. The fists were not so well disguised by installing integral driving lights in them. It was an improvement over the wing, and hardly noticeable to some, but still an imperfect solution. The rear bumpers continued to be ugly hang-on devices, often lifted from far less interesting cars. Bumper mods became easier over the years, though. It wasn't because they got any better or that the rules were changed, but because of the same factor that made everything else easier: the

11. Meanwhile, at Lamborghini

government was overwhelmed. By the mid–1980s, practically any installation that could appear to reinforce the existing nose was enough to get the nod from the DOT. Most companies that were converting a Countach would just install a mild steel framework inside the plastic nose piece and that was good enough for the DOT. Technically it did little or nothing to actually protect the car from a bump, but by then filing the paperwork on a car had become just a question of keeping up appearances.

Successfully getting a Countach through the EPA test procedure, however, could be quite expensive and technically challenging and it was of course getting worse with each year. Since the test sample was supposed to begin as the car was being started from cold, and a Countach was not an easily started car, the car often produced enough HC during the first minute to fail the entire test. Every time the engine popped back or tried to stall, which it did frequently during the warmup period, the car belched a mass of unburned HC out the exhaust before the catalysts were hot enough to function. Getting the engine to start quickly and continue running smoothly was difficult, but absolutely necessary for a successful test. Some technicians approached that problem by installing a device to kick the throttles open and immediately rev the engine up to about 3,000 RPM as soon as it started in order to quickly warm up the catalysts. But the days when a Countach could get through a lab test while retaining its original rows of carburetors didn't last long, and converters soon found themselves scrapping carburetors in favor of fuel injection as the 1981 regulations came into play. They needed the more precise fuel mixture control afforded by fuel injection, as well as the ability to contain the fumes.

Passing the evaporative emissions part of the test (the hot shed) was difficult for any car with multiple carburetors—practically any of the earlier Italian sports cars—because each air intake and bowl vent was another escape point for gasoline vapors. Fuel would also condense in the intake and seep out around the throttle seals and evaporate, leaving no trace except for a failed test. So technicians trying to pass a carbureted car built steel boxes that completely enclosed the carburetors and contained the fumes for the duration of the test. Vacuum-controlled doors at the engine air intakes opened when the engine started and closed when it was shut off. Complicated solutions like this could work up until 1981, when the regulations practically cut all the emission levels in half including the evaporative emissions sampled in the shed.

By 1980, there were enough Bosch injected cars on market that it was possible to buy the components for a complete fuel injection system in the spare parts aftermarket. It was just a question of determining the most appropriate components for the application. Some of the first fuel-injected Countachs to see the inside of a lab were built using the components for two BMW 323 six-cylinder engines. There were a number of other permutations, but the Bosch Continuous injection system of the type employed by Mercedes and Ferrari turned out to be the fuel system of choice for anyone trying to do an emissions conversion on a Countach. Everything went on in pairs: two fuel pumps, two accumulators, two fuel distributors, two throttle bodies, etc. The V12 engine was set up like two six-cylinder engines.

Jas Rarewala's conversion business had been through several iterations before he became focused on Lamborghini. He had been with Dan Morgan at American Specialty Corporation doing conversions, including one on a Lamborghini that showed up in *Road & Track*. Morgan eventually left the company and Rarewala renamed it Automotive Compliance International. But it wasn't long after that he and Trefor Thomas formed a new company and called it Lamborghini of North America. Lamborghini was foundering at the time. They had been teetering on the financial edge since 1978 and finally went into bankruptcy in early 1980. They would not have been able to build any cars at all, except that the owners of two of the Italian Lamborghini Dealerships were keeping the factory running by financing the supply chain for some of the parts.

According to a series of letters on a Lamborghini internet forum attributed to Jas Rarewala's partner, Trefor Thomas, the story of Lamborhgini in America is not what the popular press has been told. A number of coffee table books tell the story of Lamborghini, but the role Rarewala and Thomas played is absent from most. A series of remarks in the forum from one Lamborghini enthusiast, referring to "some guy in California" who was "butchering" Lamborghinis by replacing their carburetors with fuel injection, brought Thomas to the surface. According to the letters, Thomas was Rarewala's partner in Lamborghini North America, as they worked on cars on a case-by-case basis. When Lamborghini went into bankruptcy, they made plans to try to buy the factory—plans that might have worked except for the unfortunate timing of political events. The account stated they had obtained financing to the tune of $15 million, but when it came time to close the deal, the banker they had engaged would not travel to Italy. The banker was an Iranian national living in the U.S. and because of the recent (1979) Iranian revolution and subsequent kidnapping of the U.S. Embassy personnel in Tehran, there were a number of U.S. government sanctions in place against Iran. The banker was afraid if he left the U.S. he would not be allowed to return. The resulting delay caused the deal for Thomas and Rarewala to buy the factory to fall apart, and opened the door for other investors to get control of the company.

The Lamborghini factory was instead sold to a young heir to a French industrialist fortune, Patrick Mimran. In the course of the factory being sold to the Mimran family, Rarewala and Thomas were able to obtain the distribution rights for Lamborghini in North America, winning the bid over several other companies because they agreed to do the research and development work to certify the Countach for sale in the U.S. and California. The Lamborghini still had neither the desire nor the facilities to do compliance work; they needed a North American distributor who would take that job off their hands.

In July of 1981 they received their first 5-liter engine from Lamborghini and began work. They based the project on Bosch continuous injection, having decided carburetors were out of the question. Because the factory insisted they not modify the body, they had to compromise on intake manifold design. The design they preferred, with much longer intake runners, would have required putting a large bump in the engine cover, so the manifold they finally used was much shorter. As part of the compromise, the camshafts were necessarily re-ground, giving them a more street-car-like profile. The 5-liter V12 was a high-revving engine and the original camshaft grind put the useful torque way up in the higher RPM range, well above the engine's operating range during the course of the federal test procedure. Re-grinding moved the torque curve into a more useful range and in addition to making the car cleaner during warm up, it made the car considerably more tractable and easier to drive in the real world. In spite of the modifications, the car still tested at 330 HP compared to the unmodified version's 375.

Countach engine bay with half of the original Weber carburetor system removed from the right side of engine, the other half still in place on the left (private collection).

One side of the Weber carburetor system that comes on the Countach. It turned out to be impossible to sufficiently control the fuel mixture throughout the test with the carburetors, so custom-built fuel injection was required to achieve EPA compliance (private collection).

Beginning construction on a handmade fuel injection system for a Countach. A jig was built to represent the top of the engine, where the manifolds would be bolted. Then the manifold was constructed by hand on the jig (author's photograph).

11. Meanwhile, at Lamborghini

Countach engine removed from the car. Here can be seen the extra heat retaining insulation wrapped around the exhaust headers. This helped the catalysts to heat up more quickly (author's photograph).

A hand made fuel injection system that was a copy of a design by Ruff Engineering (author's photograph).

Another view of the same (author's photograph).

Author's design, Countach fuel system partially installed (author's photograph).

11. Meanwhile, at Lamborghini

Looking at the fuel system from under the wing (private collection).

Their system obtained a certificate from the EPA, and from the more rigorous CARB. In July of 1982, Rarewala appeared in the *New York Times* business news posing next to a Countach under the headline "Finally, an American Countach, at $95,000" announcing that Lamborghini was prepared to start selling their cars again in the U.S. Rarewala made casting molds for the manifold, and sent the whole package, including a DOT and EPA converted car, back to Lamborghini. But the first factory-built, fuel-injected car still wasn't delivered until 1983.

Meanwhile, if you were an American who wanted a Countach, you could travel to Europe and buy one, or you could order one in America from Rarewala. It was still a fairly small operation: he and Thomas would travel to Italy, pick up a car at the factory, and drive it to Frankfurt to be shipped to the U.S. Then, at his shop in California, he could federalize the car and deliver it to the buyer in about three months' time.

Even when the factory was producing fuel-injected Countachs using their design, they couldn't build them fast enough to satisfy the market, so they continued to federalize cars from their business in LA, along with a number of independent gray market dealers. Rarewala and Thomas were fitting the cars according to the designs and specifications submitted to the EPA for their small-volume certification, which was necessarily a time consuming and expensive operation. But they were proud of their system; it worked well and was safe and reliable. Despite Lamborghini North America having distribution rights, there were still other Lamborghinis coming into the states through independent importers, and the other gray market operators were also retrofitting their cars with fuel injection.

But this was the period of the big boom in the gray market. The EPA was not scrutinizing applications as they had been and some of the labs were manufacturing results allowing cars to pass that shouldn't have. The independent operators took advantage of the loose and slippery environment to take shortcuts in their work that, if tested by the rules, probably would not have been successful. These shortcuts enabled them to "finish" a Countach in a matter of a week, instead of the three months Lamborghini NA said they required for proper conversion. When one of the Lamborghini factory reps in LA—a man who, according to the Thomas letters, was poorly equipped to assess the quality of the work—learned of the difference in time and cost between Lamborghini NA's certified conversion and the one-off gray market work, he was said to have recommended to the factory that they bypass Lamborghini NA altogether and import their cars through gray market channels.

Thus began a struggle for control of the North American market that ended with Lamborghini taking back control of U.S. distribution, and Rarewala and Thomas retaining only the rights to the Orange County, California, market. As a consequence, there were a number of gray market Countachs hitting the street with shabby conversion work. When the owners had trouble with their cars—some of them even caught fire because of poor catalyst location—they found there was nobody ready to stand behind the cars or offer any kind of warranty protection. Lamborghini's reputation took a beating, and there were a number of lawsuits flying around, including one by Rarewala over the right to appoint dealerships, which continued to be an issue even after Chrysler bought control of Lamborghini in 1987.[3]

So, Lamborghini's 10-year affair with the gray market pretty much ended in 1987. With the purchase of Lamborghini by Chrysler, many of the lessons of the gray market sunk in; and now that Lamborghini had a rich parent, they could spend some money developing models for the U.S. Subsequent cars designed and built by Lamborghini were done with the U.S. and world markets in mind, and the demand for federalizing Lamborghinis, except for a few leftovers that were floating around, faded away.

12

The Factories Push Back

Up until about 1982, when the gray market had just been moving in from the economic fringes, European car makers and their authorized dealers had looked at the gray market shops and dealers with a sort of amused tolerance. Like the EPA in the seventies, the car makers really didn't want to be bothered. Ferrari and Lamborghini weren't suffering any loss from the rise of unauthorized imports. In fact, they'd been enjoying their fairly cozy relationship with some conversion shops because they were making cars that they didn't offer to the States anyway. And the only way those cars could be sold at all in America was through the gray market channels. So Ferrari wasn't severely affected; the only downside occurred for the American dealerships, who only had 308s for sale when buyers were looking for a twelve-cylinder model. Lamborghini's production was so low, they barely participated in the U.S. market at all, so they had no need to be offended by the gray-market importers either, though they echoed the same litany that came from other makers, that the poor work by some of the conversion shops was likely to give their cars a bad reputation.

It was, of course, the shift in the value of the dollar and the sudden spike in gray market imports that got the factories' attention. As long as the number of imports hovered around 3,500 per year or lower, they shared the sentiment of the regulating agencies in that there weren't enough cars crossing the border to justify much action. But in 1982, when the number of direct imports jumped to almost 9,000, eyebrows were raised, and the factories and their dealer networks really started to feel like they were missing out on something.

There was plenty of talk that Mercedes and its German siblings had only themselves to blame. To begin with, the surge in the dollar's value against the mark should have been accompanied by a drop in sticker price at the dealerships. But dealers did not adjust their prices to reflect reduced cost to them, and instead pocketed windfall profits. Additionally, many of the European car makers had continued to build U.S. versions of only their most profitable cars, leaving many of the more exciting models they produced out of the U.S. market. They had underestimated the resourcefulness of the American car buyers and, in the eyes of many, were reaping what they had sown. The philosophical angle was little comfort to the car companies however, and they looked around to see what measures they could take to stop, or at least slow down, the flow of unauthorized imports.

Mercedes and the rest began to lobby Congress for some kind of legislative relief. But much to their chagrin they learned that, in the U.S. legal system, Congress could not simply raise a mighty hand and stop the flow of cars at the border. The gray market had not emerged overnight and could not be quickly shut down either. There would have to be committees, studies, proposals, bills, etc., and these things take time. And they learned many congressmen were disinclined to do anything about the gray market at all, simply because, like many other wealthy Americans, they enjoyed the products of the direct importers—gray market cars were parked in the Capitol's underground parking garage.

Carmakers based in countries where the government had more direct control over businesses and commerce found the American attitude towards passing legislation against the gray market frustrating. Unlike the domestic manufacturers, they hadn't spent the last decade lobbying for this or that rule change, so they were unfamiliar with the way the American government worked, or didn't work depending on whose side you were on.

Not finding the cooperation they wanted in the halls of Congress, Mercedes took their troubles to the ultimate American authorities: the insurance companies and the banks. In many cases they were able to flex a little financial muscle and persuade the banks it wasn't in their global best interest to offer financing for gray market cars. For the insurance companies, they put on their consumer safety hat and explained that, since so many cars had not been properly modified, they should all be regarded as potential hazards to life and property, and therefore should not be insured. There was in fact, little for the insurers to be concerned about. The models that were popular among the importers were mostly the big sedans that were quite safe and practically the same as the U.S. versions, save a few details that would not likely result in serious injury. While it was true that there were some fires because of incorrect location of the catalytic converter or because a fuel vent line was installed incorrectly, and they were always a big sensation in the press, actual occurrences involving Mercedes were far less common than it would have appeared.

Nevertheless, some of the major insurers complied with Mercedes' wishes. Mercedes supplied a list of serial numbers for the insurers to use to identify the "bad" cars, and when they turned up, they declined to cover them. The hope at Mercedes was that gray market cars would acquire a reputation for being difficult to finance and impossible to insure and people

12. The Factories Push Back

would stop buying them. But the insurance market and the banking industry were far too big and diverse for their efforts to be all encompassing, and they only succeeded in making it a little more inconvenient for gray market buyers to secure financing and insurance.

They didn't stop there. They instructed their dealers not to supply replacement parts for the same "bad" cars, hoping they could start rumors that the cars were impossible to service. This also had far less effect than they hoped. New car buyers often weren't concerned with parts availability as they were likely to dispose of the car before it became old enough that repairs became an issue. And persons seeking parts found that Mercedes' barrier to replacement parts was not very solid. While the dealers might refuse to service a car (and many of them bucked Mercedes' wishes and serviced them anyway) there were in most major cities and many minor ones, garages that were perfectly capable of servicing the gray-market cars and what they could not buy in the aftermarket, they could still obtain through subterfuge. The dealer parts departments might have had instructions not to supply parts for certain serial-numbered cars, but in most cases, the parts on the shelf for the American versions of those cars were identical. An independent garage owner could simply provide the parts department with the serial number of a U.S. car that he knew to be the counterpart of the car in his shop and the factory parts would be delivered same as always. Of course, there were cases where parts unique to European models were needed, but when this happened the parts were still available through independent suppliers who were happy to make the sales Mercedes had decided to forgo.

The early efforts of Mercedes, BMW and the other European car makers didn't really put a dent in the increasing flow of independent imports, but they kept up the pressure on Congress. Congress continued to be less than helpful, but the EPA had their own agenda and was considering making a few changes. They published a notice in the Federal Register in 1983 that proposed several options they were considering for future action. But this time they did not suggest they were considering lifting the direct import requirements altogether. By 1983 they had begun to realize there were more than a few cash-flush car nuts in the country who were looking for new opportunities, and were they to lift the regulations altogether, there was no limit to the possible number of direct imports they would be seeing. They did, however, again suggest they might consider shutting down the gray market altogether by allowing only the importation of cars that had been certified by the original manufacturer. By announcing hearings on the subject, they again invited all interested parties to come and say whatever they had to say.

The EPA was leaning toward continuing to allow the modification of cars but increasing the regulation of the modifiers. They wanted very much to stop the trend that was putting more and more paperwork on their desks; likewise they wanted to take measures to improve the quality of the work they were approving. There would be no more backyard conversions or one-offs by the family mechanic. Under the new rules, only modifications done by companies that held small-volume certificates would be approved by the EPA. Reasoning that obtaining a certificate from the EPA required a fair amount of engineering expertise and mechanical know-how, they rightly felt this step would go far to raise the bar for the quality of work that was being done.

With all this talk about new legislation, some of the more prominent conversion shops, realizing the nature of their business was going to make enemies among the rich and powerful in the auto industry, banded together to form the AICA (Automotive Importers Compliance Association). Initially headed by Benjamin Jackson and consisting of some 55 members, AICA was first and foremost a public relations group. The idea was that, by unity, they could present an image of professionalism that would be more credible, and by pooling their resources, they could retain lawyers and spokespersons to defend against automakers or consumer groups legislating them out of business. As a group, they acknowledged that there were some bad apples out there in the conversion shops and with the formation of AICA they asked the public to trust them to police the business without bringing in the feds. They talked a lot about standards and ethics but how much real effect they had was questionable. It was like the Chamber of Commerce or Better Business Bureau of the conversion industry. Membership in AICA gave an air of respectability to a business without really affecting their product. The AICA meant that there was a body to which an unhappy customer could complain, and if there were enough complaints, a business' membership would be revoked. But there were few consequences beyond being dropped from the club.

AICA was at its best when defending the conversion shops in the public forum. Up until then, when the EPA or DOT held hearings to talk about possible rules changes, individual shops that thought it was in their interest would send someone to Washington to speak up. Usually, this person was a shop owner, not a lawyer or a public speaker. AICA representatives spoke the language of government and knew all the buzzwords. They spoke of an industry that employed tens of thousands across the country that should be preserved in the name of the health of the economy. They became the go-to guys for the press whenever there were articles written about the gray market, always ready to provide a counterpoint for the stories of sleazy operators and shoddy workmanship. And they issued lengthy written statements and sent representatives to Congress whenever new bills were coming up that affected the direct importers.

12. The Factories Push Back

Their arguments in favor of the gray market importers were plausible: modifiers have to individually test every car that goes through their doors, while the manufacturers only have to test a few samples; manufacturers use compliance with U.S. standards as an excuse for higher prices and elimination of the direct imports would remove competition and allow them to drive their prices even higher; spot tests of the manufacturers' U.S. version cars had shown that many of them did not pass the federal test procedure. The list went on, and for every protest that the factories leveled at the converters, AICA spokespersons were ready with a quick counter.

So, it wasn't much harder for a gifted speaker to paint the car manufacturers as the bad guys than it was to abuse the independents. When the price difference between a gray market car and the authorized version could hover around 20 percent, it left a lot of people thinking the profits being brought in by the American dealers were excessive. The dealer's official story was that the markup was needed to support the service and distribution network that buyers of luxury European cars had come to expect. That espresso machine and leather furniture in the showroom weren't going to buy themselves after all.

Whether anybody really cared what the dealers did with their money was clearly a moot point. As long as a car buyer could save thousands of dollars by circumventing the authorized dealer network, that was what they were going to do. Some gray market dealers even rubbed salt in the wounds by setting up showrooms on the same street as the authorized dealers. It was no longer necessary to broker a deal over the phone and travel to a seedy warehouse at the port to pick up your new gray market import. Now a customer could walk into a sparkling new showroom, pick out a car from an inventory, and arrange and sign for financing just like they would at the authorized dealerships. They could even bring their cars back to be serviced in fully equipped workshops staffed with factory trained technicians who had jumped ship from Mercedes, BMW, or Porsche.

Mercedes and its siblings slowly came around to the truth that they were not going to solve the problem of the gray market by winning the hearts and minds of the buying public. Their only hope seemed to be in convincing Congress that it was in their best interest to stop or at least slow down the flow of independent imports. Although making that argument persuasively enough to spur action might be difficult, it was clear that something needed to be done. With the EPA and the DOT completely overwhelmed with applications for clearance, it could not be argued that things could continue as they were.

The year 1985 saw the peak of gray market imports—over 60,000. The number was large enough to get *everybody's* attention and 1985 became a very important year in the gray market. For the years up till then, the EPA and DOT had been publicly acknowledging that policing the gray market imports was a problem, and more and more examples were demonstrating just how out of control things were becoming. Al Mardikian's ongoing troubles with the California State Attorney General's office were becoming a serial comedy in the press. Abuses of the system were clearly rampant and many of the gray marketers were taking advantage of the government agencies' huge backlogs of work by submitting only token paperwork, knowing that it was likely that it would be rubber stamped in frustration when it finally crossed someone's desk.

But even while the government agencies were complaining about how the volume of gray market cars had long surpassed their ability to screen them and auto dealer associations were complaining loudly about the damage the direct importers were doing to their "legitimate" business, another news item leaked out that seemed to demonstrate how little sympathy the European car companies were likely to find among the high levels of the U.S. government.

In the spring of 1985, the staff of the Reagan White House was preparing for a presidential visit to Germany. The purpose of the visit was discussion of the imbalance of trade that was a result of the unusually strong dollar—the very imbalance that was causing the gray market to thrive. If the auto dealers were expecting any relief as a result of the visit, they were soon disappointed when it came out that then Deputy White House Chief of Staff Michael Deaver and nine other White House staff members who were in Germany to make advance preparations for the trip purchased BMWs for their personal use and had them shipped back to the States. They were not only able to take advantage of the lopsided exchange rate, but also of a BMW policy to give discounts to persons holding diplomatic passports. In this way they were able to buy the new cars for about half the retail price at the U.S. dealers.[1]

As scandals go, it was a small one. When asked about the deals the staff had gotten on their cars, the White House issued the statement that Deaver and his pals had done nothing illegal or immoral, which was quite true. But it was something of an embarrassment and the White House made it clear that it wasn't going to happen again.

So, with White House staffers and congressmen all enjoying gray market bargains while publicly arguing about putting a lid on it, anyone watching the Capitol for signs of what was to come was getting mixed signals. The only thing to do was business as usual. The dollar was at an all-time high against the mark, and thanks to all the media coverage, more Americans than ever were lining up to get their new European car from the direct importers. The conversion shops were enjoying more traffic than ever, and many were hiring more workers.

12. The Factories Push Back

Like a mining boom town, thousands of new businesses sprang up to take advantage of the surge in independent imports. The aftermarket was flooded with ready-made bumper and door reinforcement kits, complete with necessary paperwork. Practically anything could be found in the advertising sections in the back of all the major automotive journals. An individual who wanted to import a car but was daunted by the government paperwork could purchase a set of forms already filled out for the make, model and year of the car they wanted to import. All they had to do was make a portfolio of photographs and send the forms to the appropriate agencies. In other cases, an importer who wanted to clear the DOT without actually making any modifications to their car could, by contacting the right persons, obtain a packet that included photographs taken of a car that had been correctly modified. DOT even acknowledged that they knew that there were a number of "picture shops" out there. But they had neither the time, the money, nor the manpower to investigate any of them.

EPA compliance, though necessarily more complicated, had for the most popular makes and models become an applied science as well and shops would sell EPA conversion "kits" that were guaranteed to pass the test. For about $1,000 more, you could buy a "certified" bolt-on kit that had been designed and built by a gray market shop and approved by the EPA—and a car so equipped did not even have to be tested. The kit's installation had to be inspected and signed off by a representative of the company that held the certificate, but that was far less trouble than taking a car to a lab for testing. "Cert kits" were of course a good option for a converter who had a used car that might not have been in top mechanical condition. Such cars were unlikely to pass the lab tests without major repairs. Engines that were burning even a little oil for instance would produce far too much hydrocarbon to successfully complete the test procedure. With the installation of an EPA Certified kit, the car could get a clearance from the EPA regardless.

Of course, the test labs had also boomed to fill the accelerating need for tests and among the new businesses selling Lambda controllers, seat belt buzzer kits and various other bits of hardware and paperwork to the new independent dealers, there were the companies who offered training, companies who for a few hundred dollars said they could train high school graduates to be qualified test lab personnel. With the millions of dollars flowing into the gray market during 1985, there was not going to be the smallest economic niche that wouldn't be quickly filled.

While the gray marketers were partying, California's Air Resources Board, after the embarrassing incident with the 27 cars they had tested, started getting aggressive with gray market operators. Having closed Mardikian's lab, they moved ahead to start investigations of others. Meanwhile, they worked out legislation that would require licensing of conversion shops in California and limit such licenses to shops that had acquired a certificate with the CARB after putting an example of a car through their 25,000-mile endurance test. In other words, if they wanted to market conversions on Porsche 911s, they had to sacrifice a 911 equipped with their system for 25000 miles to the CARB before they would be permitted to sell conversions on 911s to the public. In addition, the new law required that the sellers of modified cars maintain warranty on the cars similar to the manufacturers' new car warranty. Modifiers were also required to maintain records on the ownership of each car so that the buyers could be notified in the case of recalls or manufacturer updates.

The new rules were expensive to follow and were intentionally rough on the smaller operators and backyard converters in the state. Many of them went immediately out of business, but that was the intent of the legislation. The lawmakers rightly figured that the shadiest operators, those who were in the business because of the outrageous margins afforded by pretending to convert a car and faking the paperwork, would be the first to drop out. Those remaining would have to pony up the funds to obtain certificates.

In January of 1985, Congress (specifically the House Committee on Commerce) had given in to some of the pressure and asked the Government Accounting Office (GAO) to do an investigation and submit a report on the state of the automotive gray market. In typical congressional fashion, the study took practically two years, and the report wasn't submitted until December of 1986. Meanwhile, the House and the Senate each had begun work on their own versions of bills designed to tighten up the screws. Their tool of choice was to work on the rules for the NHTSA and modify the provisions of the original Highway Safety Act to squeeze out the sections dealing with "provisional" imports. The first House version, HR 1004, was very broad reaching:

> To amend the National Traffic and Motor Vehicle Safety Act of 1966 to establish procedures under which *any person* may petition for an investigation (including testing and inspection) regarding any automobile manufacturer's certification of compliance with vehicle safety standards, and permit suspension of importation of vehicles pending the outcome of the investigation.

It didn't take long for the car makers and dealers themselves to realize that it had a large potential for backfiring. In fact, it gave a very good example of how difficult it can be to write legislation that achieves what is desired. While the law's intent was to enable the legitimate dealers and original manufacturers to blow the whistle on any gray market operator and shut down his business pending investigation, the phrase "any person" meant gray market dealers could do the same to the manufacturers. In a statement to the House Ways and Means Committee, the Department of Commerce pointed out that the law "would permit complaints that neither cite a specific safety hazard nor provide any data substantiating the complaint."[2] Under HR 1004, a gray market car dealer would find that he had just as much right to suggest that Mercedes was importing non-complying cars, and insist that their importation be stopped until an investigation was complete. Fortunately for everyone involved, HR 1004 didn't live very long. It was replaced shortly thereafter with other versions also to amend the Highway Safety Act but lacking the vague provision for the whistleblowers to make trouble.

In an effort to see the new bill make it through Congress, the National Automobile Dealers Association (NADA) and the American International Automobile Dealers Association (AIADA, not to be confused with their gray market opposite, the AICA) sent representatives to testify before the House in support of the new bill. It was spring of 1985 and it was shaping up to be a bumper year for the gray marketers. There was, as of yet, no sign of things letting up. Gray market imports had already surpassed the numbers of 1984 and the year was only half over. All the organizations on both sides of the issue agreed in their estimates that if the trend continued, they could expect to see 100,000 or more independent imports in 1986.

In page after page of testimony, charts, and diagrams, representatives for the authorized dealers argued for stamping out the gray market importers couching their discontent with the current system in concern for the safety of the motoring public. They condemned the gray marketers saying that 99 percent of the gray market cars did not fully comply with the laws of the country, and that the work performed by the converters not only failed to provide the required passenger protection, but frequently created additional hazards. They went on to quote a report from the department of the treasury that claimed that these modifications frequently converted the car into "an explosive time bomb."

To be fair to the converters, their cars were usually not the death traps that their detractors made them out to be. Modifications to meet the DOT standards usually had more to do with saving the insurance companies money by protecting the car's nose and tail from superficial damage in the event of a low-speed crash than they had to do with saving the occupants from certain death. Not that there weren't flagrant offenses. In some cases a crash victim might be in more danger in a poorly modified car than they would in one that hadn't been modified at all. The most serious offenses respecting safety that occurred in the course of DOT conversion usually involved the door beam installation. Properly installed tubular beams could in fact prevent intrusion into the passenger compartment during a low-speed impact. But if not correctly mounted they not only failed to do their job; they could become a potential hazard in the event of a high-speed impact. If the beams were properly attached with rated hardware, they posed little risk. But in many cases door beams were installed using sheet metal screws in place of substantial bolts. A tubular beam that was not secure could tear loose from the inside of the door and become itself a dangerous protrusion into the interior of the car. Photos were of course supplied of the installation, but personnel reviewing the packets, if they had time to look at the photos, might not have the know-how to identify a weak installation. Other shops preferred to only provide the *appearance* of modification to the doors which they then photographed for the DOT. One much-discussed example involved a car that, when closely examined, turned out to have painted black wooden broom handles installed inside its doors, rather than alloy-steel beams.

Ironically, the discussion of gray market time bombs cruising the highways was taking place in Congress over the laws regulating the importation of cars that did not meet the NHTSA safety regulations. But it was the modifications performed to satisfy the EPA that had the most potential for disaster and the EPA made up their own set of rules. Most of the hazardous installations involved poorly thought-out catalyst location, too close to fuel lines or other flammable materials. Sometimes the catalysts were placed too close to the floor of the car. Without shielding, the heat of the catalyst was sufficient to start the car's carpets smoldering. Other times there were errors in the placement of the fuel tank vent lines installed to comply with the EPA's evaporative emissions regulations. Installation of the evaporative emissions control system often meant running a fuel tank vent line from the tank in the rear to the engine compartment. The tank vent line, when properly installed, was usually made of the same materials and installed alongside the primary fuel line. But some converters would skimp in the materials and installation of the vent line, and while a car so fitted could still pass the lab test, poor vent lines could lead to problems. AIADA's statement to Congress included a by then well-known and often repeated anecdote of a young woman who burned to death in her Mercedes because that same tank vent line ruptured in a crash and spewed fuel onto the hot catalyst. One has to wonder how many congressmen, after hearing the testimony, rushed their gray market Benz or BMW to their mechanic to check its potential for bursting into flame.

The arguments of the manufacturers were cogent, but there were a few in Congress who remained suspicious of their efforts to stamp out what appeared by comparison to be a few small businesses. However, when those few small businesses combined to import 40,000 cars into the U.S. in 1984, and were showing far higher projections for 1985, the AIADA told Congress that they should be considered as one.

12. The Factories Push Back 153

The illogic of the present system is best demonstrated by assuming that a businessman went to the EPA and the NHTSA and asked for permission to enter 50,000 imported vehicles a year into U.S. commerce. The automobiles would not comply with safety and emission standards, but the businessman assured the agencies he would modify them after importation and submit evidence that such modifications had, indeed been carried out.

Unquestionably, the agencies would deny his request. Pointing out that federal law demands that such vehicles be thoroughly tested by the manufacturer for compliance before their importation, that the assembly lines be available for random checks, that the cars be subject to unscheduled testing before sale, and that the vehicles be available for re-call by the manufacturer in the event they were found not to be in compliance according to the certification.

Yet these same agencies are permitting the wholesale importation of non-complying vehicles in volume, simply on the grounds that they are being imported by a few score entrepreneurs rather than by a single corporation or individual. Such hair splitting does not make sense, either from a legal sense or as a matter of logic.[3]

Other representatives of the mainstream auto industry added their testimony. Mercedes' representative told about the factory purchasing a gray market Mercedes and inspecting the details of the conversion work.

First, they cited that the car was licensed and on the road within two weeks of importation and before any paperwork had even been submitted to the EPA and the DOT and prior to any evidence of approval of the car by the respective agencies.

When the paperwork was finally received by the DOT, it was determined that the photographs submitted did not match the work actually performed on the car.

And "of the 33 applicable safety standards involved, 15 required no modification to the vehicle in its non–US configuration for compliance purposes. One standard was satisfied by the addition of a label. Of the 17 standards which the vehicle does not satisfy in its non–U.S. configuration, no effort whatsoever was made to bring 10 into compliance. Finally, modifications performed for the remaining 7 did not achieve compliance."[4]

Of course, Mercedes and the others were in a bit of an awkward position. They certainly couldn't use language that made it appear that the cars were not safe if they didn't comply with U.S. regulations. What would that say about the cars that they sold in the other world markets? They focused, rather, on the idea that they were victims of unfair trade practices because the government had established two classes of retailers: one who was subject to a $10,000 fine for even tampering with the emission controls on a vehicle and one who could sell with impunity cars that did not comply with either the safety or emissions standards of the country.

The fact that Mercedes found they could buy a car in the gray market that didn't come with any substantiating paperwork was echoed in the GAO's report when it was finally issued. The hearings were proceeding through the summer of 1985, but the report, commissioned by Congress in January of '85, wouldn't come out until December of 1986. The findings of the report eventually confirmed many of the things that the factories and authorized dealers were saying were true. Investigators chose the Houston Customs Authority as an example, because of the high volume of cars coming through that port. Studying HCA's files, they found an agency that had pretty much lost control of the situation.

In August 1985, the U.S. Customs district office in Houston had a backlog of 1456 nonconforming vehicles, dating back 10 months, that had not been forwarded to the EPA or the DOT. They had a backlog of 3,896 bond release letters dating back to November and August 1984 that had not been processed. As a result, Customs initiated enforcement action on cars that had been released. There were 1938 cases where the time limit had elapsed, and Customs should have sent letters to the importers to return their cars for exportation.[5]

One importer had entered a vehicle at the Houston port on May 24, 1984. The NHTSA and EPA had notified the district director on December 19, 1984, and on January 15, 1985, that the car had been demonstrated in compliance and the bond could be released. However, on June 7, 1985, Customs sent the importer a notice saying the car had to be redelivered to customs for export, and that they had to pay a fine of $2,800. Then on August 20, 1985, they sent a letter telling the owner to disregard the last letter.

Stories of customs bungling went on and weren't confined to Houston. Like the EPA and the DOT, customs offices couldn't just hire on the additional personnel needed to make things run more smoothly, they just had to stack the papers up and get through them as they could. Different ports of entry dealt with the problems in their own way, and as with the labs, some ports earned whispered reputations as being "easier" than others and became more popular. Offices at some ports addressed the problem by raising the bond requirement. In some states, the agencies were allowed to require a bond as high as three times the declared value of the car. Those who could did so because it made them less popular as a port of entry for the gray marketers and therefore reduced their paperwork burden.

Customs offices were growing tired of playing the middleman in the gray market game and they said as much to the EPA and the DOT in a letter in January of 1984. The Deputy Commissioner of Customs suggested that instead of Customs trying to track down cars that the EPA or the DOT had a problem with, those agencies themselves should take on the responsibility of recovering any cars that they were concerned about. Naturally neither the EPA nor the DOT was interested in adding to their own administrative burden, so they came up with a number of their own excuses as to why they thought this was a bad idea. By 1985, though, Congress seemed not to be able to make up their mind whether the gray market was good or bad, and those involved in the administration of the rules were growing tired of the whole affair.

13

An Inaction of Congress

When 1985 began, Congress tried to look like they were going to do something about the booming gray market. With the market mushrooming and the press changing sides, for some members of Congress it seemed like a good time to appear concerned. January had seen the launch of the GAO investigation, and in February of 1985 they started to work on the new bills for the NHTSA. Each year they had to authorize funds for the agency, and it was during the writing of these authorizations that changes in the laws could be made. They announced hearings on the bills, and everybody wanted to have their say. Mercedes was there, as were representatives for NADA. Their buddies the American International Automobile Dealers Association (AIADA) were also represented. To add to the confusion, there were two Mr. Jacksons present on opposite sides of the issue.

Benjamin Jackson, head of AICA, came to Washington to continue to plead for self-regulation. He knew that things were not going their way anymore. The side that the press was taking lately wasn't helping matters so AICA was ready for a compromise.

Michael Jackson, then president of Euro Motorcars, an authorized dealer for a number of European brands, showed up to testify about the flood of gray market cars in the U.S. Like most gray market opponents, he took the safety angle, testifying that failure to comply with U.S. safety regulations constituted an unsafe condition. NADA, publishers of the used car value "blue book," sent a survey out to car dealerships and service departments regarding the gray market cars they had seen in their shop. They got about 400 responses back describing the condition of the cars. The survey consisted of a long checklist where the service departments checked whether certain pieces of equipment were indeed on the car when it was inspected. The results only confirmed what they had suspected in the first place, that most of the cars had either not been converted at all or had been deconverted to some extent. Some 33 percent of the cars inspected had no catalyst installed and 57 percent had no oxygen sensor. Various other categories told different stories, but the end tally indicated that of the roughly

400 cars inspected, 110 of them had no emissions equipment at all installed and 54 had no safety modifications. Overall, of the 400 cars surveyed, only four appeared to be in full compliance.

Jackson cited some specific examples seen in the service department of his own dealership including a car with rubber fuel vent lines mounted next to a catalyst, the very same condition cited as the cause of the now famous Mercedes fire that had killed a young woman, and another with the catalyst welded in so close to the floor that the carpet was smoldering, causing the customer to complain of fumes in the car.

Robert McElwaine, President of the American International Automobile Dealers Association, while winding up to present a number of other survey results which pretty much told the same story as the NADA survey, took a jab at Dianne Steed, NHTSA's administrator. He pointed out that during her confirmation hearings in 1983 when she had been nominated to direct the agency, she said of the gray market, "This activity is under active consideration and is being pursued vigorously." Yet, from the time of her confirmation, the number of gray market imports had quadrupled.[1] Now, two years later, during the 1985 hearing she again appeared before the committee and said that the agency was now "looking into the gray market problem to see if there was a potential problem there." The committee chairman quipped that by NHTSA's standards that *did* constitute vigorous pursuit.

Describing through his testimony what sort of car a buyer in the gray market might expect, McElwaine said gray market vehicles may have been wrecked or stolen, may have a questionable title and no warranty, or may have been manufactured two or three years earlier and been sold to a dealer as a new car. Cars with speedometers that had been converted from KPH to MPH invariably had their odometers set to zero when installed. Any one of these cars might later be seized by Customs and turned into a large, expensive coffee table.

Ben Jackson came on to defend the converters and of course took the angle that the government was attempting to stamp out a thriving segment of the economy because of a few bad misconceptions. He pointed out that AICA was composed of about 300 businesses that counted for about $1 billion in sales and suggested that the dealers' objection to the direct imports was all about lost sales, citing an example of a car that could be bought, bonded, shipped and converted for about $19,000 yet sold on a dealer's lot for a suggested retail of $32,000.

Ben Jackson offered a threefold explanation for the apparently large number of unmodified cars on the streets, mostly blaming the owners. Citing exemptions allowed to foreign nationals who were only going to be in the States for a year or less, he suggested that a number of foreigners were coming to the U.S. and selling their cars for a large profit, then returning home. There was no system of tracking in place that would prevent that from happening. He went on to explain that many car owners upon taking delivery of their cars proceeded to have the modifications undone, again no responsibility of the converter. Thirdly, he suggested that many cars were being operated illegally prior to their pending conversion so they were also showing up in the surveys done by Mercedes and NADA. Jackson's position was that the survey results were misleading because they didn't take any of these different categories of cars into account. While Jackson's explanation for the number of badly converted and non-converted cars found may have been implausible, he shot a few holes in the factories' claim that their primary motivation was an altruistic concern for public safety. Mercedes for instance took the position that it was the additional cost of building a U.S. compliant car that accounted for the large price difference between a U.S. and German market car. Jackson pointed out that the DOT had information indicating that the additional cost to the factory of building a U.S. version of a 500SEL was about $450. Additionally, Mercedes had begun marketing emission-controlled versions of the car in Europe in response to some states offering a tax incentive for buying a catalyst equipped car. The car they sold was practically identical to the U.S. version and if placed on the dyno was likely to pass the U.S. FTP with no trouble. Mercedes offered the emission-controlled cars in Germany for the equivalent of about $700 more than the standard model. So, citing a difference in cost of about $1,200 between a U.S. version and a European version, how could they account for the 20 to 30 percent difference between a car bought in Europe and a car purchased from an American dealer?

Everybody knew the regulation problem revolved around a lack of funds. During the hearings, an official with the NHTSA explained the burden that would result if they were required to do an inspection of the cars that came in through gray market channels. He explained that under ideal conditions, one inspector could be expected to process 4 cars in a day. At the then current rate of importation, he said that would require the addition of 40 full time positions at the DOT.

AICA took the position that if the cars were more carefully scrutinized, the DOT would find that most of the work was good and wouldn't require any additional action. They advocated adding the personnel and studying the packets more closely, saying that the gray market would pay for it. They proposed a schedule of user fees to be assessed on each conversion, a fee for a DOT conversion and a separate fee for an EPA conversion; the funds to be used to pay the regulatory agencies for their time and trouble. While the idea of adding another cost to the process of importing a car wasn't very attractive, the remaining shop owners considered it preferable

13. An Inaction of Congress

to enduring the passage of a law like the one in California and they were ready to compromise to stay in business.

Following the testimony of the big names came a small business owner, Lothar Shuettler. Mr. Shuettler had a small German repair shop in D.C. and had been performing conversions for about a year as a supplement to his repair work. The cars he worked on were imported by individuals, on a case-by-case basis. Shuettler made a compelling argument to the committee that he did good work, the forms were filled out correctly, and the cars that left his shop were in full compliance with the law. He invited the members of the committee to his shop to view the process for themselves. Shuettler's position was that the only explanation for the large number of non-compliant cars being on the streets was that the DOT and the EPA were not doing their job. Referring to the exhaustive paperwork that had to be turned in on each car, he opined that the DOT must not even be looking at the applications that came in and the EPA must not be making any effort to police the labs for so many cars to be approved without actually being in compliance. He asked if the government's incompetence in enforcing the law were really justification for wiping out the entire industry.

Shortly after the committee adjourned without any action came the embarrassing incident with the White House staff and their BMWs. The House and Senate both continued to hold hearings throughout the spring and summer of 1985, inviting the usual suspects, and hearing what mostly amounted to different versions of the same testimony. The 99th Congress was able to ride out the year without agreeing on any action, while the gray market had its best year ever. Importing record numbers of cars that year and making record profits, with Congress's inaction in 1985 the gray marketeers were given a free pass for another year without being troubled by new legislation.

The gray market import figures for 1985 peaked at a little over 60,000 cars and 1986 started out pretty strong. But even though the lawmakers had decided to postpone any new rulemaking, things started to slow down. Congress and their lawmaking however had less to do with the decline than did forces that were beyond anyone's real control. The market's rapid rise had been brought about by a combination of those forces and they were starting to swing back in the other direction.

While the imbalance between the dollar and the mark was the primary driver in the big boom, the original incentive that birthed the compliance shops was the reluctance of the factories to make U.S. versions of some of their most exciting cars. If their adventures taught the factories nothing else, it taught them that the American appetite for cars was vast, and that Americans would pay whatever it took to have the cars that they wanted. Their original estimations that building U.S. versions of certain cars would not be worth the required investment just weren't accurate. Mercedes learned from the SEC model that some of the features they had only offered only on European versions of their cars, such as airbags and antilock braking, were in high demand in the States. Ferrari learned that Americans would not be satisfied to buy only V8s when there were V12s to be had across the ocean. And Lamborghini learned that if they were going to build the most outrageous sports cars in the world, and produce enough of them to sustain the company, they were going to need the American market to sell them.

In 1984 Ferrari had replaced the BB 512i, the final version of the Boxer, with the Testarossa. The name was lifted from a legendary 1950s sports racer that had been dubbed "Testa Rossa," meaning red head, for the trademark red camshaft covers on the cylinder heads. The Testarossa was built for the American market from the beginning. The body had been built to U.S. DOT specifications, the nose and tail being strong enough to support impact absorbing bumpers. The bumpers themselves were gracefully integrated into the bodywork of the car. The engine had slightly reduced compression, making it a little easier for the factory-equipped Bosch K Jetronic fuel system to tame the exhaust. But the Testarossa was proof that a car built to the U.S. specifications could still be an exciting car.

The body of the car was genuinely something new, its most noticeable feature being the six horizontal slats on each side, beginning in the doors and extending beyond the cockpit to large air scoops just in front of the rear wheels. It looked like no other sports car being made at the time but seemed more graceful and less scary than the Countach. Orders for the car far outpaced the factory's ability to produce them, and soon the waiting list for delivery of a Testarossa was more than a year long.

Some buyers who already had their orders in found they could sell their place on the waiting list for tens of thousands of dollars and happily did so. Other buyers found demand was so high for the new Ferrari, they could sell their used ones for thousands more than the price of a new one—a whole new headache for the authorized dealers. Buyers travelling to Europe had as much difficulty getting their hands on a car as they did in America, but if they were successful, the federalization was a minimal problem since the Testarossa had been built as a world market car. Of course, the Testarossa was not a 512, and some U.S. buyers were still importing used Boxers from overseas, but the introduction of the Testarossa to America changed the landscape of the Ferrari market.

Lamborghini was still building the Countach, but in 1986 they finally had a factory-built U.S. version for sale. The U.S. Countach was fitted with the Bosch k Jetronic fuel system, with the manifolds developed by Rarewala for his converted cars. The trouble was they still couldn't build the U.S.

version of the car as fast as people wanted to buy them, so there was still a fair amount of traffic among the converters. In spring of 1985, Lamborghini introduced the Countach Quattrovalvole. Essentially the same car with a few body modifications and the same engine with four valve cylinder heads, it was also available in U.S. trim, which also came with the Bosch Continuous Injection System. The Quattrovalvole still looked very much like its older sibling, though it carried some extra aerodynamic clothing. But since it was aimed at American buyers, it came with much of the hardware in the nose and tail that the DOT required.

By 1986 the gray market was less about buyers wanting a specific car that was not offered for sale in the U.S. than it was about the price or availability of the car. Business was still strong among established shops, but it had leveled off and fewer new businesses were popping up. Competition for the remaining customers grew, a conversion shop could still make a profit, but it wasn't the outrageous profit that they'd known before. The smaller and less professional and efficient operations started to disappear when they saw their margins shrinking.

And their margins were shrinking drastically. The cosmic forces that had come together to bring about the lopsided exchange rate between the dollar and the mark were shifting—the dollar had begun to decline in the fall of 1985. While Mercedes and certain members of Congress were trying to figure out how to stamp out the gray market with legislation, the imbalance that had supported it was shifting back and the gray market was beginning to show signs of weakening all by itself. During 1986, business went on as usual, but with the fall of the dollar in Europe the prices that dealers and brokers were paying for cars was going up. The gap was steadily narrowing between the prices at the authorized dealership and the independent importers and orders were falling off. The earlier predictions of 100,000 cars per year coming in through gray market channels in 1986 were proving to be overly optimistic, or pessimistic depending on which side of the fence you were on.

Of course, 1985 had been a bad year for U.S. Customs. They had been the unwilling middleman throughout the whole gray market affair and the administrator had said as much to his counterparts at the EPA and the DOT. After being overwhelmed to the point of losing control in 1985, he finally threw in the towel and in February of 1986, Customs informed the agencies that they weren't going to play anymore. They said that they were modifying their policy to inform each importer that they had 180 days to bring a car into compliance; failing that, they had 30 days to return the car to the port of entry for export, leaving the responsibility up to the importer. If the importer had any requests for additional time or other mitigation, they were to take it up with the respective agency that had a problem with the car. Customs would assume that if they heard nothing from the EPA or DOT within a year, the car was OK with them and they would release the importer's bond and clear the car, placing the entire responsibility for timely processing of the paperwork on the EPA and the DOT. In other words, just when Congress and the factories were acting like they were going to tighten the screws on the gray market, the message from Customs was that they weren't planning on making things any harder for the importers.

For some, 1986 was business as usual. Some of the major shops had invested heavily in building their business. They had put up buildings and showrooms. Those who had invested in new showrooms and test labs had a lot of equipment to pay for. They weren't going to let what they saw as a temporary slump in orders run them out of business. Other operators, by accident or design, had avoided the big investments. When the first signs of weakening in the market were beginning to show, they folded up their tents and moved on to their next big enterprise. Many a car buyer who had issues with a gray market car they purchased only a month before, from what had seemed to be a thriving dealership, told tales of going back to talk to the dealer only to find an empty building.

To make matters worse, the press had completed their turn-about. During the boom of 1984 and '85 hundreds of new operators had entered the conversion business. Many of them had no inhibitions about quality and they pushed the cars through the shop as quickly as possible. Since then, the buyers of these cars had experienced a variety of troubles and when they couldn't get any satisfaction, they became very vocal. They wrote letters to people in the industry, and most effectively, they wrote letters to the automotive press. By 1986, it was hard to find any news item with anything good to say about gray market. Buyers were no longer ill-informed of the risks afoot when buying a car from a direct importer. Every major newspaper or news weekly had published some caveat about buying gray-market. Members of the automotive press were doing their own investigations, interviewing customers and even buying gray market cars so they could evaluate and write about them, and the news that came out usually wasn't very flattering. Although these writers were not coming out in favor of stamping out the gray market—they were after all car enthusiasts and saw the value in maintaining the alternate channels for importing certain cars—to the average buyer looking for a bargain, they gave stern warning. The warnings had their impact on the market. While some buyers might have been willing to take a chance to save twenty percent on a new car, saving five or, with luck, ten percent might not seem worth the risk.

In California, the changes in the laws actually had a positive effect for the more solid of the gray market dealers. Their new laws required the converter to obtain a certificate from the California Air Resources Board for each and every model of car that they wanted to convert. If a buyer wanted to bring in a Mercedes 190, for example, he had to locate a shop that held a certificate for a 190. Continuing in the conversion business meant the shop had to do a small-volume certification, complete with mileage accumulation and durability tests for every type of car that they wanted to process. Additionally, they were required to maintain a warranty on their work, and to have some kind of warranty insurance to cover customer issues if the shop went out of business. There were also record keeping requirements that would allow the shop to locate the cars that they processed in case of a future recall by the manufacturer. Running a gray market shop now required a very serious investment. While the new laws were indeed a big hassle for the conversion shops, they served to weed out the smaller operators. The new laws drove a large number of shops right out of business in a very short time, so those left standing after the change had to deal with less competition for the far smaller volume of cars that were coming over the border.

As far as the rest of the states were concerned, the laws stayed pretty much the same throughout 1986. Everybody knew there was a change coming, right down to the lowly technicians who spent their days welding in the telescoping door bars. But the conversion shops that were still standing as they watched Washington with trepidation had to be more concerned about staying in business here and now than about the changes in the future. Larger concerns were laying off people as the flow of cars from the ports slowed to a trickle and 1986 saw the number of gray market imports cut in half without any new legislation at all.

14

The Market Winds Down

While the experts had predicted over 100,000 cars a year coming in through the gray market, history only proved them half right. Over 150,000 gray market cars made it into the U.S., but that was the total of nearly ten years. The market had peaked in 1985 with a little over 60,000. In 1986 the number dropped by half and in the rest of the decade, gray market imports wound down about as quickly as they had grown in the earlier half of the eighties. The changes in the rules were partly responsible, but it was the realignment of the dollar to the mark that really brought the end. What the factories had been losing sleep over, the gray market edging their dealer networks out of business, never occurred. Not because of their campaigns to scare the public away from the gray market dealers, or because of their efforts to get Congress to stamp them out with new laws—the gray market died mainly of natural causes.

Even with the gray market in a death spiral, Congress continued to work on the problem. The GAO report that had been commissioned in 1985 finally came out in December of 1986 about the time the 99th Congress adjourned so there was no one around to look at it. The report spelled out its conclusions plainly on the title page "Auto Safety and Emissions: No Assurance that Imported Gray Market Vehicles Meet Federal Standards." The report described the trials of Customs, NHTSA, and EPA officials in trying to cope with the number of cars crossing the borders and asking for papers. The news had already broken through the various other sources, but the GAO report made it official.

Congress finally got together and made some big changes with the 1987 NHTSA re-authorization bill. The Imported Vehicle Safety Compliance Act of 1988 included various amendments to the 1966 Traffic Safety Act to tighten up the loopholes through which the larger number of gray market cars were coming. The amendments, like so many in the past, were built around the California laws that had changed in 1986.

The new law established the title of Independent Commercial Importer (ICI) for businesses that were considered qualified to do compliance modifications. It made it illegal for individuals or small businesses to bring in non-compliant cars unless they were registered with and approved by NHTSA and the EPA. Then, when the car was brought in, the ICI had to submit a proposal to the NHTSA describing how they intended to modify the car. The modifications had to be approved by the NHTSA before they were done. In addition, NHTSA would publish annually a list of specific models of cars that they felt could not be modified to satisfy the safety rules. Cars on their list could not be imported and modified, period. By placing a car on the list, they were saying that they believed the basic structure of the car was not strong or stiff enough to be modified to meet the crash standards, don't even ask.

By regulating the conversion business to registered ICIs, the officials were narrowing down the list of people they were supposed to keep an eye on. Before that law was made, anybody that could contact a broker and buy a car could be responsible for the conversion work. Even if the NHTSA had wanted to inspect the cars in situ, they would have had to send out inspectors to travel to thousands of locations. By making importers register, they deliberately placed a substantial burden on the players, hoping to reduce the number of converting establishments to a hundred or fewer so that they could better keep track of them.

The changes the EPA made to their rules were along the same lines. The one-time personal exemption went away as of June of 1988. Companies who wanted to work as ICIs had to get a small-volume certificate from the EPA. If the cars they imported were less than six years old, they had to be modified according to the certificate. Cars more than six years old could still be modified and tested as before, but they could only be modified by an ICI meaning the shop had to hold at least one certificate to be qualified to do the work. The expected result of the rules change would to be to drive the smaller players out of business. Completing a certificate with the EPA involved investment of more time and money than many of the smaller operators were interested in investing so businesses that were built around the convert-and-test clause were soon to find themselves shut out. The new rules were to be gradually phased in over the next five years to give the shop owners who could, time to do the development work that would be necessary to stay in the game.

Had the dollar remained as powerful as it had been in 1985, no doubt those who were making a fortune converting and selling cars would have taken the trouble to adapt to the new rules, but gray market imports just weren't worth the trouble anymore. There was no money in independently shipping cars across the ocean unless the work was subsidized by a lopsided exchange rate. The only cars that were worth that kind of trouble by 1990 were special cases, rare cars, collector cars. There wasn't enough money in wholesale gray market conversions to keep anyone in business anymore.

A few more determined operators, mostly on the west coast, stayed open doing research and compliance work for small manufacturers who wanted to sell in the U.S., much like the original purpose of Dan Morgan's American Specialty Company. The SMART car, now marketed by Mercedes, owes its American debut to one of the few remaining conversion shops, G&K Conversion of Santa Ana, California. Other shop owners who chose to keep the doors open kept their businesses together by shifting their focus to classic and antique imported cars.

For many of the owners of the 100,000 plus cars that had been brought into the U.S., there was still a legacy of paperwork and hassles. The more popular models that had been brought in by the major players: the Mercedes and BMW models that were shipped in volume and particularly cars converted by those who bothered with obtaining EPA certificates could be largely trouble free. They were not the "explosive time bombs" that the lobbyists had described but instead were perfectly functional cars with a few minor differences. Even so, the emission control systems installed at the conversion shop rarely stood the test of time.

Systems built around Bosch components, usually abbreviated versions of the factory installed systems, could function well for years. Others, built around aftermarket Lambda boxes made by the Johnson Company and all the knock-offs, usually didn't last long at all. As soon as any drivability problems started showing up, whether they had anything to do with the emission controls or not, disconnecting or bypassing the systems was usually the first response of a mechanic trying to deal with a mysterious symptom. From the standpoint of the operation of most cars, deleting the emission controls had little noticeable effect but could become an annual problem when it came time for state inspections.

The late 1980s saw many states pass new emissions inspection laws. It was all part of a new EPA policy of identifying areas with the worst air pollution and encouraging states to take their own measures to mitigate the problems. These new inspection laws ranged from a cursory glance over and under the car to check for the components on a list, to the IM 240 test which employed some equipment and procedures very similar to that which was used by the test labs, and all measures in between. Most states employed crude computerized systems that sampled the exhaust of a stationary car and tracked the car through a statewide network The people involved in writing the rules for the new emissions tests originally gave little or no thought to gray market cars, so their lists of serial numbers and emissions equipment programmed in most often were made from lists provided by the factories. Many owners of gray market cars found themselves facing blank stares as technicians attempted to input the serial number of their car into a computer that was not programmed to recognize it, or as a technician looked for emissions systems components that weren't even there. Some states offered waivers of different kinds for car owners who would have to spend large amounts of money to correct whatever was wrong that would keep the car from passing an actual tailpipe test, but most of the waivers did not apply in the case of catalysts or other emission controls that were not present or had been removed from the car.

Owners whose cars were brought in under the EPA exemption for cars five years old or older also found themselves in an awkward spot. Even if they could produce the paperwork from the EPA saying the car was exempt from the rules, they might find it hard to find anyone to look at it. Emissions inspections were in most cases a kind of loss-leader operation for a garage. The money that the shop was allowed to charge for the inspection was rarely enough to compensate for the time spent inspecting a car. They performed state inspections primarily to get the more profitable repair work that came with them. It wasn't on any technician's agenda to try to find someone at the Department of Motor Vehicles on the phone who could explain how to process an EPA exemption. In many cases, gray market cars got their ticket the same way they got into the country, with a wink and a nod from a technician who knew the customer and didn't mind checking a few boxes on a form saying he'd seen something that wasn't actually there.

In later years, after many complaints, the people who wrote the rules for the states found ways to accommodate the different exemptions and changed their computer programs to recognize the vehicle identification numbers of some gray market imports. And that helped lubricate the process for the people who were lucky enough to have cars that had been properly converted, but it wasn't any help for a car owner who tried to get a car inspected that was never actually modified. More often these cars stayed on the road only by one kind of subterfuge or another.

The best way to deal with the annual inspection problem was to make it someone else's problem: to sell the car. This was one of the big factors affecting a gray market car's value. During the time of the gray market boom, the early to mid-eighties, emissions inspection programs in the states were relatively slack, so the original purchasers and usually the second owners of the gray market cars didn't encounter much trouble with their state's annual inspections, it wasn't until later in the decade, and after most cars had moved a few notches down the used car chain that the implications started to sink in. Car owners who had been breezing through state inspections in past years were shocked to find that suddenly, this year, their car didn't have the required equipment to pass. "Why did they change the rules all of a sudden?" I was asked by one angry customer who had just learned his car didn't have what it took to pass inspection. I replied that it wasn't so much that the rules had changed, it was more like they'd brought in new referees.

Then there were the cars that had never actually been cleared at all but had just fallen off of the radar. These cars couldn't be legitimately titled, so their fate was to be endlessly resold, with the old promise of the paperwork coming in the mail. Usually there was an accompanying story that held some other explanation of why the price on the car was so low, a story good enough to keep the prospective buyer excited about what a rare deal they had stumbled across. Owners who were acquainted with the automobile business sometimes dealt with the title problem by buying a wrecked car and using its title, taking advantage of the fact that once a car is inside the country, officials rarely look at its VIN unless it's suspected to be stolen or otherwise involved in criminal activity. I encountered one case as late as 1991 of a 1986 Porsche 911 that a regular customer at my garage had bought. He brought the car to my shop a few days after buying it for an assessment of what service it needed. After checking the car out and noticing a few of the telltale signs, I called him at his office and asked him if he realized that he'd bought a gray market car. Like many people, he didn't know what I was talking about, so after I explained what it meant, he asked if it was a problem. I replied "That depends, did you get a title, or did you get a cock and bull story?" At that point he launched into a long explanation of what the disposition of the title was supposed to be and after about a minute, I interrupted him and told him that what he'd gotten was a cock and bull story, and it was likely that the car had never actually been titled and it would be a good idea to try and undo whatever deal he'd made. Fortunately for my customer, the man he bought the car from was a licensed dealer and was therefore responsive to threats of legal action if he didn't offer a full refund for the car. Had the customer bought the car from a private owner, it's likely that he would never have recovered his money.

Cars like the 911 in question continued to float around the automotive world like illegal aliens. They could find a home for a while, but usually had to engage some form of minor deception to get a license to stay on the road. For this reason, the more mundane gray market cars, the Mercedes and BMW sedans that didn't have good papers, usually became parts cars well before their time. It's no secret that a car can be worth more money when sold piece by piece to garages than its market value as a whole car, and that was particularly true of a car whose value had taken a beating because of its origins. Engines, transmissions, body parts and other expensive pieces were mostly interchangeable with some "legitimate" model. There were a few differences in some details, but rarely something an imaginative mechanic couldn't adapt to. In this way, thousands of gray market cars were absorbed by the U.S. car business one piece at a time.

14. The Market Winds Down

Cars that were properly federalized usually remained on the road for a normal life span. Some states were more friendly to them than others, more by accident than by design. States with sparse populations and little in the way of air pollution problems had far less demanding annual inspections so as the cars got passed from owner to owner, it was natural for them to gravitate towards less urban areas. In such a state or county, it was little more trouble to own a gray market Benz than it was the factory version, and a car enthusiast who knew the ropes could take proper advantage of the poor resale value and drive a gray market luxury car on the cheap. Inspections in the right place weren't much of a hassle and most import mechanics who'd been around during the eighties knew the tricks for obtaining parts for the more mainstream cars.

For the other cars, the story ended much differently. The gray market began around a special class of car: The 12-cylinder Ferraris and Lamborghinis that had become forbidden fruit because of the new regulations. Renault's R5 Turbo and Porsche's 930 were cars that enthusiasts wanted to buy for their own sake, not because of a bargain brought on by a temporary economic glitch. The reasons to own those cars were still there, long after the financial advantage was gone, so they fared better in the market than the German family-style cars. Cars like the Ferrari BB 512 that were only ever imported through gray market channels were still just as valuable and if they were well maintained they appreciated in value. A gray-market Countach was often considered more desirable than one of the rare U.S. versions because the nose and tail retained their original fine lines. U.S. version cars built by Lamborghini had awkward looking concessions to the bumper regulations on either end. Those gray market cars that *had* been altered at least sported removable hardware and could readily be returned to original condition.

DOT's new rules, the ones that took effect with the Imported Vehicle Safety Compliance Act of 1988, had tightened the screws down pretty tight for anyone still interested in importing non-complying cars for modification. First, they had to make the investment to become one of the registered importers on the list. Then they had to petition the NHTSA for permission to modify a car if it was not already on the list of cars approved. With this petition they had to pay a fee so the NHTSA would be funded to review the material and make a call. That fee started at $1,560 for cars that were similar to certified versions, and went up to $2,150 for cars that were not, so in this way DOT was now getting a piece of the action that was nearly as much as the cost of the DOT conversion during the boom years.

But with that act there came a merciful stroke of the pen for the true car enthusiasts: Cars more than 25 years old at the time of import would no longer have to be brought into compliance as of January 1, 1993. This

Porsche 930, a turbocharged version of the 911 available in the U.S. only through the gray market. The bodies were mostly identical but required door reinforcement in the U.S. Many were imported under the one-time EPA exemption. For those that weren't, the engine was not difficult to bring into line using Porsche 911 equipment (private collection).

of course didn't mean much in 1993 or the years immediately following, because the 1968–1973 cars were not required to have much in the way of safety equipment to begin with. The addition of seat belts and changing a few lights was all that was needed. But with the turn of the century, cars that would normally have required bumper installations and other major work were home free. The old Countach or 512 Ferraris could cross the border without raising any eyebrows. Those used exotic cars that had been well preserved and living in other parts of the world could be happily sold to American car collectors without issues.

The EPA was also playing along. Having finally figured out what a can of worms they had opened with the one-time exemption for five-year-old cars, they closed that door in 1988. By then, it had been 20 years since the first emission controls had been required on cars, so they wrote in a 20-year-old car exemption, beginning with 1968 models and moving up with each year. So as with the DOT, a collector could select his old European classic carefully and bring it right into the States with little trouble.

With the new changes in the law, the EPA and DOT were grudgingly letting bygones be bygones. By the early 2000s many of the cars that had caused such a stink during the early 1980s were now legal as the family station wagon. While the idea of buying a 25-year-old car has a limited appeal in general, certain enthusiast publications are printing lists of interesting cars that become legal each year for their readers to consider searching out and importing. There's not much to recommend buying a 25-year-old Mercedes or BMW sedan, but well-preserved Ferraris and Lamborghinis are bringing sometimes ten times their original price or more, depending on the model, and are big with the collectors who now don't have to cross paths with the government.

There is still a trickle of exotic cars crossing the borders via the few remaining converters. Occasionally there will be a surge in traffic of the more mundane cars between Canada and the USA as those countries' economic balance shifts. Since most of the standards of the two countries are now the same, as with many other countries, there is little in the way of modification to be done. Mostly it's just a paperwork headache. Occasionally you'll read a horror story in the automotive press of the buyer of a new Ferrari not yet certified for the states and his interminable battle with the Feds, but at this point that's the way the Feds want it. By making the process difficult and expensive, they keep the paperwork off of their desks. Persons considering importing a non–U.S. version car today should do their homework carefully, as much of the time it's just not worth the trouble. Nostalgic views of blockade running and pretending to be some kind of smuggler pirate aside, the days of sneaking one in under the nose of the man are long past.

15

Lessons of the Gray Market

It's easy to see when researching any government action how, over time, regulations tend to snowball. The Federal Register, the publication where the government records its daily business, has grown from a few thousand pages a year during the first half of the 20th century to thousands of pages a day in current versions. Washington is used to handing out rules, and presuming those rules are being followed. And each year they make exceptions and amendments to iron out whatever problems may pop up with *this* phrase or *that* wording. There may sometimes be a need to leave a loophole in the rules for certain exceptional cases. Surely nobody thought there would be any harm in letting a few unauthorized cars into the country provided the owner agreed to take certain measures. But what was supposed to be a few simple exceptions written into the rules for special cases was never expected to turn into an entire industry.

America is proud of its free-market economy. There is clearly no economic motivation as reliable as giving an individual the opportunity to make a profit. And when a new market opens up, it's no time at all before thousands of enterprising citizens are lining up to get a piece of the action. Americans also love cars. They love buying and selling them, driving them, modifying and customizing them, and just showing them off. One of the most popular home businesses in the country is the back-yard garage or the front lawn used car lot. Anything that has to do with cars in the U.S. quickly becomes big business, so it should come as no surprise that things happened just as they did.

What did come as a surprise was just how powerless the government is to enforce regulations once you turn up the volume. The laws respecting the sale of cars in the U.S. were supposed to be guidelines for manufacturers of automobiles to follow, not a vehicle inspection program. When the rules were written, along with the exceptions that caused all the trouble, no one considered that it might be necessary to allow for money and personnel to monitor the rules. It took practically ten years for the government to get a handle on a boom that no one had anticipated.

15. Lessons of the Gray Market

The most significant legacy of the automotive gray market is that the government's lack of power or will to enforce the rules was exposed. The three agencies charged with regulating the importation of cars—Customs, NHTSA, and EPA—each at one time or another demonstrated that in the face of increasing numbers, they were unable to perform at a satisfactory level. The gray market worked much the way a large campaign of civil disobedience might to expose weakness in the power structure, except for the case that the importers who were cheating at least made an effort to appear that they were following the rules. By 1985, when the numbers of applications were way out of hand, it became the case that all anyone in the government was really interested in was getting the piles of paperwork off their desks. They suspected that much of what was going on was fraudulent, but it appeared that as long as you pretended to follow the rules, the agencies would pretend to care. In the long term, that really didn't matter much with respect to cars. In a market where tens of millions of cars are sold each year, 150,000 cars over 10 years isn't really much of a dent. Some cars had dirtier exhaust than they should, some had fires and other issues, and many bargain hunting car buyers became victims of scam artists or just someone's incompetence, but none of that is of great significance years later. In the end, the automotive gray market was more of a dark comedy show that, taken in the right perspective, revealed something far more important.

What is important is that we realize from this how flawed our regulatory structures can be. We have the Federal Aviation Administration to regulate aircraft maintenance and keep planes from crashing. We have the Nuclear Regulatory Commission to inspect and regulate nuclear powerplants. And with industries producing hazardous wastes by the ton, we depend on the EPA to ensure that our air and water are safe and not needlessly polluted. Those perils associated with living in an industrial society are kept at bay by a network of regulatory agencies many of whom are responsible for things far more consequential than whether your car has the right kind of turn signals. We like to assume that each of those is doing its job diligently and efficiently, but the experience of the automotive gray market shows us that if the budget isn't there, the personnel cannot be hired. If the personnel are not available, then the regulations may as well not exist at all.

In any government regulated commerce, any field where careful attention to the details is important for the health and safety of people, it can become true that the amount of money to be made is proportional to what you can get away with. An aircraft maintenance company can process more planes by playing a little fast and loose with maintenance procedures. A construction company that's building a nuclear reactor can save time and money by cutting corners in construction or repairs. A hazardous waste processing facility can skip a few chemical tests that determine whether a batch of waste can just be spread out on the ground or has to be transported to an incinerator. Any of these things can be going on at any time without any apparent signs until there is a major failure.

Most of the time, the people involved in these activities are just like the workers in the gray market shops: Just wage earners, glad to have a job, and willing to bend the rules a little or look the other way if it means their day will go easier. When the man from the government comes by, everybody tightens up their act for a while; when he's gone, it goes back to business as usual. When something goes wrong—when an airplane crashes or a power plant fails because someone took a maintenance shortcut or when there is a chemical spill because the containers haven't been inspected in years—scandals will erupt and when the whole story comes out, often as not it's a story of regulations being ignored, and overworked inspectors who can't possibly pay more than token attention to any of the facilities under their charge.

In cases like this we have to depend on the integrity of the people on the ground in business for our very health and safety. The good news is that on an individual basis, most people want to act in others' best interest. But when wrapped tightly in the layers of large corporations, individual ethics can be easily smothered. Regulation is a poor substitute for integrity but when one fails, all we have is the other. When both fail, it can mean disaster.

So, the business of Congress is to write the rules. Sometimes the rules make sense, just as often they don't. The real world usually lives somewhere in between. Congress members themselves are just as likely to succumb to a party ideology and take measures that are less helpful to the public than they are for an individual politician's career. It has even become a tactic among lawmakers that, when they are defeated in principle by the passage of legislation that charges an agency to enforce rules they or their contributors don't like, they can later come in the back door and emasculate that agency by defunding it in the name of saving taxpayer money. The end result is that the industry that is supposed to be under strict regulation can point to the agency building and say, "There are the controls, you have nothing to worry about," but without the funding, without the staff in place, there is no regulation.

Fifty years after the state of the environment was declared a national emergency and the EPA was authorized under the pen of Richard Nixon, the United States has arguably the best air and water quality of the industrialized nations. This shift did not happen because of the benevolence and good will of the companies that had brought about the pollution. It happened because of carefully crafted laws based on scientific research, careful inspections and enforcement, and it happened because of the scientific innovation that these laws brought about. Americans have always had a love-hate relationship with their government and healthy discourse requires that it always be that way, but as our population grows, and we want and need more and more, it becomes more important that we have certain structures in place to keep us from killing each other with our own carelessness or poisoning ourselves with our own waste products and industrial by-products. What the experience of the gray market should teach us is how agencies like the EPA or the DOT, or just as importantly the NRC or the FAA, can easily be overwhelmed and become paper tigers when they are treated like political footballs, taken for granted and not properly funded.

How much regulation is enough will always be the subject of discourse. Most industry leaders like to say that if Congress will leave them alone and allow them to police themselves everything will be fine. Those people are well represented in the government. But also well represented are the people that insist that industry can't be trusted and should be carefully watched. It's their job to argue those points probably until the end of time. Hopefully some kind of compromise is periodically reached that will keep most of us working at our respective jobs without being poisoned by the air we breathe or by our tap water at home. But if we are to learn anything from the automotive gray market, it is that while it may be true that some rules are not worth the writing, if any regulation is to be taken seriously, follow-through is everything. If something requires inspection, there must be inspectors to do the inspecting. If there are forms to be filled out, there has to be someone on the other end whose job it is to read those forms. Because if no one is there to do the oversight, a free market will call your bluff every time.

Chapter Notes

Chapter 1

1. "Ecology: Menace in the Skies," *Time*, January 27, 1967.
2. Elinor Langor, "Pollution Politics: LBJ Retreats on Opposition to Measure Curbing Pollution from Automobile Exhaust," *Science*, April 1965, 611–613.
3. "Bargaining Over Auto Safety," *Business Week*, January 1967, 35.
4. "Auto Safety: Nader vs. General Motors," *Science*, April 1966, 47–50.

Chapter 2

1. Ron Wakefield, "Automotive Safety," *Road & Track*, Febrary 1972, 86.
2. James M. Flammang, *Standard Catalog of Imported Cars 1946–1990* (Lola, WI: Krause Publications, 1992), 529.

Chapter 3

1. "Lotus Super Seven," *Road & Track*, October 1970, 88.
2. Francis Armstrong, "Letter to the Editors," *Road & Track*, March 1961, 6.
3. John Lamm, "One Man's Battle: Doing It Yourself Can Be an Exercise in Frustration," Road and Track, 1974, 78.
4. Fred Gregory, "Buying Exotics," *Motor Trend*, July 1978, 89–90.
5. Interview with Steve Barney, December 14, 2012.
6. Tom Cotter, *The Vincent in the Barn: Great Stories of Motorcycle Archeology* (Minneapolis: MBI Publishing, 2009), 38–39.
7. "Ferrari Berlinetta Boxer," *Road & Track*, March 1978, 38.
8. Trefor Thomas emails: https://www.flickr.com/photos/37210452@N06/7004882089/in/album7215762927474738/, accessed March 23, 2016.
9. Thomas Bryant, "Freedom of Choice," *Road & Track*, March 1976, 74–77.
10. Thomas Bryant, "Ampersand," *Road & Track*, January 1977, 101–103.

Chapter 4

1. Code of Federal Regulations, 1981, Title 40, Section 86.077-8; 078-8;079-w8;080-8;081-8.

Chapter 5

1. Karl Ludvigsen, "The Incredible Thinking Engines," *Road & Track*, February 1977, 77–80.
2. Patrick Bedard, "Revenge of the Nerds," *Car and Driver*, May 1985, 81–91.

Chapter 6

1. Federal Register, vol. 45, no. 141, 48812, July 21, 1980.
2. *Ibid.*
3. *Ibid.*, 44813.
4. *Ibid.*
5. Patrick Bedard, "Someone Doesn't Want You to Have the Car of Your Dreams and It Isn't The U.S. Government," *Car and Driver*, September 1981, 80.
6. Bedard, "Someone," 80.
7. Bedard, "Someone," 82–83.
8. Bob Hover, and Allen Cowan, "One Man's Skirmish: The Mercedes That Wasn't a Bargain," *European Stars and Stripes*, February 9, 1984, III.

Chapter 7

1. Telephone conversation with DOT official, April 27, 2011. The official preferred to remain anonymous.

Chapter 8

1. Mike Knepper, "Does the Gray Market Measure Up?" *Motor Trend*, June 1986.
2. Telephone conversation with a former conversion technician, September 3, 2011. The technician asked to remain anonymous.
3. Conversation with Peter Krause, February 8, 2011.
4. Conversation with former technician, September 3, 2011.

Chapter 10

1. William Marbach, and Jeff Copeland, "How to Tame a Wild Ferrari," *Newsweek*, January 11, 1982, 54.
2. Jean Wright, "He Stocks Cars for a Fast Lane Lifestyle," *Orange County Register*, April 5, 1983, B1, B5.
3. Jeff Baily, "Newport Auto Dealer Turns to Chapter 11 in Legal Fight," *Orange County Register*, November 17, 1982, E11, E16.
4. Jean Wright, "2 Million Dollar Caper: Victims Tell Judge About Stolen Valuables," Orange County Register, January 20, 1983, 172.
5. Wright, "Fast Lane Lifestyle," B1.
6. Federal Register, vol. 50, August 29, 1985, 35123.

Chapter 11

1. "Road & Track Road Test: Lamborghini Countach S," *Road & Track*, December 1978, 38–41
2. Ro McGonegal, "A Rack of Lamborghini," *Motor Trend*, May 1980, 34–38.
3. Trefor Thomas emails: https://www.flickr.com/photos/37210452@N06/7004882089/in/album72157629274747368/, accessed 3/23/2016/.

Chapter 12

1. William Safire, "It Seems Unseemly," *New York Times*, March 18, 1985, A19.
2. Douglas Riggs, General Council, Letter to House Ways and Means Committee, June 24, 1984.
3. Senate Hearing 99–21, before the Committee on Commerce, Science, and Transportation, April 30, 1985, 230, 231.
4. Senate Hearing 99–21, 161.
5. GAO Report, Auto Safety and Emissions: No Assurance that Imported Gray Market Vehicles Meet Federal Standards," 9(1986) (GAO/RCED-87-29) 28, 29, December 1986.

Chapter 13

1. Senate Hearing 99–21, before Senate Committee on Commerce, Science, and Transportation, April 30, 1985, 88.

Bibliography

Books

Cotter, Tom. *The Vincent in the Barn: Great Stories of Motorcycle Archeology*. Minneapolis MN: MBI. 2009.

Dron, Peter. *Lamborghini Countach: The Complete Story*. Ramsbury, Marlborough, Wiltshire, UK: Crowood. 1990.

Duguay, Jean. *How to Import a European Car: The Gray Market Guide*. Chalotte, VT: Williamson Publishing. 1985.

Flammang, James M. *Standard Catalog of Imported Cars 1946–1990*. Lola, WI: Krause. 1992.

Marchet, Jean Francois, and Peter Coltrin, *Lamborghini Countach*. London: Osprey. 1981.

Newspapers

Baily, Jeff. "Newport Auto Dealer Turns to Chapter 11 in Legal Fight." *Orange County Register*, November 17, 1983, E11, E16.

Barnhart, Bill, and Sally Saville Hodge, "Such a Deal: A Mercedes for the Budget Conscious." *Chicago Tribune*, March 29, 1985, B1–B2.

Brown, Warren. "Euro Motorcar's Jackson Breaks for Mercedes Benz of North America; Man Behind 'Gray Market Bill' Moves Up," *The Washington Post*, March 26, 1990.

"County Firm Refines Fine Cars." *Orange County Register*, November 3, 1981, 6.

Dawson, Adam. "Company Accused of Faking Pollution Tests on Autos." *Orange County Register*, May 1, 1987, D6

Dawson, Adam. "Fraud Is Charged in Auto Tests," *Orange County Register*, May 23, 1985, C6.

Dawson, Adam. "OC Man, Nephew Guilty in Case Involving Fake Auto Emissions Tests." *Orange County Register*, August 10, 1985, B9.

Holusha, John. "Unauthorized Sales Up for Cars from Europe." *New York Times*, March 4, 1985, D1, D4.

Hoyer, Bob. "Carmakers Blame Economy for Gray Market Slump." *European Stars and Stripes*, April 1, 1986, 9.

Hoyer, Bob. "The Gray Market, Dollar Rise Gives Car Fad a New Impetus." *European Stars and Stripes*, February 28, 1985, 8–9.

Hoyer, Bob. "Gray Market for Foreign Cars Losing Steam as Dollar Drops." *European Stars and Stripes*, February 19, 1986, 2.

Hoyer, Bob. "Legal or Illegal There's a Boom in Importing and Converting Cars." *European Stars and Stripes*, February 8, 1984, II–IV.

Hoyer, Bob, and Allen Cowan, "One Man's Skirmish: The Mercedes That Wasn't a Bargain." *European Stars and Stripes*, February 9, 1984, III.

Mateja, James. "It's a Rough Road in the Gray Market." *Chicago Tribune*, November 24, 1985, D2, D10.

"Mushrooming Demand Spurs Imports Firm to Expand." *Santa Ana Orange County Register*, January 21, 1982,118.
"OC Man Sentenced in Auto-Test Scheme." *Orange County Register*, November 11, 1985, 21.
Safire, William. "It Seems Unseemly." *New York Times*, March 18, 1985, A-19.
Stuart, Reginald. "Auto Group Fights Anti-Theft Plan." *New York Times*, August 22, 1985, D4.
Tabios, Eileen R. "Finally, an American Countach, at $95,000." *New York Times*, July 4, 1982, F17.
Wright, Jeanne. "He Stocks Cars for a Fast Lane Lifestyle." *Orange County Register*, April 5, 1983, B1, B5.
Wright, Jeanne. "Newport Exotic Car Dealer Target of FBI Bankruptcy Fraud Inquiry." *Orange County Register*, August 11, 1983, B3.
Wright, Jeanne. "2 Million Dollar Caper: Victims Tell Judge About Stolen Valuables." *Orange County Register*, January 20, 1983, B1, B5.

Automotive Journal Articles

"Ameritech 308 Turbo." *Car and Driver*, August 1981, 16.
"AMG Mercedes Benz 500 SEL, the Running Mother of All Rocketships." *Car and Driver*, April 1983, 95, 96.
Armstrong, Francis. "Letters to the Editor." *Road & Track*, March 1971, 6.
"Auto Safety: Nader Vs General Motors." *Science*, April 1, 1966, 47–50.
"Bargaining Over Auto Safety." *Business Week*, January 7, 1965, 35.
Bedard, Patrick. "Revenge of the Nerds." *Car and Driver*, May 1981, 81–91.
Bedard, Patrick. "Road Test, Ferrari 400I." *Car and Driver*, December 1982, 47–50.
Bedard, Patrick. "Someone Doesn't Want You to Have the Car of Your Dreams, and It Isn't the US Government!" *Car and Driver*, September 1985, 81–91.
"BMW 745i, the Ultimate Autobahn Cruiser?" *Road & Track*, March 1982, 142–144.
Bohr, Peter. "Buying a Car in Europe, How to Do It and Why." *Road & Track*, March 1984 166–173.
Bryant, Thomas. "Ampersand." *Road & Track*, January 1977, 101–103.
Bryant, Thomas. "Freedom of Choice." *Road & Track*, March 1976, 74–77.
Bryant, Thomas. "New Italian Exotics: Lamborghini's Revised Countach and the Future Ferrari Cavallino." *Road & Track*, May 1985, 162–163.
Bryant, Thomas. "Qualifying Exotics, How to Satisfy Uncle Sam." *Road & Track*, December 1978, 43, 46.
Buckley, James. "Why the US Doesn't Need Mandatory Seatbelt Interlock Laws." *Motor Trend*, January 1975, 62.
Ceppos, Rich. "Lamborghini Countach 5000 Quattrovalvole, Welcome the Big Red Vacuum Cleaner." *Car and Driver*, April 1986, 38–42.
Classified advertisement. *Road & Track*, November 1984, 199.
Classified advertisement. *Road & Track*, September 1985, 173.
"Clean Air Bill Dies, Industry in Limbo." *Science News*, October 9, 1976, 231.
Cockburn, Alexander. "On the Capitalist Road, Will the President Keep His Promise to Make the World Safe for Gas Guzzlers?" *Car and Driver*, December 1982, 104, 105.
"Countach vs Ferrari 512." *Road & Track*, February 1982, 32–39.
Ethridge, John. "Phase II Catalyst System, Better Driveability, Fuel Economy, and Lower Emissions." *Motor Trend*, November 1978, 81.
"Ferrari GTO, Those Legendary Letters Ride Again." *Car and Driver*, September 1984, 39–43
Frere, Paul. "Porsche 917 K, the Fastest Car Ever Registered for the Road." *Road & Track*, September 1975, 56, 57.
Gregory, Fred. "Buying Exotics." *Motor Trend*, July 1978, 89–90.
Gregory, Fred. "A Chip for the Old Block, Computer Technology Will Make Cars Better, Safer and More Efficient." *Motor Trend*, October 1978, 110–115.
Hill, Phill. "Ferrari GTO." *Road & Track*, August 1984, 38–45.
Hilton, John. "Buying a Car in Europe: Because Getting Around Is Half the Fun." *Car and Driver*, December 1985, 91–9.

Hogg, Tony. "Now You Can Buy a Morgan in the US." *Road & Track*, January 1977, 100, 101.
Kimball, Steve. "Adiabatic Engines." *Road & Track*, December 1985, 132–144.
Knepper, Mike. "Does the Gray Market Measure Up?" *Motor Trend*, June 1986.
"Lamborghini Countach 5000S Quattrovalvole, Still Crazy After All These Years." *Road & Track*, March 1986, 50–52.
"Lamborghini Jalpa, the Bull Charges Back with Excitement to Spare." *Road & Track*, November 1982, 32–38
Lamm, John. "One Man's Battle: Doing It Yourself Can Be an Exercise in Frustration." *Road & Track*, March 1974, 78.
Langor, Elinor. "Pollution Politics, LBJ Retreats on Opposition to Measure Curbing Pollution from Automobile Exhaust." *Science*, April 30, 1965, 611–613.
"Lotus Super Seven." *Road & Track*, October 1970, 88.
Ludvigsen, Karl. "The Incredible Thinking Engines." *Road & Track*, February 1977, 77–80.
Marbech, William, and Copeland, Jeff. "How to Tame a Wild Ferrari." *Newsweek*, January 11, 1982, 54.
McGonegal, Ro. "Lamborghini, a One-of-a-kind Street Legal Countach S." *Motor Trend*, May 1980, 34–38.
McGonegal, Ro. "A Rack of Lamborghini." *Motor Trend*, May 1980, 34–38
McGonegal, Ro. "Save the Whales." *Motor Trend*, January 1980, 60–63.
McKibben, Jon. "Special Import Cars, Gray Market, or White Knight?" *Road & Track*, March 1983, 46, 47.
"Mercedes 500 SEC." *Road & Track*, January 1984, 118–120.
"Mercedes 500 SEL, the Controversial Flagship of the Fleet." *Road & Track*, May 1985, 47–49.
"Miscellaneous Ramblings." *Road & Track*, July 1981, 34.
Orme, Ted. "Washington Report." *Motor Trend*, January 1978, 9, 10.
Orme, Ted. "Washington Report." *Motor Trend*, February 1978, 4, 5.
Orme, Ted, editor. "A Conversation with Joan Claybrook." *Motor Trend*, August 1978, 102–107.
Orme, Ted, editor. "Washington Report: EPA Ends One Time Exemption." *Motor Trend*, January 1988, 24.
"Renault 5 Turbo 2, Son of Renault Turbo, Overdosed with Steroids." *Road & Track*, February 1984, 141, 142.
Richards, Richard. "Removing Smog Gear: The Legal Aspect." *Motor Trend*, April 1975, 104, 105.
"Road & Track Road Test: Lamborghini Countach S." *Road & Track*, December 1978, 38–41.
Sherman, Don. "Ann Arbor Hosts a Boxer." *Car and Driver*, June 1981, 99–103.
Sherman, Don "Lamborghini Countach 5000 S, Life in the Whips and Chains Lane." *Car and Driver*, December 1983, 36–39.
Smith, Kevin. "Ferrari GTO: This Is Italian for Grand Touring Omnipotent." *Motor Trend*, August 1984, 84–89.
Wakefield, Ron. "Automotive Safety." *Road & Track*, February 1972, 86.
Wakefield, Ron. "The Regulated Automobile Part 1: Noise and Emissions." *Road & Track*, April 1980, 169–177.
Wakefield, Ron. "The Regulated Automobile Part 2: Safety and Fuel Economy Regulations." *Road & Track*, June 1980, 72–81.
"Will Lamborghini Make It?" *Road & Track*, June 1980.
Witzenburg, Gary. "Reeling in the Red Tape." *Car and Driver*, September 1981, 30.

Government Documents

36 Federal Register, December 3, 1971, 23092.
37 Federal Register, February 1, 1972, 2432–2433.
37 Federal Register, November 15, 1972, 24314–24315.
38 Federal Register, February 27, 1973, 5281.
38 Federal Register, August 21, 1973, 22509.
39 Federal Register, March 21, 1974, 10602–10603.

39 Federal Register, March 25, 1974, 11134.
39 Federal Register, March 27, 1974, 11334–11339.
39 Federal Register, December 23, 1974, 44246–44254.
39 Federal Register, December 31, 1974, 45360–45380.
45 Federal Register, July 21, 1980, 48812–48813.
50 Federal Register, September 9, 1985, 36838–36856.
Code of Federal Regulations, 1969 CFR Title 49 Part 355, 186–188.
Code of Federal Regulations 1972 CFR 40 part 85, 221–278.
Code of Federal Regulations 1981 Title 40 section 86.077-8; 078-8; 079-8; 080-8; 081-8.
Code of Federal Regulations, 1984 CFR Title 40 Part 85, 202–264.
Douglas Riggs, General Council: Letter to House Ways and Means Committee, June 24, 1984.
GAO Report Auto Safety and Emissions: No Assurance that Imported Gray Market Vehicles Meet federal standards, 9 (1986) (GAO/RCED-87-29) 28, 29, December 1986.
"Hearing Before the Committee on Commerce, Science and Transportation, United States Senate," February 21, 1985, April 30, 1985, S Hearing. 99–21.
"Imported Vehicle Safety Compliance Act of 1987" US House of Representatives, November 10, 1987, Report 100–431.
"Motor Vehicle Safety Authorization Act of 1987," US House of Representatives, September 26, 1987, Report 99–833.
"Remarks by Matthew Ronaldo, US House of Representatives, on automobile Gray Market Act of 1985," *Congressional Record*, February 6, 1985, 2014–2015.
"Remarks by Thomas Bliley, Jr. US House of Representatives on Gray Market Cars," *Congressional Record* June 12, 1985, 15539–15541.
"Report on "National Highway Traffic Safety Administration Authorization Act of 1985," May 14, 1985 (Legislative Day April 15, 1985), Report 99–48.

Interviews

Conversation with Al Bloodworth, March 5, 2011.
Conversation with Peter Krause, February 8, 2011.
Telephone conversation with a former conversion technician, September 3, 2011, under request of anonymity.
Telephone conversation with a former DOT official, April 27, 2011, under request of anonymity.

Internet Resources

Thomas, Trefor. Emails accompanying classified ad for "The Countach That Saved Lamborghini" https://www.flickr.com/photos/37210452@N06/6858764988/in/set-72157629274747368/, accessed March 28, 2016.

Index

ABS (Antilock Brakes) 94
AIADA (American International Automobile Dealers Association) 81, 151, 152, 156
AICA 146, 147, 151, 156–158
air bags (SRS) 94, 101, 160
air flow meter 75
Air Pollution Control Act of 1955 9
air pump 19, 20, 33, 39, 55–59, 70, 99, 101, 106, 107
Alfa Romeo 81
AMC (American Motor Corporation) 17, 109
American Specialty Corporation 43, 136, 166
Amerispec 41, 42, 78, 82, 83
anthropomorphic dummies 13, 48
Armstrong, Francis 31, 177
Austin Healey 18
Automotive Compliance Center 43, 83
Avanti 18

Barney, Steve 38, 39, 41, 42, 177
Bloodworth, Al 105, 106, 182
BMW 70, 71, 73, 74, 76, 81, 84, 85, 90–95, 101, 105, 106, 111, 136, 145, 147, 148, 152, 166, 168, 171
BMW 325 71, 95, 105
BMW 745i 74, 180
bond 34–36, 64, 79, 86, 96, 154, 157, 162
Bosch 22, 58, 67–76, 107.109, 135–137, 160–162
British Leyland Motor Corporation BLMC 18–21
British Motor Corporation BMC 18
British Motor Holdings 18
Buick 17

CAFE rating 74, 93, 105
Caiti, Alfred 38, 39, 43
camshaft 7, 19, 21, 34, 58, 61, 100, 137, 160
Car and Driver 33, 41, 75, 177, 180
Carter, Jimmy 5, 89
carbon monoxide 10, 53, 55, 116
catalyst 19, 59–63, 67–76, 92, 99, 101, 103, 105–108, 110–112, 123, 135, 139, 142, 152, 156–158, 167, 180
catalytic converter 33, 59, 60, 62, 63, 99, 128, 144

cert kit 106, 108
certificate 61, 62, 64, 65, 79, 80, 82, 105–108, 141, 146, 149, 150, 163, 165
chassis dynamometer 53, 113, 114, 120
Chevrolet Cavalier 49
Chinetti, Luigi 41
Chrysler 17, 142
Citroën 22–24, 35
Clean Air Act 10, 11, 29, 53, 54, 66, 82, 83
closed loop 66, 69, 70, 106
Code of Federal Regulations 113, 177, 182
compliance shop 1, 5, 28, 35, 66, 82, 159
compression 19, 57, 58, 60, 61, 100, 160
constant volume sampling (CVS) 53
control pressure 69
convert and test 63, 64, 107, 165
Corvette 61
Countach 1, 7, 8, 25, 27, 29, 40, 43, 44, 56, 62, 133–142
Cruise, Tom 42
Customs 28–31, 34–38, 42, 61, 64, 78–80, 84, 86, 87, 96, 154, 157, 161, 162, 164, 173

DC Johnson 72
Department of Transportation 13, 15, 31
dial in 91, 111, 114, 117, 119
dilution tunnel 114, 115, 117
Dr. Laverne 121, 122
DOT 13, 15, 16, 17, 23, 24, 29, 34, 36–40, 42, 13, 45–51, 61, 62, 64, 66
durability factor 64, 105
dyno 63, 75–77, 109, 112, 114–118, 120–124, 158
dyno driving 122

E Type 21, 22
emission control 12, 13, 19, 21, 39, 42, 51, 54, 61, 62, 64, 72, 77, 98, 100, 105, 112, 125, 166
emission standards 18, 20, 27, 53, 54, 70, 71, 79, 109
emission testing 77, 98, 112–114
endurance test 62, 150
Environmental Protection Agency (EPA) 10, 12, 29, 32–40, 42–43, 45, 46, 51, 53, 54, 59–64, 76, 78–88, 90–92, 94, 96–98, 105–115, 117–120, 122, 124–126, 129, 131, 133,

183

184 Index

135, 138, 141–143, 145–147, 149–162, 164–170, 173–175, 181
Euro Motorcars 156
evaporative emission control EVAP 12, 54, 55
evaporative system 106, 116
exhaust gas recirculation (EGR) 19, 58, 70, 99, 101
exothermic reaction 59

Federal Aviation Administration (FAA) 173
federal test procedure (FTP) 33, 63, 74, 77, 87, 91, 113, 115, 137, 147
feedback 66–77
Ferrari 26, 29, 38–42, 44, 46, 48, 62, 70, 71, 80–83, 96, 99, 104, 128, 130, 133, 136, 143, 160, 171, 177, 178, 180, 181
Ferrari Compliance Inc. 128
FIAT 26
Fink, Bill 44, 45
firing off 63
500 SEC 94
512BB 40, 41, 42, 44, 133, 160, 169, 170
Ford 14, 17, 32, 39, 43, 67, 86, 89, 113
Ford, Gerald 89
frequency valve 69, 70–72, 107
Fritz, Richard 40–42, 82, 83, 99, 133
fuel distributor 71, 136
fuel injection 22, 58, 67–71, 107, 135, 136, 138, 139, 142

G&K Conversion 166
gas guzzler tax 93
GM (General Motors) 15, 17
Gordon, John 85
Government Accounting Office (GAO) 150, 154, 156, 164, 178, 182
grams per mile (GPM) 11, 53, 57, 116, 117

hot shed 116, 135
House Ways and Means Committee 150, 178
HR1004 150, 151
Hutchinson, Phillip 80
hydrocarbon (HC) 10, 12, 35, 53–56, 59, 61, 67, 108, 115, 116, 117, 124, 135, 149
hydrogen sulfide 60

IM 240 166
Independent Commercial Importer (ICI) 164, 165
Isis Imports 44, 45
Iso Rivolta 43

Jackson, Benjamin 146, 156–158
Jackson, Michael 156, 179
Jaguar 18, 21, 22, 81
Johnson, Jeff 31
"Johnson" Box 72–75, 112; *see also* lambda box

K Jetronic (K jet) 68, 70, 73, 107, 160

lambda 69–74, 77, 107, 111, 149, 166
lambda box 72, 107, 166
lambda sensor 70; *see also* oxygen sensor
Lamborghini 1, 7, 8, 26, 27, 29, 39, 40, 43, 44, 46, 49, 62, 80, 133, 134–143, 160, 161, 169, 178–182
Le Car (R5) 24–26, 169
lead 60, 61; *see also* tetra ethyl lead
lead free (unleaded) fuel 60, 115
Long, William 81
Los Angeles 9, 45
Lotus 29, 31, 177, 181

Mardikian, Albert 42, 44–46, 82, 83, 129–133, 148, 149
Maserati 1, 2, 26, 33, 44, 81
Maserati Ghibli 33
McElwain, Robert 157
Mercedes 5, 17, 44–46, 58, 68, 70, 71, 74, 81, 85, 86, 90–94, 101, 105–108, 126, 136, 143–145, 147, 151–153, 156–158, 160, 161, 163, 166, 168, 171, 177, 179–181
MG 18–32
MG Midget 19
MGB 19
Mimram, Patrick 136
modify and test 32, 62, 64, 78–80, 99, 110
Morgan (automobiles) 32, 33, 37, 39, 44, 45, 181
Morgan, Dan 43, 136, 166
Motor Trend 103, 177, 178, 180, 181
Motor Vehicle Pollution Control Act of 1965 11
Motronic 73, 74

Nader, Ralph 13–15, 177, 180
National Automobile Dealers Association (NADA) 151, 156–158
National Highway Traffic Safety Administration (NHTSA) 18, 182
National Traffic and Motor Vehicle Safety Act of 1966 31, 150
New York Times 43, 141, 178–180
nitrogen oxide (NOx) 10, 11, 53–55, 57, 58, 63, 66, 67, 71, 101, 105, 115–117
Nixon, Richard 11, 89, 174
Nuclear Regulatory Commission 173

Offenhauser 45
Olson Laboratories 33
one time exemption 81, 83, 84, 86, 87, 90, 98, 170, 181
oxidize 106
oxygen sensor 68–73, 75, 76, 100, 107, 156; *see also* lambda sensor

parts per million (ppm) 53, 54
Pokony, Michael 42
Porsche 30, 42, 44, 51, 70, 73, 76, 81, 82, 84–86, 90, 147, 150, 168–170, 180